MEN POSSESSED
BY GOD

Frontispiece. THE MEETING OF ST. ANTHONY AND ST. PAUL OF THEBES

MEN POSSESSED BY GOD

THE STORY OF THE DESERT MONKS
OF ANCIENT CHRISTENDOM

JACQUES LACARRIÈRE

Translated by Roy Monkcom

1964

DOUBLEDAY & COMPANY, INC.

GARDEN CITY, NEW YORK

Translated from *Les Hommes Ivres de Dieu*
© B. Arthaud, Paris, 1961

Published in England as *The God-Possessed*

Library of Congress Catalog Card Number 64-13885
Translation copyright © 1963
by George Allen & Unwin Ltd
All Rights Reserved
Printed in the United States of America
First Edition in the United States of America

FOREWORD

Men Possessed by God deals with a certain period of Christianity, in the course of which there took shape in the East a very special religious phenomenon. The period is the fourth century and the phenomenon is the appearance and increase of the early communities of ascetics and monks in the desert wastes of Egypt, Palestine and Syria. This book, therefore, treats of Christianity at a time when its history and that of mankind had been intermingled for three centuries. Why, in a certain part of the world and at a certain moment in history, did men feel the need to shun towns and establish hermitages in the deserts? Who were these men and how did they live? And what was the outcome of this experiment, both for those who took part in it and for the generations which followed them? Such are the main questions dealt with in *Men Possessed by God*.

The first question is answered in the two chapters headed: '*Why Asceticism?*' At first sight, there is nothing stranger than to find thousands of men giving up the world and its advantages, with every human social interest, in order to live in the heart of the desert and follow an existence as remote as possible from the natural conditions which are befitting to men. But such a phenomenon is only apparently strange. It has often happened during the course of history that one society or another has created 'anti-societies', made up of every kind of rebellious spirit: outlaws and robbers but also hermits, monks, sages and the like. In the present instance, the communities of ascetics and monks organized in the Egyptian deserts—on the fringe of the secular world—are ascribable to this phenomenon, the justification for which is first and foremost a religious matter: if the ascetic leaves for the desert, it is not with the object simply of breaking with secular society; his chief concern is to re-discover God, even to await him there, since Christ's coming upon earth is ever expected. The whole phenomenon can be understood only from this choice on the part of the ascetic, from his basic undertaking with respect to a Future which must shortly put an end to the history of the world. All around him he sees nothing but a doomed reality, and to this hopeless death-agony of the world he reacts by suppressing in its turn, within himself, everything which links him to that world, whether in mind or body. To these basic options, which are defined in the first chapter, '*The End of Time*', must be added the particular facts of history as described in the second chapter, '*The Great Transition*'. The 'world' whose death-throes the ascetic glimpses from the silence of the desert is synonymous with Egypt, for Egypt is his birthplace and the land where the first Christian hermitages and monasteries are established. This contact, or rather this clash, between the great symbols of Christianity and the oldest civilization known at the time, a civilization harassed by the image of Death and the Here-after, explains many of the aspects of Egyptian monasticism. The ascetic or the monk is at the meeting-point of two bewildering and contradic-tory influences, that of the Past, burdened with its dead and its gods, which obsessed ancient Egypt and continues to torment the imagination in solitude, and that of the Future, a dramatic, violent Future, the end of the world. It is not surprising that the ascetic, a prey to these two temporal influences, should seek so earnestly to forget history and live a timeless existence.

The central part of the work consists of five chapters under the title: THE GOD-POSSESSED. It deals with the second question: who were these men and how did they live? It is a matter of anecdotal record, in the strict sense of the word, in which the texts have been allowed almost complete freedom to 'speak for themselves'. An important hagiographical literature did, in fact, begin to develop in fourth-century Egypt, Palestine and Syria, around this experiment and these remarkable men: bio-graphies of ascetics, for the greater part the work of their followers, or collection of maxims pronounced by the 'old ascetics', pilgrims' records, travellers' eye-witness accounts, etc. These texts are rich enough in anecdotes, historical notes and factual evidence to constitute both essential documentation and literature proper. This part is therefore rather a succession of biographies of the great ascetics: St Anthony (in the '*Star of the Desert*'), Paul of Thebes and St Pachomius (in the '*Field of the Saints*'), St Macarius and his followers (the '*Trials of Exile*'), St Simeon Stylites ('*Closer to Heaven*'), with which it has been considered sufficient to intersperse a few commentaries in order to give history and legend their appropriate shares in so far as it is possible to do so.

The assessment of the value of this experiment is made in the three chapters grouped under the heading: '*Dying in the Land of the Living*'. Truth to tell, it is less a matter of an assessment than of a critical re-flection on some of the aspects and consequences of this unparalleled experiment. The general results are known: monasticism, originating in Egypt, spread to Palestine and Syria, reached Cappadocia, Greece and then the West. On the individual plane, such assessment is a more difficult operation, first and foremost because it inevitably presents contradictory aspects. A complete break with the world is not undertaken with impunity, one does not fast for years, hidden in the gloom of a cave or exposed to the scorching sun, without one's personality becoming completely upset. This trial, endured for a lifetime, finally brings about in the ascetic certain psychical phenomena to which the writings bear surprising witness. Those weird shapes which appear to the hermits during their meditations by night or in the full glare of the noonday sun, those fiends, the fantastic creatures that come to tempt the ascetic and are described in the chapter, '*The Face of Satan*', form the inevitable pageantry of those who have thought they were free of the world for all time, but have been unable to rid their minds of aggressive or alluring imagery, aggressive in the case of temptations, alluring in that of miracles. Such miracles, briefly considered in the chapter entitled '*The Face of Satan*' are the inevitable accompaniment of the temptations. Against the burden imposed by the dead, the old gods and the world which they have spurned—in short, the bewildering demands imposed by the Past—they set the dazzling vision of the hopefully awaited Future of a differently constituted mankind, in which time, weight, matter and language are transformed: the ascetic who walks on the waters, raises the dead, halts the sun in its course, speaks with wild animals or sees what is invisible, already believes that he lives in the bosom of the celestial city, with the body, the mind and the powers of a new man. Finally, beyond these temptations and miracles, which are but the 'spectacular' aspects of life in the desert (in the strict meaning of the term), spectacular and illusory as they are, another and more secret assessment is indicated. What other reality was in fact achieved by certain ascetics? Were they really 'dead to the world'? Did they find that *hesychastic peace*, that silence of heart and thought, which was their ultimate objective? For this, one must consult the few texts from those exceptional, outstanding desert mystics: Evagrius Ponticus, John Climacus, Macarius the Elder. The texts are quoted in the last chapter '*To be like the Angels*'.

Let it be clearly understood that in this work, which deals with an experiment concerning history and sociology, as well as the Egyptian and Christian religions, we have never at any moment considered that its Christian character gave it a value or provided evidence superior to all others carried out in different places, at other times, and within the scope of other religions.

Paris, April 1961

CONTENTS

CONTENTS

DYING AMONG THE LIVING

ILLUSTRATIONS

MAPS

INTRODUCTION

There is nothing intrinsically unusual in cutting oneself off from the world and breaking with contemporary society or in thinking, with the Hermit, that the answer to the problem of human destiny can be found only outside that society, in solitude. It is an attitude which may even be considered natural, in so far as any highly developed society almost inevitably produces an antisocial 'fringe' ranging from the hermit to the outlaw. It may cause surprise to find the hermit here placed on the same level as the outlaw, but in fact there is nothing to distinguish them radically in their attitude towards society: whether they are socially rebellious or 'religiously rebellious', both are essentially at odds with the accepted order.

It may even be said that from the moment the decisive step is taken it is often easier for the recalcitrant to pass from one rebellious state to the other (to become a hermit, for instance, after being an outlaw) than to become reinstated in a social group with which he has deliberately broken. That is a truth long confirmed by popular tradition and by history, as witness the many tales of *Robber turned Monk* and the texts of the lives of the Desert Fathers, in which former outlaws have become hermits.

A breaking away from society is, then, very natural, in so far as the history of each 'civilization' includes 'anti-societies' of its own making. But if we have elected to confine our illustration of the phenomenon to a certain time and place, it is because in fourth-century Christian Egypt, with the departure of thousands of men for the deserts, it reached an extraordinary pitch of violence and vividness, with lasting results (which persist even today) by raising up in the wastes of Upper and Lower Egypt the first monasteries known to Christian history.

Of what does the phenomenon consist, then, as it is found in fourth-century Egypt? It can be defined in a single word: anchoritism. From the Greek *anachoresis*, meaning 'departure', the word signifies avoidance of the world, renunciation of the society of men and the adoption of a life of solitude. It is first and foremost a social (or rather antisocial) attitude which only later assumes religious meaning. The anchorite is primarily a man who shuns the world for one of many different reasons.

Hundreds of peasants, slaves and thieves, in Graeco-Roman Egypt, fled to the deserts in order to escape payment of taxes, to be free of their masters or to avoid legal action. They became *anchorites*, they went 'underground'. Two centuries later, thousands of Christians did likewise, fleeing from the towns to escape persecution. When, from the fourth century onwards, other Christians thought of withdrawing to the desert so as to live a life of asceticism and meditation, they were naturally referred to as anchorites; and the term has never quite lost its original sense of 'rebel' or 'recalcitrant person'.

It is, therefore, a purely negative attitude—or, at least, appears to be so—since embracing the life of an anchorite implies in the first place an escape, a breaking away, a denial of society. But one knows quite well that anyone who escapes to a life of solitude does not necessarily break with all social values or cease to remain a social being. The anchorite certainly flees to the desert to escape from the temporal community to which he belongs, but to become part of a spiritual community which includes all Christians, living or dead, saints and martyrs, and all who live or have lived, since the time of Adam, according to the law of the 'true' God, the God of the Old Testament and the New. The anchorite holds aloof from his contemporaries and rebels against his own century only to join the ideal, timeless community of Christians from all ages. And so this essentially antisocial attitude, which consists of breaking with actual, living society, paradoxically enough ends by creating a new society on the fringe of the old, true desert communities (hermitages, lauras, monasteries, coenobia), earthly likenesses of the celestial City. Even the word 'monk' itself is paradoxical, since it originally meant a man living alone (from the Greek *monachos*, 'alone') and later came to signify any man living in the body of a religious community.

Of the thousands of men who, in Christian Egypt, chose to live apart from the world and time, history has recorded two names in particular: St Anthony and St Pachomius. St Anthony was the historical promoter of this escapist movement from society, the first to think of breaking completely with the world in order to devote himself to a life of asceticism. The second, St Pachomius, knowing nothing of St Anthony or of his experiment, left in his turn for the deserts of Upper Egypt and with his own hands built the first monastery known to Christian history.

When one thinks that half a century later, when St Anthony and St Pachomius had died, there were already hundreds of anchorites and monks established in the deserts and that in the succeeding centuries monachism and asceticism spread to Palestine, Syria, Persia, Mesopotamia, Cappadocia, Armenia and the lands of the West, the distance between the personal adventure of these two men and its repercussions upon history seems immeasurable. There is exemplified the inevitable two-sidedness of all great historical events, those which reveal a mysterious coincidence between a man's free decision and the dormant needs of his time. Anchoritism is both a collective phenomenon, perfectly understandable and even foreseeable for anyone who knows the religious atmosphere of the East in the fourth century, and a personal phenomenon, the spontaneous adventure of a small number of men who decided to leave the world and face the hazards of asceticism and the desert. It is this adventure in particular, the individual aspect of the phenomenon, that is recorded in all the extant texts and documents concerning the life of the ascetics and saints of the desert: *Life of St Anthony* by St Athanasius, *Life of Paul of Thebes*, the first hermit, by St Jerome, *Life of St Pachomius and his follower Theodore*, *Historia Lausiaca* by Palladius, *History of the Monks of Egypt* by Rufinus of Aquileia, *Institutions of the Fathers* and *Conversations with the monks of Egypt* by Cassian, *Apophthegms of the Fathers*, *The Spiritual Meadow* by John Moschus, etc. These texts describe the vocation of some saint or anchorite, his sojourn in the desert, his fasts, mortifications, miracles and his struggles against temptations, but (since it is not their purpose) they never deal with the phenomenon and its full significance in a comprehensive manner.

Before getting to the heart of the matter and describing the incredible way of life of the 'god-possessed', we must examine the roots and the extensive range of this strange phenomenon: it was not without deep, compelling reasons that so many Christians broke with their time, leaving their possessions, their families and their 'worldly' lives. We must acknowledge that it was a particularly exciting undertaking in the history of mankind, this attempt on the part of an organized body of men to develop on the fringe of the secular world an ideal type of society: the monastic communities established by St Anthony and St Pachomius, and an ideal type of human being: the desert saint.

John Climacus, an ascetic of the seventh century, writes: 'The monastery is an earthly heaven, and we must therefore be as angels.' Was it, then, to become angels that St Anthony, St Pachomius and the thousands of their imitators went to the deserts of Egypt and the East, there to lead a monastic existence which made the greatest possible demands upon human strength and endurance?

WHY ASCETICISM?

CHAPTER 1

THE END OF TIME

When the first monks and anchorites settled in the Egyptian deserts in the fourth century, Christianity had in fact become the official religion of the Roman Empire. The persecution of the Christians had ceased, the number of conversions was rapidly increasing and the famous Edict of Milan, proclaimed some years earlier by the Emperor Constantine, allowed Christians freedom to practise their religion. Traces of paganism subsisted in many parts of the *orbus romanus*, but it was no longer the representative religion of the Empire, the history of which was henceforth inseparable from that of the Church. After an interval of fifteen centuries, this seems quite natural, but it is in fact rather surprising when one considers that, originally, nothing was more at variance with Christian vocation.

The purpose of the new religion, as preached by Jesus and propagated by the Apostles, was not to conquer the temporal world and establish a place for itself in History, but rather to announce that the Kingdom of Heaven was at hand, bringing with it the end of the world. Like all great religions, Christianity first made an impact upon its devotees by effecting a fundamental change in the relationship between man and time. For the Gentiles—or Pagans—living in a Time cycle in which religious ceremonies, festivals and sacrifices unflaggingly perpetuated the same original events, within a repetitive (and therefore endless) universe, Christianity brought the sudden, distressing revelation of progressive Time, which evolves and passes, of a growing universe and therefore one capable of *coming to an end*. Is not one of the themes frequently to be found in the words of Jesus the fact and the imminence of the end of the world? The universe is soon to cease to exist, for Jesus, having come once on earth 'to fulfil the prophesies', will return a second time to bring the history of the world to a close. The destruction of Jerusalem—also frequently foretold—will be but a preliminary to the final cataclysm in the course of which 'the sun shall be darkened, and the moon shall not give her light, and the stars shall fall from heaven, and the powers of the heavens shall be shaken'. Then 'shall they see the Son of man coming in the clouds with great power and glory. And then shall he send his angels, and shall gather together his elect from the four winds, from the uttermost part of the earth to the uttermost part of heaven'.[1]

It is difficult to imagine the impact which such ideas might have had on the masses of the age, whether they were Jewish and for generations had been fully prepared for the Event by the Prophets and Apocalyptic writers, or whether they were Gentile and were suddenly confronted with the hitherto unsuspected vision of a universe dependent on Time. The impact must have been all the greater since it was a matter, not merely of a warning, but of the *imminent* end of the world. The generation of those who hearken to Jesus 'shall not pass till all these things have been fulfilled' and the Event will be so sudden that 'he which is on the housetop' will not have time 'to come down to take any thing out of his house'. The Son of man will appear with the speed of lightning, 'coming out of the east and shining even unto the west'.[2]

How could one live in this perpetual dread of annihilation? How could one help watching day and night for the preliminary signs of the Apocalypse? And, as the end of the world was expected at any moment, how could one disregard the responsibilities, the commitments and the values of this life? It was all the more difficult because this prediction was the theme incessantly discussed throughout the first century by Christian preachers, including St Paul. To those who asked him when and how the Last Judgement would take place, St Paul replied in the *First Epistle to the Thessalonians*:

'We which are alive and remain unto the coming of the Lord shall not prevent them which are asleep. For the Lord shall descend from heaven with a shout, with the voice of the archangel, and with the trump of God: and the dead in Christ shall rise first: then we which are alive and remain shall be caught up together with them in the clouds, to meet the Lord in the air',[3] a prophecy which was to have such an effect upon those to whom the apostle preached that the same Christians ceased all work and lived in idleness while awaiting the impending event.

The exciting eschatological atmosphere of the first century became

---

[1] Matthew 24, 29-31; Mark 13, 24-27; Luke 21, 25-28.
[2] Matthew 24, 34, Mark 13, 30, Luke 21, 32. In Matthew and Mark this prediction is also related to the destruction of Jerusalem. In the minds of those who listened to Jesus these two events were clearly connected, the destruction of Jerusalem being but the premonitory indication of the end of the world.
[3] I Thessalonians, IV, 15-17.

more widespread in the ensuing centuries and is most certainly responsible for much unreasonable and extravagant behaviour, such as the appeal to martyrdom, the obsession with virginity, and asceticism and the escape to the deserts. This attitude has the basic characteristic of being a radical denial of the world, which is easily comprehensible if the world is destined to extinction from one day to the next. It is of little importance whether at any particular epoch the emphasis is placed upon the Martyr or at another time upon the Ascetic or Anchorite, for the attitude depends upon a complete disinterestedness in life here below and results from disorders of the mind due to the fear, distress and exaltation of the End of Time.

An example may be given: Since, with regard to the preliminary indications of the fate of Jerusalem, Jesus had said 'Woe unto them that are with child, and to them that give suck in those days!' many young women remained virgins and numerous couples engaged in virginal or apotactic marriage (living together without sexual relations) so as not to be surprised in impurity or pregnancy at the Last Judgement. If supplementary proof is required of this link between concern for virginity and the fear of the end of the world, as it operated in many minds, here is a very revealing quotation from St Hippolytus, Bishop of Rome, taken from his *Commentary on Daniel* written at the beginning of the third century:

'A bishop, who was a pious and modest man but who placed too much trust in his visions, had had three dreams and began to prophesy: "Know, brethren, that the Last Judgement will take place within one year. If what I tell you does not come to pass, have no more faith in the Scriptures and do as you please." At the end of a year, nothing had happened; he was abashed, the brethren were shocked, *the virgins got married* and those who had sold all their possessions were reduced to beggary.'

The strange thing is that this concern with asceticism and virginity, which had come about from specific motives, persisted in certain cases, even when the motives no longer applied, that is when one ceased to believe in the impending end of the world. Thus, in the fourth century, when the Roman Empire had become Christian and when belief in the end of the world was subject to severe testing (for one wonders how God could destroy a Kingdom which in the future was to be his), certain writers extolled virginity and continence for the purpose of *hastening the end of the world* by extinction of the human race. 'The world,' writes a certain Dositheus, 'began with marriage and will end through continence.' And Basil of Ancyra, the fourth-century Christian writer, adds in his *Treatise on Virginity*:

'Now that the world has everywhere flourished and borne its fruits (an allusion to the Emperor Constantine's recognition of Christianity) and the earth has been peopled to such an extent that it can no longer contain its huge population, now that the prediction of the Lord's coming has been made and those convinced by his teaching will beat their swords into ploughshares and their spears into pruning-hooks, now that no nation shall lift up a sword against another and there shall be no more war, the body shall flourish through virginity and shall not fall into corruption.'

Obviously, Basil of Ancyra displays a little ingenuousness when he imagines the future of the new Christian Empire in such a peaceful light. But a curious aspect of Christian thought in the early centuries is observable in this text: the idea that procreation is justifiable only to make good the losses sustained in wars. Now that the Empire, thanks to Constantine, has become Christian and God's law prevails upon the earth, men, having now no reason to fight, have likewise no need of procreation. It is the duty of one and all to remain virgin or chaste; in other words, every Christian must play his part in hastening the extinction of the human species. Which is, clearly, the best way of not giving the lie to the Prophets and the Scriptures!

It may seem surprising that such a belief should have endured intact for centuries (since it is found again in the sixth century), for each generation could testify to its futility. Indeed, it is pointless to be always watching the skies for signs of the end of the world, to rub one's eyes each morning to see if the sun is becoming dark and each night to see if the stars are falling, when nothing comes of it. All through these early centuries, sun, moon and stars continued serenely on their courses. But such a belief as this, being by its nature irrational, has no need of rational proof. The moment one believes in the imminent end of the world, everything, from the most terrible happenings to the most harmless (a war, an earthquake, but also a too cold winter or an unusually hot summer), is interpreted as a sign of the end of time. If, in the general state of tension, a man should rise up and declare: 'God has inspired me and revealed to me the day and the hour of his coming', the multitude will run towards him, prepared to take his word. Thus, in Phrygia in the second century, a certain Montanus, in the company of two women,

Priscilla and Maximilla, for seven years in succession prophesied the imminent descent of the New Jerusalem upon the earth, without the slightest waning of public enthusiasm and credulity.[1] He even specified the exact spot where the Holy City was to come down, viz. the plain of Pepuza, in Phrygia, and everyone waited patiently in the plain for the descent of the celestial city, while listening to Montanus's prophecies.

> Man sleeps, while I keep watch.
> And now the Lord takes away the heart of each man,
> To replace it with another.
>
> (Montanus, *Oracle V*)

Long after Montanus's death, his prophecies continued to shake the multitudes they collected, since very many Montanistic churches were formed throughout the Christian East and some of them were still in existence at the end of the fourth century.

Through continuous watchfulness one comes a little later on to believe that one sees the Holy City actually come down from heaven, this time in Judea.

Towards the end of the second century, Tertullian writes in his treatise *Against Marcion*:

'Moreover, the Holy City of Jerusalem appeared during the course of the Eastern expedition, which took place in recent years. Even pagans, who were in Judea at the time, declared that every morning for forty days a town which seemed to come from the sky took shape in the air. It was equipped with walls which vanished in the full light of day. It is in that city that the saints will live in spiritual bliss after the Resurrection.'

What is more, whole multitudes in the third century, acting on their belief in rash prophets, set out for the deserts, believing they would see the Christ, whose coming was ever expected.

'A bishop of Syria,' further writes St Hippolytus in his *Commentary on Daniel*, 'persuaded many brethren to make their way to the desert, with their wives and children, where they expected to find the Christ. For several days they wandered about the mountains and along the roads and were very nearly arrested as robbers by the Governor. He was prevented from doing so by his wife, who was a Christian.'

Obviously, these are extreme cases. Belief in the imminent end of the

[1] According to the Apocalypse, a new Jerusalem was to come down out of heaven at the end of time: 'And I saw the holy city, new Jerusalem, coming down from God out of heaven, prepared as a bride adorned for her husband.' (XXI, 1-2.)

world did not always compel Christians to wander in the deserts or to spend seven years waiting in the plain of Pepuza. But beliefs of that sort are the more firmly held just because they are vague and because, with the conviction of immediate and tangible proof to come, their endless power of exaltation does not diminish. And if supernatural signs are lacking, if nothing spectacular, such as an invasion, an earthquake or an eclipse, occurs to confirm the probable end of the world, one falls back upon more natural, everyday indications. Thus, from the second half of the third century, when the exaltation and frenzy of the first two centuries have lessened and the question has, so to speak, lost some of its urgency, the notion of a universe stricken in its vitals by a single act of God's will, a universe destroyed by action from outside, logically gives place to that of a universe threatened from the inside, a weary world which contains within itself the causes of its own destruction.

'Who cannot see,' writes St Cyprian of Carthage in a letter to Dimitrianus, 'that the world is already in its decline and no longer has the strength and vigour of former times? There is no need to invoke scriptural authority to prove it. The world tells its own tale and in its general decadence bears adequate witness that it is approaching its end. There is less rain in winter to encourage the growth of seeds; springtime is not now so enjoyable or autumn so fruitful; the quarries, as if from weariness, give less stone and marble and the gold and silver mines are already worked out; the land remains untilled, the seas lack pilots and the armies are without men; there is less innocence in the courts, less justice in the judges, less concord between friends, less artistic sincerity, less moral strictness. Do you think that anything which is in a decline can be as vigorous as it was originally? Everything which is approaching its end must of necessity wither away. We see children who are already quite white; their hair dies before it can grow and they are stricken with old age at the beginning of their lives. Thus, everything in these days is rushing to its doom and is affected by the general debility.'[1]

---

[1] These children, 'stricken with old age at the beginning of their lives', were really german babies, which St Cyprian must have seen for the first time at this epoch and whose hair—white at birth—developed its colour with the years. In a passage of his *Politics* (273), Plato had, with regard to the end of the Golden Age, already pictured this reversal of time, when animals begin to get smaller and old men to become young again and return to the womb. In Plato, this reversal was due to the gods' withdrawal from their creation. The universe, left to itself, regresses towards its primary stages until everything vanishes. Men are old at birth and die as babies. Now, this text by St Cyprian was written at a time when analogous ideas were coming to light in Christian minds: the ideas that God had withdrawn from this world and the universe, left to itself, could only fade and die.

In other terms, the end of the world, in St Cyprian's text and in the perspective of his day, is no longer an object of terror or wild hope, a source of anarchy or irrational conduct as in the time of St Paul and Montanus, but on the contrary an object of meditation, a source of reasoned consideration of man's end on the earth. Then it becomes comprehensible why the early centuries of Christianity attributed such great importance to the Martyr, the Ascetic and then to the Anchorite and the desert Saint. It is because each of them, by his antisocial attitude and his rejection of the moribund world, appeared as the only 'answer', the only possible solution to the sufferings of a society which saw within itself its own doom.

By leaving for the Egyptian deserts, in the fourth century, far from a world condemned by God, the 'God-possessed', without being aware of it, merely resumed the old, original dream of Christianity: living for ever remote from the world and History, while awaiting the New Kingdom of Heaven. But to live a life of solitude was not enough to ensure the Anchorite's salvation. In this respect, the outlaw, compelled to live for years in the desert in order to escape the justice of men, would be just as deserving as he. Equal or identical as regards their attitude to society, they differ profoundly when consideration is given to the values which inspire them. For the Anchorite, these values are to be found wholly in another world, and it is they which decide his choice of action. Now, these values demand a *complete* dissociation from the secular world. Breaking with society implies breaking with everything that identifies and justifies man in that society, everything that makes him a social being; knowledge, culture, possessions, family, marriage, procreation. Renunciation of society also implies renunciation of the flesh, which is the reason why the Anchorite is necessarily an Ascetic.

Pursuing this thought further, one discovers a still closer relationship between asceticism and anchoritism: these two types of behaviour are not only antisocial, but anti-natural. Contrary to the myth of the *noble savage* which so greatly stimulated the imagination and thought of the eighteenth century, that of the *noble desert saint*, as it appeared in Christian literature of the fourth and subsequent centuries, extolled the rejection of nature in all its aspects. Living in society is as natural to man as eating and procreation (which the fourth century writers understood perfectly well). The retirement to the deserts was therefore at no time a return to any sort of 'natural' or wild life but, on the contrary, was a seeking after a way of life as anti-natural as possible. The anchorite practised a strict asceticism and lived under conditions which were, in a material sense, *inhuman*. He clearly showed his partiality for a restrictive existence: staying in caves or desert holes, inside hollow tree-trunks like a recluse, or on the top of a pillar in the manner of the stylites. In short, he persisted in living under material and spiritual conditions which were *artificial*. The forbidding of speech, for instance—very frequently to be found in the desert—or even the invention of an artificial language by an anchorite for the purpose of communicating with his followers,[1] clearly indicate this concern to break completely with the aggregate of habits and relationships which make up secular social life. It is almost all the essential attributes of man *in this life* that are in question, the better to prepare the individual for the other world to be established by Christ's second Coming, in which the parts played by the body, by society and by language will be changed.

This may all appear to be abstract, or at least theoretical, and it is true that the facts are not often presented so directly in the texts and supporting evidence relating to the 'God-possessed'. It is a question of the underlying meaning, the fundamental aims in the phenomenon and unconscious motivations (present in almost all the participants, for a certain number of them, like Macarius the Elder, John Climacus, Evagrius Ponticus and Diadochus of Photike, clearly foresaw these motivations and defined them with the greatest exactness). The different 'models' of behaviour offered for the admiration and consideration of the Christian multitudes during the first four centuries clearly tend towards the ideal type of man—or superman—the desert Saint, who seeks in mind and body the realization of the new man referred to by St Paul. These 'models' are the Martyr Saint, the Ascetic Saint and the Anchorite Saint.

It remains to define briefly what is meant by asceticism, since there will be frequent allusion to it in this book. The term asceticism and its practice, which are by no means the invention of Christianity, were used in the early centuries to indicate very different, and even contradictory, conceptions and attitudes.

In its proper sense, asceticism (from the Greek *askèsis*: exercise or gymnastics) is a physical and mental training by which man may achieve greater self-control. The word has always held something of its original meaning: an attempt at self-mastery, acting first upon the body and through the body. An ascetic is one who 'exercises' his body like an athlete, and the fourth-century Christian writers made no mistake about that: in describing the asceticism of the anchorites of Egypt they made use of sporting terms, speaking of 'performances', 'feats', fasting

[1] See the case of Pachomius and the 'Language of the Angel', p. 83.

'records', and quite properly naming the desert saints *athletes in exile*.

It is obvious that by adopting a much earlier technique and way of life, derived from paganism and Judaism, Christianity could not avoid a certain amount of misunderstanding. Such misunderstanding soon made its appearance, at the beginning of the second century, when consideration was first given to the basic principles and the nature of asceticism. It was then realized that it was not merely a practical method of achieving self-mastery but also a spiritual attitude adopted in the light of God's work, a kind of *judgement* passed on the body, on Creation and on the part allocated to them in man's salvation. It was then that circumstances worsened, for a great number of Christians in fact considered the flesh and all Creation (the world, matter, etc.) as bad in themselves and the personification of Evil. This conception was heretical since orthodox dogma (lacking, moreover, in definition until the occasion of these 'heresies'; which indicates that they were essential) held that the world and Creation were the work of God, originally good (since God did not create Evil) but perverted as a result of Satan's revolt and of original sin, that is through the transgressions of the rebellious Angel and of rebellious man. The flesh, matter, the world or society, *are* not intrinsically Evil, but have *become* the prey of Satan and of Evil. In other words, from the orthodox viewpoint the flesh and, generally speaking, matter are glorified in so far as they are considered capable and worthy of embodying the Spirit (for is that not the real meaning of Incarnation?), whereas, for the various heresies that appeared from the second century onwards, matter was Evil and could not serve to house the Spirit. It is easy to see that any theory that treats the world as the product of Evil and the body as unworthy to contain the Spirit, inevitably comes to a denial of the reality and even of the possibility of Incarnation. (How could a deity be embodied in anything incapable of receiving the Word?) And it came also—in order to explain the existence of Evil—to create a distinct entity of God, outside itself; in other words, to divide the universe into two opposing principles: that of Evil (responsible for Creation) and that of Good. From the second century, it was the case with all the heresies which for that reason were called *dualist*: Gnosticism, Manicheism, Marcionism, etc. The creation of matter and the world was attributed to a bad demiurge and not to the supreme God; which explains that everything which binds man to the world—the pleasures of the flesh, social ties, possessions, even marriage and procreation—were utterly forbidden and condemned. The moment this world is identified with Evil, is it not man's duty to refuse all collaboration with it and to break all laws established by the demiurge and by men since they merely confirm the original injustice? Such was the assertion of many Gnostics in the early centuries. Carpocrates, one of the leading Gnostics of the second century, writes: 'Man must break all laws because they are the work of Evil.' His son Epiphanius, who died at the age of seventeen and was buried with divine honours in Greece on the island of Cephalonia, adds in his treatise *On Justice*:

'One sky stretches above the earth and encompasses the whole of it. The night displays her stars for all. God makes the sun to shine upon the earth so that all may see it equally, for no man has the right to deprive his neighbour of his share of light. These are the laws which teach men to act against the laws. The special laws break and destroy communion with divine Law.'

This was obviously an antisocial attitude (but all heresies were in the first place antisocial ferments, clandestine churches in opposition to the established Church and even to Authority, which justified in advance all condemnations and all massacres, every power, whether spiritual or temporal, profiting by it). It was an antisocial attitude, and particularly systematic. If one really wishes to overcome the world, it is not enough to stand against it as it is; one must also impede its future progress, prevent the increase of Evil and oppose procreation, whence the obsession with continence and virginity, which was so characteristic of the early centuries and, as has already been seen, led some to preach the sheer extinction of the human race! Does not God himself, in the view of certain heretics, consider the world to be suspect and evil, since he is preparing for its destruction?

It can be seen how, in such an atmosphere of ascetic rivalry, these ideas, whether heretical or not, could lead to extremes of behaviour. Therefore, in the course of those centuries, certain sects, such as the *Encratites* (from the Greek *encrateia*: 'ascendancy over oneself'), are seen to put the ideas into practice, to forbid the consumption of wine and meat, sexual relations, marriage and procreation. 'Man,' writes a certain Severius, 'is the work of God down to the waist and the work of the Devil below.' Since no evangelical text takes account of such a conception of man, the Gospels and the Acts of the Apostles will be re-written in order to provide some authoritative basis for such prohibitions. That is the partial explanation of the origin of certain apocryphal writings like the *Gospel according to the Egyptians*, the *Apocryphal Acts of St Thomas* and *St John*. 'Be not concerned with marriage or with children', says Christ in the *Apocryphal Acts of St*

John and the *Gospel according to the Egyptians*: 'I am come to put down the works of woman. The time will come when the body, that garment of shame, shall be trodden under foot, when there shall be no more male and female.' St John in his *Apocryphal Acts* proclaims that 'union between man and woman is a crime' and that a woman should prefer to die rather than 'perform such abomination'.[1]

Thus, the practice of asceticism—in the sense in which it was taken—could be something very different from a contemplative attitude and calm meditation upon man and his destiny. It could take the form of antisocial ferment, a source of disturbances and dissensions, even of massacres and condemnations—a very powerful spiritual weapon against the society of the day, a 'protest' carried to extremes against the conditions imposed by God and society.[2] But how, in practice, can 'good' asceticism be distinguished from the 'bad', or, if one prefers it, orthodox asceticism (which rejects the body, while not believing it to be synonymous with Evil) from heretical asceticism (which holds that the flesh and matter are the embodiment of Evil)? It is an essential distinction, even vital, since for centuries it resulted in condemnations and persecutions and continually brought bloodshed to the history of Christianity. It was practically an impossibility to renounce the world *completely* (and therefore renounce certain fundamental rules of social life) without soon finding oneself in the position of a rebel. That is why the chief heretical movements of History: the Gnostics, Manicheans, Arians and Monophysites, and later the Paulicians, Bogomili and Albigenses—to whom denial of the world meant also denial of temporal Authority—were the object of mass persecutions and exterminations. One may very well wonder whether this method was the right one, since the extermination of thousands of men who hold that this world and its laws were Evil itself could not but strengthen their views!

The question was of the greatest importance—as much because of its dogmatic consequences as of its effect on society—and immediately the Empire became Christian and bishops were able freely to hold their Councils, it was one of the very earliest subjects for debate. It was certainly not an easy question, as there was no *a priori* means of distin-

---

[1] The Encratites, in spite or perhaps because of the extreme nature of their prohibitions, played an important part during the early centuries of Christianity. They had many followers and formed themselves into churches with a hierarchy of bishops. There was even an Encratite monastery. This heresy lasted until the fourth century at least, since the Council of Gangra, in 342, anathematized 'whoever despises a woman living with her husband on the grounds that she cannot enter into the Kingdom of Heaven or refuses to take part in acts of worship in the houses of married people'.

[2] Rather like non-violence in India, from the nineteenth century onwards.

guishing between heretical asceticism and orthodox asceticism. It there-fore soon became necessary to have recourse to empirical, sometimes arbitrary criteria for judging asceticism. Thus, there was nothing intrinsically heretical in abstaining from eating meat or in practising continence; but the general suspicion with which the Gnostics, the Manicheans and the Encratites regarded flesh meant that, from the fourth century, it became difficult to refuse meat during the course of a meal without being suspected of heresy. Did a monk who refused a piece of meat do so from motives of purification and sacrifice, in order to be pleasing to God (the orthodox attitude), or because he formally condemned flesh and considered it to be the work of the Devil (the heretical attitude)? To settle the question, it was officially decided during the Council of Ancyra that 'priests and monks might abstain from meat on condition that they first tasted and ate a small piece of it'. Having thus provided proof of their orthodoxy, they were free to leave the rest of the meat untouched on their plate. If one but tasted a piece of meat, albeit unwillingly, it showed that flesh was not held to be the Devil's creation. Some monks, however, with dubious intent, refused even to eat vegetables cooked with meat. Had they the right to refuse? No. Such intransigence revealed dualist notions and the Council of Ancyra threatened to condemn them as heretics.

Such, during the first four centuries, was the eschatological and ascetic atmosphere before the exodus into the Egyptian desert by thousands of men, both ecclesiastics and laymen. Belief in the imminent end of the world, now inevitable since the world contained the causes of its own destruction, and ascetic rivalry which regarded asceticism as a weapon against society as much as a purely spiritual exercise; it can be seen how far man had ventured in self-denial or self-assertion. An asceticism which goes to the lengths of wholesale rejection of procreation, even if it is 'heretical', is one of the most extreme and desperate attitudes ever adopted by man, as far as his possible future *on earth* is concerned. And since this doomed universe, this world, condemned by God him-self and everywhere revealing the stifling presence of Evil, is henceforth unable to guarantee the survival and the salvation of man, he must go elsewhere in search of them: he will become an Ascetic or an Anchorite, in a spot where the world may best be forgotten—in the barrenness and calm abstraction of the deserts.

2. ST. ANTHONY'S DESERT

3A. ST. ANTHONY'S MONASTER[

3B. ANCIENT TOMB IN
UPPER EGYPT

CHAPTER 2

THE GREAT TRANSITION

'A time will come when it will appear that the Egyptians have worshipped their gods in vain. These gods will leave the earth and return to heaven and Egypt will be abandoned. This holy land, the land of sanctuaries, will be covered in sepulchres and be shrouded in death. Egypt! Egypt! Of thy beliefs only incredible stories will remain to future generations. There will be nothing left but words on the stones to tell of thy pious acts!'

ASCLEPIUS

This calm abstraction of the deserts could be provided by Palestine, Syria, Libya and Egypt, for those who renounced the world. Why was it Egypt that became the chosen land for asceticism and anchoritism?

Before this question is approached, one thing must be made clear: the texts which tell of the life of the 'God-possessed' in the desert and to which reference will be made in this book are mostly Greek texts written by Greeks: the *Life of Anthony* by Athanasius, the bishop of Alexandria, the *Historia Lausiaca* by Palladius and the *History of the Monks of Egypt* by Rufinus of Aquileia. The two other most important texts: the *Life of Paul of Thebes, the first hermit*, by St Jerome and the *Conversations with the Monks of Egypt* by Cassian were written in Latin. But writing Greek implies thinking Greek. All the texts in question, designed for an informed public speaking Greek and Latin, naturally transcribed into their own language the teachings, the sayings and the peculiar mentality of the men of the Egyptian deserts. Now, these men were neither Greeks nor Romans, but Egyptians: Anthony, Pachomius, Macarius the Elder, Poemen, Pierius, Serapion, Horus, Paphnutius, Onuphrio, Shenute, Pisentios, all the great names of Coptic Christianity, were of Egyptian origin, born in Egypt of Egyptian (and very often pagan) parents. They spoke neither Greek nor Latin, but Coptic, the demotic form of the traditional Egyptian language. What is more, they were mostly of peasant stock and belonged to the class of fellahin which had no contact (unless it was through constant revolts) with the Greeks and Romans in occupation and long perpetuated the traditions, the forms of worship and the mentality of the Egypt of the Pharaohs. It is essential to make the distinction here and now, for otherwise one is liable to fail to grasp in its original entirety the remarkable phenomenon which was the birth of monasticism in Egypt. By its origin and in its scope it was a purely Egyptian phenomenon, the revival in changed forms of a past and a civilization which, although believed dead, had in fact never ceased to exist and to grow despite centuries of foreign occupation.

GRAECO-ROMAN EGYPT

When Anthony and Pachomius left for the desert, Egypt had for more than eight centuries ceased to be an independent country. Alexander the Great's landing in the fourth century BC and the incorporation of the country into the Roman Empire during the thirty years before Christ had made Egypt first a Hellenized territory and then a Roman province; but that does not mean that the land had become Greek or Roman. It does not appear that Egypt ever underwent a change, in depth, because of the influence of her different invaders, especially in the religious field (the most important aspect here), since the bulk of the population: peasants, fellahin and craftsmen, remained faithful to their ancestral gods.

Naturally, after several centuries of occupation, the Greeks had an influence on certain aspects of Egyptian life. The foundation of Alexandria, which for a thousand years became the intellectual centre of the East, the introduction of certain Greek deities (Dionysus at the time of the Alexandrian campaign and the Eleusinian goddesses under the Ptolemys), the establishment of schools of science and philosophy in Alexandria and the creation of a class of Hellenized Egyptians, speaking both Greek and Egyptian, were all important. But this Greek presence in Egypt was felt only within a class which the Greeks themselves had helped to form, an urban class of Hellenized Egyptians, a wealthy, cultured intelligentsia, the only one capable of leaving concrete evidence of Greek influence. On the other hand, the real Egypt, the Egypt of the peasants, craftsmen and priests, was always unsubmissive to Hellenism. The proof lies in the fact that relations between Greeks and Egyptians remained rather superficial, the Greeks of Egypt being predominantly traders, artisans and officials, whom the Egyptians treated as foreign elements in their country. For their part, the Greeks never took the Egyptians very seriously. From the first the country seemed so strange and unusual to them that they saw in their surroundings something comic, as did the Europeans in China or Japan in the last century. 'Because of their form, the tombs of Memphis they called *pyramis*, that is "bread-rolls", those of Thebes *syrinx*, that is "flutes", the great stone pillars standing before the temples were called *obeliskoi*, meaning "roasting-spits", and the terrible denizens of the Nile were known as *crocodiloi*, a name which stood for "lizards" in their own tongue!'[1] The Egyptians were polite to them. In their eyes the Greeks were regarded as boisterous folk, rather frivolous, lacking in religious sense, a scatter-brained, childish people. (Remember the famous remark made by an Egyptian priest to Solon, as reported by Plato in his *Timaeus*: 'You Greeks will always be children. When will the Greeks grow up?') In short, Greek and Egyptian maintained fairly free but superficial associations, yet remained mistrustful and a little contemptuous of each other.

The Roman presence in Egypt was even less effective than that of the Greeks. Rome treated Egypt like a country apart, a land differing from the other provinces of the Empire in its customs, its way of life, its gods and even its position on the southern limits of the *orbis romanus*, to such an extent that it never achieved the administrative status of a Roman province but was just occupied territory and the personal property of the Emperor. Whereas the Greeks lived alongside the Egyptians without actually mixing with them, the Romans merely crossed into Egypt. Moreover, what does a glance at the map of Roman Egypt discover? All the towns founded by the Greeks: Alexandria and Naucratis in the Delta, Arsinoe in the Faiyûm region and, higher up the Nile towards the Nubian frontier, Aphroditopolis, Oxyrhynchus, Antinoe, Hermopolis, Lycopolis, Ptolemais, Coptos, Thebes and Syene. Of all these towns (or rather metropolises, as they were called) only one was Roman: Antinoe, founded by Hadrian after the death of his favourite, Antinous. It is because, in fact, Roman penetration did not go beyond Middle and Upper Egypt. 'Rome,' writes Victor Chapot, the principal historian of Roman Egypt, 'was never concerned to establish in Egypt a *limes*, or frontier strip, a network of roadways and small forts such as she maintained so carefully in Arabia. In fact, the Roman occupation zone always stopped short at the southern borders of The-baid, Nubia being no more than a protectorate.' In Upper Egypt the presence of the Romans was sporadic. At the very most, documents record that in such and such a town, at a certain time, appeared a Roman desert patrol riding camels. The Romans themselves seemed to be almost non-existent, appearing only as soldiers and officials stationed in the Delta and a few important towns, and had no contact with the

[1] Adolphe Erman: *The Religion of the Egyptians* (Payot).

population or the rest of the country. Rome occupied Egypt, but was inactive there and could make little of it. She contented herself with putting down the revolts which were always breaking out and with squeezing from the country as much wealth as possible by imposing heavy taxation upon the millions of fellahin. 'All Egypt,' writes Victor Chapot, 'had to bleed for the Romans.' This country, situated at the frontiers of their world, was for them incomprehensible, a hostile land surrounded by disquieting deserts and indomitable nomadic tribes.

It may seem that too much consideration is given to mystery and exoticism, but to belittle these factors would be to underestimate the Egyptian contribution to Roman culture; for this land—so little appreciated by the occupying Romans—became a real craze with the people of Italy. From the Roman or Pompeian viewpoint, Egypt was not a wheat-producing country inhabited by stupid natives but a land of wisdom and learning, the realm of occult traditions and of magic. Its mysteries, its indecipherable symbols and its picturesque monuments, were imbued with the exotic and the miraculous. This does not mean that the Romans had formed any exact notion of Egyptian civilization and wisdom; it was merely suspected that behind the gods with animals' heads and the hieroglyphics, as in the shaven heads of the priests of Isis, there were hidden dreadful secrets. Proof of this is found in the popularity enjoyed by the Egyptian religions, especially the cult of Isis, in the first century BC. A whole cultured aristocracy developed a craze for Isis, with its mysteries and its priests, and for such strange, hitherto unknown religions, and the emperor Tiberius was obliged to suppress these cults, to have a few priests crucified as an example and to banish some thousands of Isis worshippers to Sardinia. All this, together with the more or less fanciful travellers' tales (for it was then the fashion for such fabulous stories, with their facile vividness, their exoticism, their wonders and miracles, the kind of story parodied by Lucian of Samosata in his *True History*), finally conjured up in secular minds a conventional picture of Egypt, to be found in the paintings of Nilotic landscapes which were 'all the rage' at that time in Rome and Pompeii. Temple and reed-hut on the Nile bank, boat and ferryman, ibis and crocodile, were reproduced times without number, like the wallpaper of our childhood days, in which a stereotyped Eastern view—with desert, camels and mosque—depicted veiled women drawing water in the shade of the palms. In the early centuries of our era the Romans had their Egypt, just as the sixteenth century had its East Indies and the nineteenth its Polynesia, earthly paradises in which are crystallized the unconscious bitterness and yearning for innocence experienced by civilizations in times of material success and conquest. The Egypt of the ibis, the sage and the sphinx, was the secret retaliation on the part of a land conquered and held down by the Romans.

The power and fascination of this fairyland of Egypt in and after the first century were such as to create a veritable surge of Roman tourists. The chief sightseeing tours were described by Diodorus of Sicily and Pliny the Younger: they included the Pyramids, the Lake Moeris Labyrinth, the Colossi of Memnon (which were visited at dawn to hear them sing) and the royal tombs at Thebes, which still bear the thousands of designs scratched on them by the visitors. And as Egypt added to the splendour of her monuments the unique attraction of her sacred animals, one did not fail to stop at Arsinoe or Memphis on the way, to throw meat to the crocodiles or to give fodder to the bull Apis (which, for a consideration, the priests let out of its sanctuary on this occasion!) An entrancing picture later to pass, naturally, into Christian Egypt. Three or four centuries later, nobody in the East was surprised to learn that Egypt was still a land of wonders. The miracles attributed to the anchorites—who walked on the waters, halted the sun in its course and raised up the dead—attracted to Egypt a crowd of Greeks and Romans who thought of themselves as pilgrims but who were in fact nothing but 'tourists' in search of Christian marvels in succession to pagan marvels.

THE END OF AN IDOL

For more than four thousand years the Egyptians worshipped the same gods. To this solid pantheon the Greeks added Serapis—a 'mixture' of Zeus, Osiris and Apis—and Hadrian gave Egypt Antinous, but nothing was fundamentally changed in the country's beliefs.

The Egyptians were themselves quite well aware of the permanence of their gods and traditions. This fact is shown by Plato in his *Timaeus*, when he puts words into the mouth of an Egyptian priest speaking to Solon: 'Our land, Solon, derives all its traditions from remotest Antiquity. Everything that has been achieved, whether here, in your country or in any other place, everything beautiful, great or distinctive that has been produced, was recorded here long ago in our temples and saved from oblivion. You have but to consider our laws, our way of life and our erudition and you will see that they are more than eight thousand years old.' A further indication is supplied in an account by Herodotus, and therefore of earlier date than that by Plato, in which Egyptian antiquity is also placed at eight thousand years. When Herodotus visited the temple of Amen-Ra at Karnak and asked the priests how long the gods had reigned in Egypt, they took him inside the sanctuary and enumerated one by one, three hundred and forty-one wooden statues: 'for every high-priest in his lifetime has his statue made, and by methodical enumeration they showed me how they had succeeded one another, like kings, from father to son, from the beginning.' Three hundred and forty-one generations amount to about eight thousand years, the figure mentioned by Plato. Even if the figures supplied by Herodotus are halved (so as to bring them in line with archaeological data), they remain sufficiently telling. In view of the age which the Egyptian priests attributed to their gods and the permanence of their beliefs and culture, they must have felt bewilderment—a bewilderment which gripped the foreign visitor at the sight of the three hundred and forty-one statues standing in line in the dimness of the temple, each of which formed a link in the chain of time. For four thousand years Egypt lived in a bewilderment of eternity, in the certainty that time was unchanging and that the gods had always reigned over this world.

And then, one day, this bewilderment was broken, for the Egyptian gods died. 'Died' is a figure of speech, for it is extremely difficult to describe—and even to grasp—in its complexity, the death of a god. When can it be said that a god is dead? When he ceases to have an official following? There is nothing to show that his followers will cease to believe in him and in his occult presence and power. In the sixth century AD, two hundred years after the official banning of paganism by the emperor Theodosius, there were still men, mystic philosophers, in the Roman world who continued to believe in the truth of the Egyptian gods. 'We know,' writes one of them, 'that the gods lived there and still live there.' A question which so closely concerns the human soul cannot be resolved from the external traces which the gods and their creeds have always left in the world, and particularly in Egypt. The only criterion by which it may be said that a god has just died is that provided by his own followers, when they become aware within themselves that he is dead and cease to believe in him. It was just such a phenomenon that occurred in Egypt, in Alexandria, during the last decade of the fourth century, on the day when the patriarch Theophilus was authorized to install a church in a temple of Dionysus. There he discovered some statuettes which he considered to be obscene, shattered them and threw the fragments to the Christian multitude. The furious pagans rebelled at this, attacked the Christians, then panicked and ran and shut themselves up in the Serapeum—the great temple of Serapis. This temple was exceptionally magnificent and had already impressed Christians like Clement of Alexandria two centuries before. But it was now neither the hour nor the century for admiring pagan temples. The Christians, urged on by Theophilus, climbed the hundred steps to the entrance of the sanctuary, burst in and then stopped short, halted by amazement and even by fear, before the huge statue of the god. Nobody dared to attack it. At last, on an order from Theophilus, a soldier grasped an axe, climbed up a ladder and set about striking at the head of the god. The idol tottered and collapsed, the crowd cried out in alarm and— a swarm of rats ran out of the gaping hole in the statue! No longer afraid, the Christians rushed upon the idol. The pagans were dismayed. Was it not stated by a very ancient oracle that the world would fall to pieces when Serapis was desecrated? Serapis was broken, yet the world had not crumbled. The Christians seized the chance to drag the pieces through the town and burn them.[1] Everyone saw in the vision of this shattered, rat-infested colossus, this dismembered god being dragged through the streets, the very image of a broken, moribund paganism. Christianity had achieved in Egypt—through violence—something which the Persians, and the Greeks, and the Romans had been unable to accomplish: the suppression of the age-old gods of the land and their replacement by a new deity.

EGYPT BECOMES CHRISTIAN

The earliest authentic documents which attest to the existence of an organized Christian community, in Alexandria, date from the end of the second century. It was also about this date that a Greek philosopher, Pantaenus, a former Stoic converted to Christianity, who appears to have travelled to India in the steps of the apostle Bartholomew (according to Eusebius of Caesarea), founded in Alexandria the famous Catechetical School, the Christian school of exegesis, later to be directed by Clement of Alexandria and Origen. The success of this establishment proves in any case that at the date of its foundation there were already in the town fairly numerous organized Christian communities—no doubt since the middle of the second century. Who were these early Christians? They were primarily Greeks, Jews, Romans, Hellenized Egyptians, members of the cosmopolitan, cultured society of Alexandria. It was among this intelligentsia that Christianity first spread—for the very good reason that it was preached only in Greek and could not reach

[1] This episode has been described—with some differences of detail—by Sozomen, *Ecclesiastical History* (VII, 15) and Socrates, *Ecclesiastical History* (XI, 29).

the mass of true, Coptic-speaking Egyptians. That situation brought its own difficulties: this refined society was, by its nature, not over-zealous, but rather tolerant and receptive of the new forms of religion. It had already accepted the Greek and Roman gods and the eastern divinities— Syrian or Zoroastrian—even if it meant 'amalgamating' them with those of Egypt. It was, particularly, a class which favoured religious syncretism, for the recruitment of the most ardent devotees of Gnosticism, neo-Platonism, neo-Pythagorism, the Hermetic doctrines and all the religious and philosophical sects which developed in second-century Alexandria. To take only one example, Serapis, whose 'death' is recounted above and who was the great god of the Graeco-Roman epoch, was a 'combination' of Zeus-Jupiter, Hades, Osiris, Apis, Dyonysus, with even a little of Amen-Ra! Besides his sanctuary in Alexandria, he had another famous sanctuary at Memphis, where he could be worshipped according to the Egyptian rite or the Greek rite and where the paths were bordered with Egyptian sphinxes, Greek sirens and statues of Pindarus, Protagoras and Plato! Such syncretic flexibility obviously has a certain fascination. It is difficult, after twenty centuries of Christianity, to imagine that the gods could be linked together in this way and not become mutually exclusive, that they could unite to form pantheons of increasing richness. The ease with which new gods could then be 'manufactured'—from old or foreign gods (a facility from which the emperors were not slow to profit for their own deification)—is perhaps a little disconcerting, but it is fundamentally only a way of showing the many ways that lead to salvation.

To return to Egyptian Christianity, it penetrated into Egypt at a time and in a social environment in which syncretic means still guaranteed the dissemination and success of new religions. This obviously represented a source of danger to the new-born Christianity: that of being absorbed, assimilated or associated with existing religions and not received as a unique and revealed faith. The fact that its preachers presented it as such made no difference at all. Christ was accepted, the new Saviour God was admitted, but as all the gods of this epoch— Dionysus, Mithra, Osiris and others (even to the deified emperors)— were saviour gods, the confusion became even greater. Even if one did not go to the lengths of carving a statue of Christ to place alongside those of Plato and Pindarus in the paths of the Serapeum, he was in any case treated as one Saviour among others, or as just a sage (which, from the Christian viewpoint, was much more serious). Among the Gnostics it was even a traditional attitude. The leading Gnostics of the age, Basilides and Valentinus, considered Christ to be a superior being, an essential entity, but not unique in their Pleroma (Creation as a whole). For instance, in second-century Rome, a woman Gnostic called Marcellina is recorded as 'having offered incense to the figures of Christ, Paul, Homer and Pythagoras', while at a slightly later date the Emperor Alexander Severius 'set out side by side in his lararium effigies of Jesus and other spiritual leaders whom he worshipped: Alexander the Great, Abraham, Orpheus and Apollonius of Tyana'.[1]

There was the same syncretic attitude in matters concerning cults and religious rites. Certain Greek and Roman circles had long adopted the Egyptian custom of having themselves embalmed and mummified. When, later, they became Christians, they very naturally continued the practice, so that the necropoles in the neighbourhood of Alexandria, from the third century onwards, showed pagan and Christian mummies buried side by side! The frontiers of death did not halt this strange mingling of cults, gods and rites, so typical of Egyptian life of the times: the Christians thought it quite natural to be buried in pagan necropoles together with the symbols of Osiris. But were they really Christians?

It can be seen how difficult it is to decide where, at this time in Egypt, 'authentic' Christianity begins and ends. If it existed, it was submerged in a profusion of sects and claimed by the Gnostics, Marcionists, Encratites, Hermetists and Judeo-Christians alike. In second-century Alexandria, where, in the words of a present-day writer, 'religions were as varied as business negotiations' and 'fashionable people changed their god as readily as others change their doctor',[2] the 'true' Christians were as yet nothing but an obscure sect, almost undetectable amidst the confusion of dogmas and deities. And it was certainly the impression received, about the year 130, by Hadrian when he visited Alexandria. He was one of the most experienced emperors in Egyptian matters and one of the most receptive of religions and truths, from whatever source. He writes to his brother-in-law Servianus, 'There you see bishops who call themselves Christians worshipping Serapis. Not a priest, whether Samaritan, Jew or Christian, who is not a mathematician, haruspex or aliptic. When the patriarch himself comes to Egypt, he worships Christ and Serapis so as to please everybody.'

THE GREAT TRANSITION

Hardly two centuries separate the time when Hadrian wrote those words and that when the first anchorites appeared in the deserts of

[1] Quoted by Jean Doresse, in *Les Livres secrets des Gnostiques d'Egypte* (Plon).
[2] Marguerite Yourcenar, *Les Mémoires d'Hadrien* (Plon).

Egypt. Two centuries, in the course of which the religious character of Egypt underwent a complete transformation. In Hadrian's day Christianity was as yet only one religion among others. Two hundred years later the whole of Egypt had become Christian: the towns were full of churches, the banks of the Nile were covered in monasteries and the deserts were peopled by anchorites. What had come to pass ? First, an event of importance: from the second half of the third century Christianity had been preached in Coptic and was spreading rapidly and substantially among the purely Egyptian population: craftsmen, administrative officials and especially peasants. Quite quickly, Christian communities formed in the interior of the country, from the Delta in Upper Egypt to Arsinoe, Thmuis, Philadelphia, Theodelphia, Oxyrhynchus, Thebes, Coptos and Syene, so that about the middle of the fourth century, according to Harnack, Egypt already had a million Christians and a hundred bishops and seemed almost won over to Christianity. We say almost because, at both ends of the social ladder, among part of the Greek and Roman intelligentsia and among a certain number of peasants, paganism lingered on for a long time, even after its official prohibition by the emperor Theodosius.

By winning over the bulk of the Egyptian fellahin, Christianity was to make great strides and become in practice the religion of Egypt. Such a sudden and far-reaching transition deserves explanation.

After all, it was not so very evident that Egypt was at all events to become Christian. The Christianization of the intelligentsia could be expected to take place by a natural, or at least acceptable, evolutionary process (since in such circles one was more ready to accept the new religions than to reject them), but it was quite different with the Egyptian peasantry. The peasants did not change gods like doctors. Moreover, since it was essentially from this poor, illiterate, rural class that the anchorites and monks were recruited, it is very important to know why they became monks.

Certain it is that in broaching so complex a problem one is very liable to error and approximation. The documents listed to date are far from shedding complete light on the subject (Coptic Christianity had few historians and there are still a number of texts to be found and archaeological excavations to be carried out) and, in particular, these documents but rarely concern the milieu which interests us here, namely that of the Coptic peasant. It cannot be denied that for an Egyptian peasant of the third century to become a Christian it meant not merely adopting a new religion but also implied more or less renouncing the old religion, with its images, symbols and ancestral rites. Between the *more* and the *less* lay the whole true range of Christianity in those times and the need for adjustment with a stupendous past so as to break with only certain of its requirements; in short, the Copt had to be given the impression that he could become a Christian *while remaining an Egyptian.*

The words *Christianity* and *Christian* had for the Coptic peasant a sense quite different from that which we attribute to them. From one end of the *orbis romanus* to the other, moreover, every converted country quickly formed its own picture of Christ, so that the history of the Church in the first six centuries was a continual struggle against heresies, a constant effort to impose upon all an identical view of Christ. The weight of the past had a profound influence on the religious sensitivity of Christian Egypt and it is evident that there was always in Coptic Christianity something foreign to our own experience. This is shown by the fact that when the Copt was able freely to choose his own form of Christianity he chose a very equivocal, heretical form: Monophysism, which from the end of the fifth century became the national religion of Egypt.

It may be wondered whether the Copts were not already heretical without knowing it, in the third century, at the time of their conversion, and whether the future history of Christianity in Egypt, in the fifth and sixth centuries, would not explain that of the third and fourth centuries. For, on later becoming Monophysites, the Copts were in no way aware of having changed the nature of their faith but, on the contrary, were confirmed in their conception of Christianity and their vision of Christ. It is very well known today that if the Egyptian peasants and monks adopted Monophysism and defended it against orthodoxy, sometimes at the cost of their lives, it was not because they had any particular light to shed upon the relationship between the Father and the Son (the great subject of the Monophysitic quarrel) but for much simpler reasons. For a fifth century Copt, becoming a Monophysite meant first choosing Egypt in preference to Byzantium and resisting the increasing inter-ference of Byzantine emperors and bishops in the problems and religious destinies of the Church of Egypt. The theological quarrels were most often the pretext for deeper quarrels (the only ones capable of having any real effect upon the illiterate peasantry), viz. political disputes which combined national sentiment with religious feeling. In the case of Egypt, Monophysism provided the means of putting into execution secession from Byzantium and of escaping once for all Byzantine imperialism which, to the Egyptians, was nothing but the old Graeco-Roman imperialism in a new guise.

Could not such an explanation be applied also to the story of Egypt's sudden conversion to Christianity (for a conversion may be termed sudden when it operates in one generation and wins for Christianity a population which had not changed its beliefs for four thousand years)? Why should not that conversion also have been a reaction due to Egyptian nationalism, quite natural in a land and people always in revolt against Hellenism? Could not Christianity have been, for the Egyptian peasant, a way to avenge himself upon a pagan culture and a pagan intruder, always considered by him to be foreign, a way to assert himself as an Egyptian against the pagan Roman Empire? Robert Amelineau, the principal historian of Christian Egypt, has answered these questions very clearly in his work on Coptic Christianity. He shows that the mass conversion of the peasantry to Christianity coincides with the great revolt by Egypt against the demands of Diocletian. These same peasants who had first rebelled against the Roman legions found themselves again facing Roman authority ten years later, but this time *as martyrs* at the time of the great persecution ordered by Diocletian throughout the Empire. In the rebel and martyr is found once again that identity of antisocial behaviour indicated in the previous chapter. The faith of the Egyptian peasant had nothing in common with that of the intelligentsia and that less solid faith of the urban middle classes. It was a firm faith, deep-seated in the individual, since the new religious feeling was intermingled with national sentiment. And for proof? At the time of the great persecution by Decius in 250, a generation earlier, when Christianity had touched only the urban middle classes of officials and small landlords, living solely *by and for* the Roman Empire, their beliefs had been put to a severe test. When persecution, such as that of Decius occurred, all the new converts immediately denied their faith,[1] whereas at the time of Diocletian's great persecution, the whole of Egypt refused to renounce its beliefs. Eusebius of Caesarea draws attention to the fact that even in the remotest villages of Upper Egypt there were mass executions and horrible massacres. In short, it would certainly appear that the extensive Christianization of Egypt may be explained as much by political motives as by religious considerations. The new religion was, for the Egyptian peasants, a historic opportunity

---

[1] 'The defection was widespread,' writes Dionysius, bishop of Alexandria, who himself narrowly escaped death. 'A large number of high-ranking persons and officials on their own account approached the Roman authorities. Called by name and invited to make sacrifice, they stepped forward, livid and trembling, as if they themselves were about to be sacrificed. Those with greater assurance ran towards the pagan altars, protesting that they had never been Christians.' (It is known that the Romans compelled all whom they suspected of being Christians to sacrifice a victim on the pagan altar. They were then given a *libellus*, or certificate of sacrifice. The first *libelli* issued in Egypt date from the end of the second century.)

which, paradoxically, enabled them to rediscover an ancestral Egypt and set it against an Egypt in Greek and Roman bondage.

As already described, the Christianization of Egypt could appear to be a rational process, the logical—one might say calculated—reaction of a population enslaved for hundreds of years and determined to have done with the pagan forces and values of the foreign Authority. But this was true only in the collective sense. Individually considered, the attitude of the Coptic peasant—whether it was a question of his conversion to Christianity, his becoming a Monophysite or leaving for the desert—was in the first place a spontaneous impulse, contrary to all rational principle. To this must be added the strangely irrational atmosphere which had persisted in the East for three centuries: belief in the imminent end of the world, the need for ascetic rivalry, the distress felt by men faced with the chaos of a universe in its death-throes and a society deemed corrupt for all time. Who knows whether, in this general confusion in the minds of the third century, the final persecution by Diocletian, which followed so closely upon the Egyptian uprising, the systematic killing which gave its name to the Great Persecution, did not appear as the obvious sign of the collapse of the world, the last chance offered to humanity to break with a reality to be henceforth unlivable?

It was in any case during those distressing years at the beginning of the fourth century that the first signs of renunciation of the world and flight into the deserts were seen. Just when the revolt broke out against Diocletian, St Anthony had left his village to shut himself up for twenty years in the fortress of Pispir, by the Nile. And it was when Diocletian's terrible persecution was raging that the soldier Pachomius was baptized and in his turn shut himself up in a hut, in Upper Egypt.

These events were not coincidences, for it was through the anchorites Anthony and Pachomius, and their imitators, that the course of Christian history was later to be set. Everything which so far, for lack of adequate individual testimony, could have been known only through impersonal documentation and had provided the setting for a collective undertaking (the Great Transition in Egypt, in the light of the Christian message) was, thanks to Anthony, Pachomius and so many others, to become an individual record, made up from the personal accounts, texts, words and thoughts of those who lived through these events and witnessed them, a record which had its beginning in a village chapel in Thebaid, when a young man of twenty, named Anthony, having listened to the Gospels, suddenly bethought himself that God no longer dwelt within the urban communities and that he must be sought in the remoteness of the desert.

HISTORY	CHRISTIANITY
100	
ROMAN EMPIRE OF HADRIAN	Christianity spreads throughout the Mediterranean.
Antonius	Martyrs and heresies.
150	
Marcus Aurelius	*Gnosticism. Encratism. Marcionism. Montanism.*
Commodius	
200	
Septimus Severius	
Caracalla	202-257 Great persecutions throughout the Empire.
Alexander Severius	
250	
Gallienus	*Manicheism.*
Aurelian	
284-305 DIOCLETIAN	
300	303-304 Great Persecution by Diocletian.
312-337 CONSTANTINE	
	313 Edict of Milan: FREEDOM OF CHRISTIAN WORSHIP.
Rule of Christian Emperors	
	End of persecutions.
	325 Council of Nicea condemns *Arianism.*
337-361 Constantius and other sons of Constantine	
350	
361-363 Julian the Apostate (pagan)	
363-378 Valentinian Dynasties	
379 THEODOSIUS	380 Christianity proclaimed State Religion.
	392 INTERDICTION OF PAGANISM THROUGHOUT THE EMPIRE.
395 Death of Theodosius	
400	
BYZANTINE EMPIRE	

EGYPT	LITERATURE
Hadrian's visit to Egypt.	
Gnostic sects in Alexandria.	
	190 Pantaenus and later Clement of Alexandria at the Catechetical School.
251 Birth of Anthony.	202 Foundation of School of neo-Platonism in Alexandria. Plotinus.
286 Birth of Pachomius.	
	Origen.
295 Revolt against Diocletian.	
305 *Anthony retires to the desert.*	
315-325 Arius preaches in Alexandria.	
318 *First Pachomian monasteries.*	
333 Birth of Shenute.	Theological works and polemics by St Athanasius.
346 Death of Pachomius.	
356 Death of Anthony.	356 *Life of St Anthony by St Athanasius.*
Macarius the Elder at Skete.	374-379 *Life of Paul of Thebes* by St Jerome.
385 Cassian and Evagrius Ponticus in Egypt.	390 *Life of St Hilarion* by St Jerome.
388 Palladius in Egypt.	395 *History of the Monks of Egypt* by Rufinus.

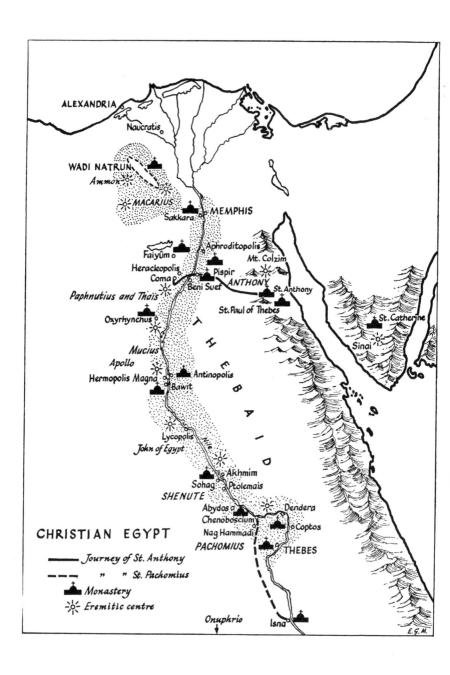

ALEXANDRIA

Naucratis

WADI NATRUN
Ammon
MACARIUS

Sakkara   MEMPHIS

Aphroditopolis

Faiyûm
Heracleopolis   Mt. Colzim
Coma   Pispir   ANTHONY
Beni Suef   St. Anthony

Paphnutius and Thaïs   St. Paul of Thebes

Oxyrhynchus   St. Catherine

Mucius   Sinai
Apollo
Hermopolis Magna   Antinopolis

Bawit

T H E B A I D

Lycopolis
John of Egypt

Nile

Akhmim
Sohag   Ptolemais
SHENUTE

Abydos   Dendera
Chenoboscium
Nag Hammadi   Coptos
PACHOMIUS   THEBES

CHRISTIAN EGYPT

———   Journey of St. Anthony
- - -   "   " St. Pachomius
⛪   Monastery
☀   Eremitic centre

Onuphrio   Isna

E.G.M.

4A. DEATH OF ST. PAUL
OF THEBES

4B. ST. ONUPHRIO

4C. SHENUTE OF ATRIPE

5A. ST. MACARIUS AND ST. ONUPHRIO

5B. ST. MACARIUS THE ELDER

THE GOD-POSSESSED

CHAPTER 3

THE STAR OF THE DESERT

DID ST ANTHONY EXIST?

It is a well-known fact that mythical characters leave behind them as many traces and are the source of as much literary material as those who have actually existed. The Greeks who followed Alexander set out to conquer the East and it was ever their belief that what they found in the foreign territories which they overran bore traces of earlier conquests by Dionysus and Heracles. They mixed the present with the past and the real with the imaginary to the extent of finally attributing the success of the conquest to their favourite god or hero, whereas the achievement was due entirely to their own efforts. For the Greeks—and probably for all ancient peoples—mythological influence was so strong that they would doubt their own existence or the reality of their surroundings, rather than contradict a truth affirmed by a myth!

On the other hand, it often happened that any historical character who, as a conqueror, inventor or legislator, had played an important part in civilization, was remembered only if he became mythical. As mythical characters finally 'take possession of' history, so historical characters become in the end an integral part of the great mythological cycles. Thus, Minos, Priam, Agamemnon, Orpheus and Lycurgus lived on the borderland of myth and history. The tendency of the mind *in the long run to prefer myth to history* in order to explain the origin of great historical events did not vanish with the coming of Christianity. The teaching of Jesus, which used examples from the Past (the great Prophets and the Scriptures) rather than the present, and referred to a mythical future (the End of the World and the Last Judgement), excited the imagination of contemporaries by its constant reference to models and facts not belonging to the present. Therefore, as the teaching spread through the Roman world and reached different peoples, greater emphasis was placed on the Saviour of the world, invested with a universal mission: 'the fulfilment of the Prophecies' and the announcement of the impending New

Kingdom of Heaven, than on the Master who had taught men to live in brotherly love *on this earth*. Such a tendency, in so far as it testified to man's systematic doubting with regard to himself, was certainly disastrous. Attributing to gods or heroes rather than to men the origin of everything which a man considered essential in the concrete or spiritual aspect of life: fire, speech, writing, laws, corn, wine, the domestication of animals, etc., probably explains why, in the first century of the Christian era, it would have been thought sacrilegious to attribute to a man—and not to a god—the revelation of the powers of the Faith.

Now, the powerful influence of the myth upon the human mind was clearly brought out, paradoxically, by those very people who, in the nineteenth century, attacked Christian history and the teaching of Jesus in the hope of finding the stamp of a man and not of a god. The methods of exegesis applied to the Gospels at that time soon revealed that it was impossible to make use of them as purely historical testimony to the life of Jesus. They gradually showed themselves to be works intended to spread a religious truth (the Messiahship and Divinity of Christ) in certain quarters of the *Diaspora* and not objective, historical accounts of the exploits of a person called Jesus. In short, the scientific methods of exegesis finally set the seal upon the already detailed character of the Gospels and the inventiveness of men in the field of narrative. And it is not so much the God as the man in Jesus that they killed, for everything in his life, his miracles and his teaching became mythical in the end. In addition, certain great Christian saints, in so far as they were imitators of Jesus, also shared his posthumous fate, and became mythical figures. Having shown men the value of Asceticism and Solitude, St Anthony became subject to the general rule applying to the pioneers of human adventure: certain nineteenth-century historians—Germans for the most part—saw in him, in his life and asceticism, a myth and nothing more. It was, of course, an exaggerated point of view but, in St Anthony's case, it brought out evidence which would otherwise have passed unnoticed. What is this evidence?

The only contemporary text on Anthony, the *Life of Anthony*, was written in Greek by St Athanasius, the bishop of Alexandria, during one of his two long stays in the deserts of Egypt, in 356 and 366, at the time of the Arian crisis.[1] This famous work, which gave the East and the West as a whole much to meditate upon and played such a decisive part in the expansion of monachism, had, until the nineteenth century, always been regarded as a biography of Anthony. Moreover, its original title was:

---

[1] 356 is the more probable date, since a Latin translation of the *Life of Anthony* by Evagrius of Antioch was already in circulation throughout the East by 370.

The Life of our father Anthony by Athanasius, bishop of Alexandria.[1] At a later date, certain historians (including Reitzenstein) showed that the *Life of Anthony* did not in fact belong to the realm of biography but to that of aretology (from the Greek *aretos*: virtue, and logos: speech, which may be translated as *edifying dissertation*), a form of writing which was very fashionable for several centuries in pagan Antiquity and which complied with precise rules of literary composition. Its aim was not to provide historical and objective testimony to a man's life but to offer the reader an edifying picture of ideal life; which is almost to say that it was the literary expression of an *ideal* model of behaviour and it was employed for the Lives of the pagan sages as well as for those of the Christian saints. The main literary processes in the *Life of Anthony* are to be found in an identical form in the Lives of sages of previous centuries, and some exegetists considered it to be a pure and simple imitation of such pagan Lives as *The Life of Apollonius of Tyana*, written by Philocrates about the middle of the third century, *The Life of Pythagoras*, written by Iamblichus early in the fourth century, The *Life of the Sophists* by Eunapius at about the same date. In these *Lives*, the sages, and later the saints, control the elements, dispel plagues, tame wild beasts, effect miraculous cures and exorcize spirits, and this makes it possible to place in proper context all the miracles, diableries and wonders which crowd the *Life of Anthony*. They are present only to fulfil the author's purpose: to edify rather than to describe, to set up a vivid picture of life in the desert, rather than to make a detailed report of the saint's activities. The *Life of Anthony* could not dispense with the literary conventions essential to any *Life* of a sage or saint: astounding miracles, great rhetorical passages on virtue and wisdom, recourse to the marvellous and the supernatural, and attacks by fiends. In short, it is the 'why' of the *Life of Anthony* that explains the 'how', and not the reverse. It must be understood that there is nothing Christian in all this fund of miracles and temptations, of conversations with angels or powers of exaltation. For the public of the day, whether pagan or Christian, no *Life* of a sage or saint could possess an *edifying* value unless it had first the quality of *amazement*, and conformed to the laws of the aretological 'genre', as strict and binding as the literary conventions which apply today as, for example, in the detective-story. Ferdinand Lot is therefore right, in a sense, when he states in his *End of the Ancient World* that

---

[1] Not *Saint Anthony*, as given in the subsequent translations, since Anthony was canonized much later. It should be made clear that in this book the term *Saint Anthony* is used when it is a question of the historical character and *Anthony* alone when, as here, his life is being recounted.

'hagiography was, in its early stages, an inferior form of literature, akin to the present-day serial-story'.

Once the edifying purpose of the *Lives* of saints is allowed, it cannot be inferred that they do not contain their share of history or truth. Nobody would dream of denying the existence of Pythagoras or the Greek sophists, even if their lives, as told by Iamblichus and Eunapius, have a disproportionate amount of the marvellous and the fantastic. Everything goes to show that Anthony did exist. It is stated in his *Life* that he undertook two journeys to Alexandria and that he took a definite stand against the Arian heresy; these facts have been confirmed by other sources. There certainly existed in the desert of fourth-century Egypt a character called Anthony, who was an uneducated Copt, but endowed with great wisdom and intelligence, and who devoted himself to a desert life of asceticism sufficiently spectacular to impress his contemporaries and prompt Athanasius to write about it. But it is equally certain that this historical character had little in common with that in the *Life of Anthony*. The proportion of historical fact contained in this Life must be estimated from the text itself and from the author occasionally, in all the detail that can be elucidated from the deeds, places and circumstances described. It is from this obscure, unconscious aspect of the work, amid the myth and legend, that can be gleaned the true story of the Anthony later to be called in the synaxaries the Star of the Desert.

What was this call of the desert in the fourth century? Quite simply, it was hearing someone say: 'Set out for the desert!' Of course, the speaker might be unseen. In that case, it was rather a question of the voice of God himself. But always, whether the appeal came from the multitude, from a friend or from God, it was a voice heard and obeyed which made the call. This concrete sense of the term 'call' no doubt supplies an explanation why, in the course of the first centuries of Christianity, certain expressions in the Gospel played so important a part in the lives of the early Christians, not merely by reason of their content or import, but because they were heard and felt as a personal appeal made to each one. It must not be forgotten that the teaching and propagation of the Gospel in those days were undertaken wholly by word of mouth, especially among the thousands of ignorant Coptic peasants converted to Christianity, and that for that reason the words of Jesus, his talks with the disciples, assumed greater significance than if they had been written in the third person. For all who, in those times, became monks or hermits, it was *the very voice of Jesus speaking to them*.

It was therefore not surprising to find the great hermits—Anthony, Pachomius and Paul of Thebes—setting out for the desert just as the result of a phrase from the Gospels, a phrase in which Jesus spoke directly to them.

One day, in church, Anthony heard the voice of Jesus say: 'If thou wilt be perfect, go and sell all that thou hast, then come and follow me.' At that time Anthony was but a youth. He had been born twenty years earlier, about 251, in a village of Middle Egypt called Coma, near Heracleopolis, of a wealthy Christian family. It is worthy of note that the two founders of Egyptian anchoritism and monachism, Anthony and Pachomius, belonged to well-to-do sections of society. In that respect they were quite different from those who followed their example, but it is precisely because they were rich that they were responsive to the words of Jesus quoted above. What did Anthony do? He sold all his possessions (his parents having died shortly before this time), distributed his wealth among the poor, keeping back only a small sum for his young sister, and turned his back on the world. So began the experiment in solitude and asceticism.

At first, it was an experiment in part only. Anthony did not leave at once for the desert. He first settled in a spot close to his native village, living there with an old man who had practised asceticism for many years. That was the current tradition: in the early centuries it frequently happened that men and women engaged in asceticism in their own homes or near their own towns and villages. Sometimes too, other people came to stay with them and formed themselves into small ascetic groups. So it was in Egypt in Anthony's day. Since asceticism was as much a mental discipline as a physical exercise, every beginner first placed himself under the guidance of an older experienced ascetic. It was only a custom, and not a rule, but it was a significant habit: one had to obey others before claiming obedience to God alone.

For some time, therefore, Anthony followed the orders of an old man and his first temptations date from this time. These temptations were fairly commonplace, not to say feeble, by comparison with those he was to experience later in the desert. It is because the word temptation covers many different possibilities and in fact has several meanings. For the moment, it is sufficient to note that these well-known temptations (which are perhaps all that we know about Anthony today) were, in any case, second-hand accounts from the pen of Athanasius. With the exception of one letter, no authentic text about Anthony remains, and the problem here is somewhat analogous to that of Plato and Socrates. Athanasius knew Anthony, at least for a time, during his first sojourn in the deserts of Thebaid when he lived with him, and it is likely that Anthony felt impelled to talk to him of his asceticism, his struggles and his experience

55

as a solitary; but it is practically impossible to discover what remains of these utterances from the *Life* written by Athanasius. Athanasius (who was Greek) was far more cultured than Anthony (who never studied pagan literature or philosophy) and, what is more, spoke and wrote Greek, without anyone's being aware if he knew Coptic or not.[1] In short, Athanasius's education and personality, and the aretological objectives which he set himself in writing the *Life of Anthony*, present many obstacles to a knowledge of the real Anthony.

Anthony underwent his first temptations, then, when he lived in seclusion near his village. He had not completely broken with society, since he often received visitors and went himself to see ascetics in the neighbourhood; which furnishes an explanation of the nature of his temptations. The Devil reminded him of 'the possessions he had left behind, the care he should have shown his sister, pride of race and love of riches, the pleasurable sensations to be found in life. Moreover, he drew his attention to the immense difficulties and hardships to be experienced in the exercise of virtue, to the weakness of the flesh and the many years he had to live; in short, he created as it were a dust-cloud of thoughts in his mind.'[2] This cloud stayed with the Ascetic like a continual remorse or regret for the past. So far the Devil was no more than a familiar, vibrant voice heard by the Ascetic within himself, mingling with his thoughts and urging his return to society. Therefore, the better to resist, he decided to leave the old ascetic one day and bury himself more deeply in the solitude of the desert.

THE EXPERIENCE OF DARKNESS

Why the desert? At first sight the question may seem absurd. Beyond the immediate vicinity of the Nile, Egypt was nothing but a vast solitude and anyone who cut himself off from the life of the towns was inevitably reduced to living in the desert. That was already happening, in the Roman epoch, to the peasants, slaves and criminals who fled from the inhabited areas in order to escape drudgery, taxation, their masters or the clutches of the law. But their stay in the desert was only transitory. In Anthony's case, his departure meant something quite different, for it was not so much the solid reality of the desert that attracted him as its symbolical reality.

---

[1] A passage in the *Life of Pachomius* shows that the festal letters of Athanasius were translated into Coptic so that they could be read in the monasteries. Why did he not write them in Coptic if, as is sometimes stated, he really knew that tongue?

[2] *Life of Anthony* by St Athanasius, translated by Arnauld d'Andilly.

Like all the anchorites who later imitated him, Anthony lived at a time and in a place deeply imbued with symbolism and biblical imagery. The whole of the surrounding material reality: desert, sky, sound, light, the everyday sensations, possessed symbolical value and meaning, seeing that in one way or another they had served as a framework for some episode in divine history. The desert was, first and foremost, an unwelcoming, sweltering place, where nobody could lead a normal human existence. There, man was naked, caught between earth and sky, exhausted by day and chilled by night, the prisoner of an abstract landscape, which bore no similarity to the familiar world. The desert was an inhuman place. But what did a Copt mean by *inhuman*? He meant: a place peopled by creatures other than men—by angels and demons. In the desert no man could live unless helped by God or his angels, no man could stay there without sooner or later having to face attacks from the Devil: he had to live with Miracles and Temptations. But through association with angels men came to be like them. What the men of the desert lost in humanity they gained in angelic properties and it is understandable that the Byzantine painters who depicted these men of Egypt on the frescoes of monasteries in Cappadocia or Greece should have represented them as beings half savage and half angel: they were given emaciated faces, tattered clothing, hair hanging down to their feet, but also the look of people lost in contemplation of another reality and flesh which was hardly substantial. All conventional Byzantine art aimed at making the great Ascetics, not impassive creatures, phantoms or illusions, but beings already belonging to a sort of humanity different from that of ordinary mortals and half-way to the other world. In all, the desert was the setting for a supreme experiment, a trial inevitably leading man out of himself, towards the Angel or the Beast, the Devil or God.

Origen, who for a long time directed the famous Catechetical School of Alexandria and was one of the most outstanding figures of the third century gave a clear explanation of the meaning of life in the desert when he compared the latter to the cave described by Plato in his *Republic*. Any man who is concerned with the truth must spend time living in the desert because by so doing he is enabled to glimpse the reality of the other world. All the illusions and phantasmagorias which crowd the *Lives* of hermits, the weird figures, the angels, demons and supernatural creatures which continually appear and disappear, make the desert a veritable *shadow-theatre*, in which the ascetic first perceives only the pale image of God: his angels and the visions he concedes, but which sooner or later enables him to grasp the extreme reality where

57

there is nothing between him and God. Time spent in the desert gives expression to the same symbol as Plato's cave—that of a temporary sojourn in the land of illusion—and this Anthony was to do in a very literal sense. Where was he to go after leaving the old ascetic of Coma and where live shut up when he reached the desert? He chose a place of darkness and phantom spirits—a tomb.

When he had taken his leave of the elder and the other ascetics, 'Anthony set out for distant sepulchres. He asked a friend to bring him bread at long intervals, entered one of the sepulchres, closed the door behind him and stayed there alone.'

With fasts, abstinences and sleepless nights, Anthony devoted himself to a life of strict asceticism in the tomb. Already, while he was in the company of the elder, his vigils had been such that 'he frequently passed the whole night without closing his eyes. He never ate more than once a day, after sunset, or on alternate days; and he took nothing but bread, salt and water. When he wished to rest a little, his bed consisted of plaited reeds and a hair-shirt, but most often he lay naked on the ground.' Here, in the gloom of the sepulchre, he was also to experience something still more terrible, which affected him as a social being: deprivation of all contact with his fellows.

It must not be thought that this solitary confinement was invented by Anthony. Shutting oneself up in a tomb for several months for the purpose of meditation was a form of asceticism already practised in pagan Egypt. It was a somewhat limited practice, which never reached the state of an institution but which had sufficient support to establish a particular class of recluses known as *katochoi*. These *katochoi* (from the Greek, meaning both 'withdrawn' and 'inspired') were priests in the service of the god Serapis and lived inside the great temple of Memphis —the Serapeum—and never saw the light of day. Some historians have been concerned to show that these *katochoi* were the forerunners of the desert anchorites, but there is no reason to suppose any direct link between these two forms of asceticism. Egypt has always shown a liking for underground caves and hypogea, for life that is dark, still and silent. These practices, whether pagan or Christian, are in any case inseparable from the Egyptian mentality, its obsession with eternity and concern to preserve for all time the physical and spiritual integrity of man. Stillness, silence, long fasts and vigils, are elements of asceticism which give man a 'living-death'. As he nears a semblance of death and approaches the frontiers of the beyond, it is perhaps possible for him to penetrate its secret and come near to hidden understanding. In a second-century text, the *Philopseudes*, to which we shall return later, Lucian of Samosata describes a pagan Egyptian sage called Pancrates, 'a great scholar, versed in all the Egyptian doctrines, *who had stayed for twenty-three years in an underground cave* where he had been initiated by Isis into the mysteries of magic'. The long sojourn in the caves, the introspection, the silence and meditation in the darkness, were a form of initiation or trial practised in the course of certain mysteries. Unless one sees in it a direct influence, there is therefore nothing surprising in the fact that Anthony—by birth and temperament an Egyptian—should in a Christian setting have made use of a form of asceticism current in, or at least known to, the Egypt of the Pharaohs.

Where, however, his experience differed from that of pagan recluses was in the fact that his purpose was not 'the revelation of magical secrets' or the acquisition of esoteric knowledge. On the contrary, he sought to forget all secular knowledge and abolish personality. Far from changing him into a 'living corpse', the experience gave him enlightenment and his trials in the darkness compelled him to fight Evil, to engage in daily, apocalyptic combat against demoniac forces.

It was in the tomb that Anthony suffered his most remarkable temptations, which have so impressed readers of his *Life* through the centuries. When one lives alone, without food or sleep, in the gloom of a sepulchre, it is quite natural that one should be tempted, should see rising up the hostile images of a world so forcefully rejected. And what sort of sepulchre was it in which Anthony lived? It was a hypogeum, one of those vast tombs in which the Egyptians buried their mummies and the walls of which were covered in frescoes and texts describing the Kingdom of the Dead: the judgement of the departed by the court of Osiris, and especially, from the time of the New Empire, the nightly journey of the Sun in the Am-Duat, the Infernal Regions, the Realm of the Dead. Let us dwell for a moment on those pictures.

Here one is faced with a strange coincidence: for what has occasioned the greatest surprise in the readers of the *Life of Anthony* down the ages is especially the riotous imagination displayed by Anthony (or was it Athanasius or the Devil himself?) during the temptations, those many strange shapes assumed by Evil to frighten him. Such imaginings were the exact counterpart of those shown by Anthony's pagan ancestors when they pictured the human, divine or monstrous creatures which peopled the land of the dead.

The wealth of imagination concerning what was monstrous, or just demoniacal and divine, was one of the chief characteristics of Egyptian civilization. To take an example: it was believed in Ancient Egypt— especially at the time of the New Empire—that, by night, the Sun

passed through the land of the dead, known as the Am-Duat. This
region was divided into twelve parts or *hours*. Each of these hours was
inhabited by an ill-assorted crowd of gods, spirits and dead men, each
of whom accompanied the solar barque (for the god sailed on the river
which flowed through the Am-Duat). Consider the figures of the third
hour, for example: there were ninety-seven of them. In the middle, on
the subterranean stream, there was the vessel carrying the Sun-God,
Amen-Ra. (Now he had the head of a ram but he changed his appearance
for each hour of the night!) Before him stood the cow-goddess Hathor.
There were three attendant barques: the first of these bore the pilots,
'their flaming faces stuck with knives', and the 'Oarsman of oarsmen',
the second and third carried a retinue consisting of snakes 'of flashing
face and eye', the *lord of the sceptre*, the *male falcon* and the *female falcon*.
On each bank, watching the divine procession, was a host of creatures.
On one side were all those who 'create the Ocean and give movement to
the Nile'; they were in order: three gods, four women, four horned and
winged mummies, four nobles, an object of strange appearance (perhaps
a papyrus stalk), in reality a living creature since it was called *he who is
full of magic*, a kneeling man named *he who brings awakening*, Anubis,
a ram dubbed *the slayer of his foes*, two eye-bearers (one male and one
female), the ant-eater god Set and a cynocephalic (in Egyptian mythology the cynocephalics are the doorkeepers of the Kingdom of the
Dead). On the other bank stood *those who cut out souls and imprison
spirits*. There were the god Orion, a god named *The Occidental*, a goddess
which rides the flame, five bird-headed creatures carrying knives, eight
Osirises and the ram-god Chnûm. There was a similar pageant for each
of the remaining hours of the Am-Duat! And these were only the gods
and creatures most in evidence, on the river-banks. Afar off, in the murk
of this strange world, the Sun-God's brilliance, like a searchlight sweep-
ing through the darkness, lit up nightmare creatures: the dead, buried
up to their necks in the sand, snakes set up on long legs like stilts, the
dragon Apophis on a high place which he gripped in his coils, men lying
decapitated or bound upon the ground (the 'enemies' of the Sun) and
others that could hardly be discerned, buried under hillocks of sand.

This funereal scene was not only visual; in any hour of the Am-Duat
was a multitude of sounds accompanying the divine craft as it sailed
along. There were cries of joy from the dead while the Sun passed
through their 'hour', followed by their groans and lamentations when
he left them, the noise of strife as the god's escort fought the enemy
lying in wait: serpents and dragons. There was the combined clamour
of the inferno: the squalling of cats, the buzzing of bees, the bellowing

of bulls, the cries of birds, each god or creature giving voice according to its kind. By a strange coincidence this is the description given by St Athanasius of the noises which accompanied the appearance of the fiends in Anthony's sepulchre: '"Let us make ready to attack Anthony in another way," said the fiends, "since it is quite easy for us to invent various kinds of mischief to do harm to men." Thereupon, this infernal band worked up such a din that Anthony's whole dwelling was shaken with the noise, and when the four walls of his cell gaped open the demons crowded in. Assuming the shapes of all sorts of wild beasts and snakes, they immediately filled the place with figures of lions, bears, leopards, bulls, wolves, asps, scorpions and other snakes, each crying out in its particular way: the lions roared as if intent on devouring him, the bulls made as though to gore him and the wolves to leap at him, the snakes slithered over the ground and darted towards him. The appearance of each of these creatures was as cruel as it was fierce and their hissing and crying were horrible to hear.'

Beyond doubt, such was the source of the fantastic ballet which, in Anthony's state of hallucination, was staged by the creatures that haunted his vigils and his fasts. For nearly two thousand years this nightmare circus had been inseparable from the Egyptian psyche. The gods of ancient Egypt became the fiends and phantoms which pestered Christian Egypt, by a transposition which has its counterpart in many other religions. According to popular beliefs on which there is no need to dwell, the old sacred monuments of Egypt, in particular the tombs— those deserted, desecrated tombs which were to house so many ascetics and anchorites—were naturally considered to be the haunts of ghosts and evil spirits. One such antique monument was the abode of 'a demon known as Bes. Many people had seen him capering about in the temple; occasionally he even came out and struck the passers-by who, as a result, became blind, crippled, deaf or dumb.'[1] Ghosts and demons which were none other than the ancient Egyptian gods reduced to the level of phantoms and which the Copts called *n'ter*, a term which formerly stood for pagan gods.

THE EXPERIENCE OF LIGHT

Anthony was to spend several months in this tomb, where he withstood the repeated attacks made by demons, and so violent were they that he felt his body was being beaten black and blue and he then lay unconscious on the ground for several hours.

[1] Adolphe Erman.

When he considered that he had meditated sufficiently in the gloom and had completed the trial by darkness, he left the tomb, came out into the light and set off for a remoter spot, where he might remain alone for all time.

On leaving his sepulchre which, it will be remembered, was in the neighbourhood of Coma, Anthony walked into the desert in an easterly direction and eventually came to a deserted Roman fort overlooking the Nile near a place called Pispir (the present township of Der el Memun). During this journey, he was tempted several times by the Devil. These were very ordinary temptations which, by comparison with those undergone in the sepulchre, showed a surprising lack of imagination. The Devil set in the ascetic's path a 'huge bowl of silver' and bars of gold. Obviously, it is always possible to furnish a rationalist explanation of this temptation: the 'gold' and the 'silver' were only a desert mirage, one of those countless brilliant stones with which the Egyptian desert is strewn and which Anthony mistook for gold during his exhausting journey in the heat of the sun. In reality, the gold plays a symbolic part here, with the object of testing—*at the very time of the Ascetic's leaving the world for ever*—his detachment in respect of this world's goods, represented in their most precious form: gold and silver.

Anthony, in any case, disdained this useless luxury, so insolently displayed in the open desert, and continued on his way. At last, on the bank of the river, he discovered the place where he was to live: a deserted fort.

'It was full of reptiles, but they made off at once as if they were driven out, and Anthony made it his abode and filled up the entrance. He had brought with him a six months' supply of bread (the Thebans knew how to make bread which would keep for a year), and there was water inside the enclosure. He went into this fort as if into a sanctuary and there he remained alone, never leaving it or seeing any of those who came to visit him. This discipline lasted a long time and he accepted bread only twice a year, when it was passed to him over the wall.'

A long time, indeed; it was exactly twenty years. During all that time he saw nobody, took nothing but bread and water and slept for only two or three hours each night. Anthony was alone, beneath the scorching sun or the starry sky. After the trial by darkness, he underwent that by solitude, engaging in the same struggle with the forces of evil. The struggle was carried on openly, in repeated attacks and phantasmagorical contests, the noise of which reached the ears of the terrified visitors obliged to remain at the gate (since Anthony refused to admit them). Anthony, surrounded by apparitions among which it was very difficult to distinguish the good from the bad, lived, prayed and fasted in this shadow-theatre. (For the anchorites, was not desert life as a whole an apprenticeship in the secret laws of an unseen universe?) For twenty years he undertook what might be termed the experiment of the Real and Illusory: to distinguish from among the many shapes which, by night or in daylight, his disordered mind conjured up around him, those which were the true signs from God. For the demons, 'inasmuch as they were ineffectual, seemed as if they were acting on a stage, putting on different faces and assuming many ghostly shapes to startle children, which testified to their extreme powerlessness and caused us to scorn them all the more. On the other hand, the good angel sent by God against the Assyrians did not need to be supported by a great crowd, to borrow strange forms or to create a great clamour, but, in the calmest way imaginable, killed a hundred and eighty-five thousand men in an instant.'

Let us pass over the strange criterion employed by Anthony in distinguishing the good angels from the demons. When, after twenty years of solitary asceticism, he had sufficiently tested himself by contact with the unseen world, he felt he was ready to have disciples and provide instruction. But, in the end, the hosts of visitors who came to him in spite of the hardships and dangers of the desert succeeded in weakening his determination to be alone. One fine day, instead of keeping them at the gate in his usual way, he decided to see them and speak with them. Then, for the first time, 'he was seen outside his stronghold by those who were coming towards him, and they were filled with astonishment to see him in as robust a state of health as he had ever enjoyed. He was not stout, as a result of lack of exercise, nor had he lost weight through fasting and fighting with the demons. His face had not changed and he had the same calmness of mind and pleasantness of manner as ever. He was neither downcast nor overjoyed, his expression was neither too cheerful nor too stern. He showed no evidence of displeasure at being surrounded by such a great throng of people or of satisfaction at being greeted and held in reverence by them. His demeanour was perfectly well-balanced and quite natural.'

He formed his band of disciples from those who decided to renounce the world and gather around him. The foundation of the first Christian community in Egypt dates from this time—approximately AD 305. This community was not yet a monastery, but at best a group of anchorites, subjected to an asceticism and a way of life which were relatively free. This first community Anthony established on the banks of the Nile, not far from the fort of Pispir, near the present town of Der el Memun.

Anthony's reputation in Egypt at this time was very great, reaching all levels of society and not merely confined to a handful of fervent admirers. People flocked to the Pispir 'monastery' and lay down across the entrance in the hope of seeing the Ascetic appear, of having him speak to them and cure or exorcize them. Already it was rumoured that an immediate cure could be effected if one but went near Anthony's 'monastery'. But Anthony would have nothing to do with the crowd, miracles or with glory; he decided once more to go further into the desert, 'to a place where he was known to nobody'.

In spite of some substantial facts, the last part of Anthony's life, after the age of sixty, hardly forms a part of human history.

After leaving his Pispir companions, Anthony stopped on the Nile bank, with no clear notion where he would go; and suddenly he heard a heavenly voice telling him to make his way 'to the inner desert'. Some Bedouins were passing at this moment, and he followed them, coming eventually to the eastern bank of the Nile near the foot of Mount Colzim by the Red Sea, at the eastern end of the mountain chain known today as Gebel-el-Galaza. There, when he had reached the height of medita-tion as well as the summit of the mountain (and it is not a play on words, for the parallel between material ascent and spiritual elevation is main-tained throughout the *Life of Anthony*), he decided to stay there for the rest of his days.

Jean Coppin, a French traveller of the seventeenth century, visited and described this famous spot where Anthony made his abode and eventually died. After leaving Cairo and travelling for several days through the desert, he came to the Wâdi Araba, at the foot of Mount Colzim, and then to Anthony's cave:

'The entrance is not more than two feet wide and four and a half feet high. This opening goes for some eleven yards into the rock but does not widen out so that two men could not pass through it abreast. At the end of this passage there are three stones placed one on top of another in a crevice of the rock to act as descending steps, and when we had gone down them we found ourselves in a cave almost circular in shape and large enough to hold about thirty people. The whole face of the rock is very high and rises naturally sheer as a wall. It continues in this way for a distance of some three or four hundred yards. The area is bare of wood, barren and rocky, traversed by a path which makes several turns, since

6A. ST. PAUL THE SIMPLE

6B. A DESERT ANCHORITE

7A. ST. HILARION

7B. ANCHORITES

it would be impossible to climb straight up it. From this spot we could observe the Red Sea lying to the east, but because it was so far distant it looked to us like a cloud resting on the ground.'[1]

This is a rather harsh description, which contrasts strangely with that in the *Life of Anthony* and that later to be given by St Jerome in his *Life of Paul of Thebes, the first Hermit*. In the *Life*, Anthony's retreat is described as a heavenly spot, an Eden miraculously preserved from the surrounding barrenness:

'At the foot of the mountain was a limpid fountain of extremely good and very cool water. Below, there was a plain, with a few natural palm-trees. As if from divine impulse, Anthony conceived an affection for this place, because it was the kind of spot indicated by the voice which had spoken to him on the river-bank. He accepted the offer of loaves from the Saracens with whom he had shared the journey, and then remained alone on the mountain, believing the place to be the abode chosen by destiny especially for him. Seeing how satisfied he was at being there, the Saracens later returned by the same route and joyfully brought him the bread. He obtained some assuagement also from the fruit of the palms.'

Begun in the dark depths of a tomb, Anthony's life as an ascetic ended in this lofty, sunlit spot, from which the Red Sea appeared as 'a cloud resting on the ground'. After his victories over Evil, he lived a virtually angelic existence, and all the episodes in his earlier life were relived in reverse: darkness became light, temptations changed to miracles, demons gave place to angels. Even the wild beasts sent by the Devil to attack him in his sepulchre at Coma, became in Colzim the meek companions of his daily life: 'At first, the wild animals which came to drink at the spring often damaged his plants and seedlings. He gently took possession of one of them and said to all the rest: "Why do you do me hurt, seeing that I do you none? Begone, and in the Lord's name do not return." And, as if this command had put them to flight, they never did return.'

The sky itself filled with angelic visions. Seated on his mountain, Anthony could watch through the clouds a panorama depicting events which nearly always held some premonitory message: unknown people coming towards him through the desert, the soul of his disciple Ammon ascending into the heavens in the company of angels; sometimes, he

[1] Jean Coppin: *Egyptian Journey* (1686).

saw himself raised up by the angels. He heard conversations being carried on by unseen speakers and witnessed strange sights: one day, when he came out of his cave, he observed a bright phantom of terrible aspect, whose head touched the sky, trying vainly to hold back the souls of the just from ascending into heaven, or the whole earth suddenly enclosed in a net spread by the demons.

The very peculiar atmosphere that surrounded Anthony's last years, the endless visions of a heaven peopled by angels and permeated by the souls of the departed, the phantoms and the demoniacal nets covering the earth, all irresistibly conjured up a picture of the Last Judgement as a man like Anthony might imagine it. Henceforth the spectacle was seen in heaven as often as on earth. Moreover, when the heresy of Arius was obtaining a hold over Egypt, Anthony left his cave and set out for Alexandria with the purpose of denouncing the peril and stated, *'This heresy is one of the last to precede Antichrist'*.

On the mountain to which he had retired, and living like Adam in paradise, he had already been accepted into heaven as a companion of the angels. And when he died, a little later, his body was saved from misplaced adoration by the living, for Anthony insisted that his disciples should bury him in a secret place, known only to them.

Apart from the *Life of Anthony*, from which the foregoing episodes are taken, there are hardly any other sources of information on the doings of this saint. The Coptic *Apophthegms* which are attributed to him (*apophthegm* is the name given to short utterances made by the ascetics) are merely a plagiarism of the speeches made in his *Life*. It is the same with the other *Lives* or other texts attributed to Anthony. A review of the Jacobite Arabian synaxary alone supplies material complementary to the life of Anthony, but it is of much later date. The Coptic synaxary, on the other hand, has preserved an abstract of the Coptic *Life* of Anthony which reveals a few differences from the Greek *Life*. These differences concern the episodes themselves less than the manner of their presentation but, through them, the reader will be able to appreciate all that divides the Coptic from the Greek. In spite of the brevity of the text, here one has the impression of being nearer to the Old Man of the desert, the true Anthony.

'When Anthony was twenty years old, his parents died. He gave to the poor the wealth they had bequeathed to him. He had a sister, whom he entrusted to the care of the nuns. He liked devotion and solitude. The term "monachism" was not known, but whoever wished to be alone went out from his village and gave himself up to his devotions. That is what great Anthony did. And Satan attacked him with the weapons of sloth and tedium: he placed beside him the double of a woman as his companion, and Anthony bore with it all.'

So Anthony withdrew to his tomb and 'Satan ordered his minions to go to him in various shapes, as wild animals, wolves, lions, snakes and scorpions, and they each attacked him to bring fear to his heart, but he laughed at them and said: "If you had any power over me, one of you would suffice." And so they went away, defeated, and dispersed like smoke, and he was left untroubled by suffering and temptations. He baked his own bread twice a year and put it to dry in the sun. Nobody might enter his abode, but remained outside and hearkened to his words.'

And as Anthony died on Mount Colzim, January 18, 356, at the age of a hundred and five, the synaxary adds: 'He lived to a ripe old age with no lessening of his vitality. He did not lose a single tooth'.

CHAPTER 4

THE FIELD OF THE SAINTS

'The existence of Paul of Thebes has been denied because he lived in hiding', writes St Jerome at the beginning of the *Life of Paul of Thebes, the first Hermit*. This was a necessary literary precaution but it did not prevent St Jerome's contemporaries or modern critics from continuing to hold doubts about the actual existence of Paul of Thebes. The life of this mysterious saint has provided historical criticism with many puzzles and they still remain unsolved. In fact, for once, everything tends to make one believe that Paul was a mythical character. There is never any mention of Paul of Thebes in the *Life of Anthony*, and even supposing that a man called Paul withdrew to the deserts of Thebaid some years before Anthony, there is little to connect him with the one described and magnified by St Jerome. Here, the aretological intention is so clear that the work cannot be taken literally.

Many commentators have even attributed malicious intentions to St Jerome. Jealous of the success of the *Life of Anthony*, he in his turn, it is thought, decided to write a saint's life and created the character of Paul of Thebes from nothing, letting him set out for the desert before Anthony so as to dispute the originality of the latter's undertaking. As a matter of fact, St Jerome wrote his *Life of Paul of Thebes* about 374-379, when he himself was living in retirement in the desert of Calchis in Syria, to the east of Antioch, and therefore some years after the Latin translation of the *Life of Anthony* by Evagrius of Antioch. In many respects Paul's life of asceticism is just an intensified copy of that of Anthony. Let it be made quite clear that no historical document mentions the existence of this Paul of Thebes, except a petition addressed in 382 to the Valentinian emperors, Theodosius and Arcadius, by the people of the town of Oxyrhynchus in Middle Egypt, and speaking of a 'blessed Paul who formerly lived in Thebaid, was as famous as Anthony and whose feast is still celebrated'. That is all that is known of him, and it is little enough.[1] All the rest, that is the *Life of Paul of Thebes the first Hermit*, is entirely due to St Jerome, but it is not possible to determine whether he indulged in a pleasant literary 'leg-pull' or whether, in all good faith, he turned to account documents known only to him. Moreover, that is not the problem. It may even be conceded that the absence of all historical fact makes St Jerome's venture still more exciting, for we can thus observe the actual birth of a myth and an ideal type of man, the desert saint. Here is found the creation of the pure material of fable, and the *Life of Paul* may fairly be considered the most theoretical, but also the most perfect, model of the life of a saint. It is from this time, also, that the theme of the *desert saint* makes its appearance in Greek, Latin, Coptic and Syriac literature, just as that of the *noble savage* graced the work of the French philosophers of the eighteenth century. It is easy to see that in this connexion the historical authenticity of characters like Anthony or Paul of Thebes matters less than the influence they exerted through their half-fictitious, half-authentic *Lives*. In view of the upheavals brought about in the East and the West by the barbarian invasions, the fall of the Roman Empire, the difficult birth of the Byzantine Empire and their effect on people's minds, the *Lives* of the desert saints supplied the comforting picture of a few men, outside the temporal world, leading an artificial existence (since it was already an anticipation of eternity or paradise) in desert places where the turmoil of wars did not reach and where only the voices of angels were heard.

The angels' voices are continually found in the life of Paul of Thebes. They are present with every detail of his existence and, like the fairies around the cradles of princes and princesses, from his childhood they create the best conditions for one day becoming a great saint: wealthy parents who die young, so permitting Paul to dispose of his inheritance and to take a vow of poverty (for, in order to be poor in the desert one has to be wealthy in the towns—that is the 'founders' ' tradition), a married sister, a pagan upbringing and training which avail him nothing and which he rejects along with his sister and his possessions.

At the age of fifteen, Paul of Thebes set out for the desert. This precocity should be noted: Anthony did not hear the 'call' until he was twenty, whereas Paul heard it when he was fifteen. So, back through adolescence to childhood, and we find the great saints leaving for the

---

[1] There also exists a Coptic *Life* of Paul of Thebes, but it seems to be just a translation or an imitation of the Latin *Life*. At least, that is R. Amelineau's thesis in his study on *The Coptic Lives of St Pachomius, St Macarius and St Anthony*.

desert at ten or even eight years of age. Already the legend was taking shape and compelling recognition.

After several days' walk in the desert, Paul came to Mount Colzim (to which Anthony withdrew), near the Red Sea, and there discovered a cave, a heavenly spot: the deserted den of a gang of conterfeiters of Anthony and Cleopatra's day. Some tools, an anvil and hammers littered the ground. Nearby, a palm-tree and a spring provided Paul with the necessaries of life: water, food and clothing. Jean Coppin writes:

'This cave is almost circular in shape and the water coming from the rock is held as if in a basin. We found some a foot above the ground and that was all there could be, since, below that level, there are openings through which the water drains away into the rock from which it comes. We also saw that the Red Sea was less than a league distant and we went up to a higher point to have a good look at it. It is about twenty-one or twenty-two miles wide as seen from the cave and we were told that it was here that the Israelites crossed it. As the day was very clear, we could see on the other side the twin peaks of Mount Sinai, although we were more than twenty leagues away. The sea lies to the east of this monastery. A few heights were observable to the west, with a little woodland, but very far off, and everything else within view was quite barren and scorched.'

It was there that Paul of Thebes lived for a hundred years, a hundred years of a quasi-miraculous existence, although St Jerome found nothing unnatural in it:

'The palm-tree of which I have spoken provided him with all that was necessary for food and clothing, and this must not be thought impossible since I take Jesus and his angels to witness that, in that part of the desert which borders on Saracen lands and adjoins Syria, I saw some solitaries, one of whom had been a recluse in a cave for thirty years and lived on nothing but barley-bread and muddy water, and another, living shut up in a tank, existed on five figs a day.'

No doubt, Paul of Thebes lived on less than that. In this cave he led an angelic life of which the world would have known nothing if, a short time before his death, God had not informed Anthony of Paul's existence. Anthony was then ninety years old, but he immediately made up his mind to go in search of him. After this episode the *Life of Paul of Thebes* becomes a kind of waking dream in the open desert.

First of all, where did Paul live? Anthony did not know and set out at random. But, for an Anthony living in the desert, this meant setting out under God's guidance. Providence watched over him and pointed the way in strange fashion:

'At daybreak, St Anthony began to walk, not knowing where, and by the time the sun had reached its zenith the air was so hot that it seemed to be on fire. Then he saw a creature which was half horse, like those which the poets call Centaurs. As soon as he caught sight of it, Anthony made the sign of the cross on his brow and called out: "Ho! Where in these parts dwells the servant of God?" Then the monster, with uncouth mutterings and disjointed, vague utterances, strove to produce sweet sounds from a mouth bristling with hairs and, stretching forth its right hand, pointed out the desired road. Then it vanished before the eyes of him who had been filled with amazement. As to whether the Devil had assumed this form to terrify the saint or whether the deserts, so prolific in monsters, had produced it, I can give no assurance.'

The reader will have noted that the Centaur appeared at high noon. Noon was the hour at which the demons always made their appearance when they wished to tempt the ascetic, to cause him to worry and feel regret at having turned his back on the world. In spite of appearances, Anthony's Centaur was none other than a *noontide demon*, one of those countless forms of temptation due to solitude endured in the blazing sunlight.

Thanks to the signs made by the monster, Anthony came to the foot of a mountain. He saw a cave, deep and dark, and in its depths a light was shining. It was the abode of Paul of Thebes. Face to face at last, the two aged men, in the middle of the desert, engaged in the following remarkable dialogue:

' "I am he whom you have sought with such difficulty and whose long white hair, encrusted with filth, hides a body shrunken with age. I am that man, about to turn to dust. But, since charity finds nothing difficult, tell me, I pray you, of the state of the world. Are new buildings being made in the towns? Who is in the seat of power at this time? And are there still men so blinded with error that they worship devils?" During this speech they saw a crow alight on the branch of a tree and then swoop gently down to the ground, placing before them a whole loaf of bread. Then it was gone. Paul began to speak: "See how God, merciful and truly good, has sent us food. Every day for sixty years I have received half a loaf in this manner, but since you have come Jesus Christ has doubled my portion as a sign of the care vouchsafed to those who do battle in his service." Then, when both had given thanks to God, they sat at the edge of a crystal-clear fountain and, each wishing to confer upon the other the honour of breaking bread, they entered upon an argument which lasted until vespers, Paul asserting that custom and hospitality required this civility to be shown by him, and Anthony declining on account of Paul's superiority in years. At last, they decided that both of them should hold the bread and pull it, and that each should have the part which broke away in his hand.'

Thereupon, after a night spent in prayer, Paul of Thebes bethought himself that his end was nigh. He asked Anthony to return home to his monastery to find something suitable for a burial. Anthony set out again (for the Pispir monastery, no doubt). He took a tunic and returned with it to Paul's cave three days later. There, he saw 'the figure of the saint kneeling on the ground, his head raised and his hands stretched up towards the sky. He thought at first that he was alive and was at prayer, and he knelt down to pray with him. But, not hearing him sigh as was his custom while he was praying, he went to kiss him and became aware that, in an attitude of devotion, the holy man, though dead, was still praying to God.'

Anthony took the body out of the cave to bury it. But how was it to be done? The soil was hard and he had nothing with which to dig. And then by chance (for everything was chance in the life of Paul of Thebes, and even in his death),

'two lions ran out of the heart of the desert, their long hair streaming above their necks. Anthony was afraid at first but, commending his spirit to God, he became as calm as if they were doves. They came straight to the body of the aged saint, stopped and, caressing him with their tails, lay down at his feet. Then they began to roar loudly so as to show him that they were praying for him in the only way they could. Next they fell to clawing the earth a short distance away, vieing with each other in throwing up the sand to both sides and so making a hole large enough to hold the body of a man. Immediately afterwards, as if asking to be rewarded for their work, they came towards Anthony, lowering their heads and wagging their ears, and licked his feet and hands. Then Anthony, realizing that they were asking for his blessing, raised his hands to heaven and said: "Lord, without whose will not a leaf falls from a tree and not a tiny bird dies, grant to these lions what thou knowest them to need." And, signing to them, he commanded them to leave.'

So died Paul of Thebes, much as he had lived. An angelic death.

A SAINT AMONG MEN: PACHOMIUS

The life of Pachomius, the founder of Coptic monasticism, takes us into a very different sort of world. Wonders and angels continue to play an important part, but they no longer constitute the only material for the saint's actions. The life of Pachomius is primarily the daily toil of a man determined to found the first Christian monasteries in the desert. The idea seemed so strange to his contemporaries that they considered it to have been inspired by an Angel.

In spite of its miraculous setting, the life of Pachomius gives the impression of a much greater authenticity than that of Paul of Thebes or Anthony. Why should this be so? There is an essential reason: the life of Pachomius has come to us through Coptic texts and the Coptic language (the mother tongue of all the 'founder' Saints, Anthony, Pachomius, Macarius and others) describes the facts and the men in a much cruder and more concrete manner than do Greek and Latin. It is above all a language of testimony and description, rather than a strictly literary medium. It lends itself much less readily than Greek to philosophical speculation and infinitely less readily than Latin to oratorical effect. What is more, Coptic was a language of translation before it became a language of expression: translation of the New Testament, the Lives of the martyrs and the countless apocryphal writings that were in circulation in Egypt from the second century onwards It was only when the first *Lives* of Pachomius were to be produced (about the beginning of the fifth century) that the Coptic tongue became a literary language properly so-called. In so doing it lost nothing of its original qualities, but remained serious, direct and thrilling in its terseness. This effect of concrete detail, of laconic expression, of plain fact, enables the Coptic writers to restore to us the spirituality of Christian Egypt a thousand times more effectively than the Greek or Latin authors, and that is why reference will be made to them rather than to the Greek writers. The Coptic language goes straight to the heart of things and people, whether it describes a dragon, a man or an angel.

The *Life* of Pachomius has come down to us in a great number of versions written in various Coptic dialects: Bohairic and Memphitic (the Delta and Lower Egypt); Akhmimic (Middle Egypt) and Sahidic (Upper Egypt).

These *Lives,* as revealed by Mgr Th. Lefort, present as a whole a certain number of variants. The matter cannot be given undue consideration within the scope of this book. It must suffice to consider Mgr Lefort's most recent conclusions and to quote extracts from the oldest, or Sahidic, version. Moreover, despite all the variants, these *Lives* agree on the essentials: the principal episodes in the childhood of Pachomius and his Code. From them can be constructed, on fairly reliable historical bases, the amazing existence of the first of the monks.

Pachomius was born in the year 286 in the village of Esneh (now Isna) in Upper Egypt, some thirty miles from Thebes. Unlike Anthony's, his was a pagan childhood, but as one would be reluctant to admit that a future saint could, even in innocence, have worshipped idols, his *Life* makes it clear that he only appeared to do so. He vomited every time he took the sacrificial wine, his stomach rejecting all sustenance offered to the idols. At twenty years of age, Anthony had the revelation of a life consecrated to God, but the opposite is true of Pachomius: he was consecrated to God *without even knowing it.* The contrast is observable in even the most factual details: Anthony heard the voice of Jesus, whereas Pachomius, on going into a pagan temple at the age of eight, heard no voice: the idols stopped speaking and prophesying. The call came to Pachomius for the very reason that *the pagan voice became silent in his presence.*

Not in the least surprised at so many wonders, Pachomius continued to grow up: when he was twenty years old, he was pressed into service in the Roman army and stationed at Antinoe. There, for the first time, he learned of the existence of people called Christians, who devoted themselves to others and suffered martyrdom rather than renounce their faith. Pachomius was impressed by their generosity and kindness. He eagerly sought their company and decided about this time to consecrate himself to the God of the Christians.

Two or three years later, when he had completed his military service, young Pachomius went south again and eventually came to Sheneset (*Kenoboskion* in Greek)

. . . 'an almost deserted village, lying in the broiling sun. He began to think about this place: there were few people living there. He made his way along the river to a small temple which the Ancients called Pmampisarapis (the place of Serapis), stood up and prayed, and the spirit of

God urged him, "Make this your abode and do battle." It pleased him to do as he was bidden and he settled there. He grew a few vegetables and some palms to provide food for himself and the village poor, or for strangers who might pass that way by boat or along the road.'

It was in this virtually deserted spot that he was baptized, but he soon decided to go elsewhere because of the excessive number of strangers who stopped to see him. He wondered where he should go. Then it was that he heard of an 'experienced ascetic' named Palemon who lived in the neighbourhood.

Palemon was living in retirement not far from Khenoboskion, on a hillock in the desert near the small Greek city of Diospolis Parva. Pachomius proceeded to this place and knocked on Palemon's door.

'The old man at once showed himself at the window and saw him. He said roughly, "Why do you knock?" His tone was rather abrupt. Pachomius answered, "I should like you to take me in." At first, Palemon took much asking. "What you seek," he said, "is no trivial thing. Many a man has sought it and failed to find it. They could not endure the life. In summer I fast every day, and in winter I eat on alternate days. I take nothing but bread, water and salt, and I rarely sleep." '

Faced with such a 'programme', Pachomius became even more insistent and in the end Palemon accepted him. Pachomius did not give up; he remained with the elder for seven years.

In these seven years he was schooled in asceticism, obedience and humility. To the fasts already mentioned was added lack of sleep, an essential point. 'Doing without sleep', 'staying awake', 'keeping vigil', were recommendations constantly urged by the great ascetics, and obviously they were to be taken in the literal as well as in the figurative sense. Sleep lured the ascetic into a world of illusion and error, into the realm of Satan. Every hour of sleep hindered his spiritual liberation. Sleep was restricted to the bare minimum and, if possible, one did not lie down to sleep, so as to avoid dreaming and the enervating effect of repose: one slept in a sitting position, squatting or even standing with one's back against a wall. In later Pachomian monasteries this rule was strictly applied: the monks always slept *seated on low seats*, instead of lying down, and Pachomius did likewise in his monastery, 'spending fifteen whole years without lying down to sleep. He used to stand in the middle of his cell, without relief except by leaning slightly against the wall, a great ordeal which he bore with the utmost patience.' This discipline in wakefulness was undertaken in the presence of Palemon; in the evening, when he returned to the desert mound at Diospolis Parva after a day of prayer and fasting, he would lie down to sleep, but Palemon compelled him to stand up and he sent him to walk for hours in the desert, carrying stones so as to abolish the temptation to sleep. For sustenance, they had water, bread, salt and cooked herbs, to which Palemon added a '*small admixture of ashes to make it more unpalatable*'.

A further detail is important: the ascetic prayed in a standing position, motionless, with his arms folded across his breast. This attitude, intended in the first place to counteract sleep, later became very common and itself constituted a particular act of asceticism, which might be termed a *stance*. This stance consisted of remaining motionless for as long as possible, with arms folded or raised and, sometimes, a load on one's shoulders. The symbolical sense of this attitude can be understood: the ascetic assumed the stillness and silence of the dead and so lost all awareness of the outside world. One day, in Syria, a certain James of Nisibis, adopting this attitude, became buried in snow without realizing it. A strange coincidence should be noted here: it was in a tomb that Pachomius first imagined the following form of asceticism:

'One evening, in the deserted village where he lived, he went underground. He placed a brick beneath his feet, stretched out his arms and, in tears, prayed to God throughout the night. The brick on which he was standing broke down because of the sweat from his body which ran over it. Indeed, there was great heat in this underground place.'

Unlike Anthony, Pachomius did not linger in the tombs. Nearly always, he practised his asceticism in the open air, in lonely spots not far from Khenoboskion and Diospolis Parva, places which were visited and closely observed by Mgr Th. Lefort, Pachomius's biographer, and more recently by Jean Doresse. The latter has noted that these places have, even to the present time, preserved the living memory of the saint:

'In the neighbourhood of Es-Seiyad (Khenoboskion), not far from the Nile, a high, massive enclosure of solid, white walls contains a few churches and chapels huddled together and overtopped by a strange-looking pinnacle with clerestories: it is the Deir anba-Palamun—Father Palemon's monastery. Further inland, near Debba, there is a similar building: the Deir el-Malak—the Angel's monastery. Between these two, which today have no monks, there lies a small inner desert which, according to the Coptic texts, was the site of the first monastic work by

Palemon and his disciple: there is still a hole to be seen there which, according to the legends, was a hermitage.'[1]

A little further off, half-way up the great wall of rock at Gebel el-Tarif are tombs of pharaohs, those where, on the authority of Mgr Lefort, Pachomius spent some time. Some of them bear Coptic inscriptions and others pagan *graffiti*, since 'this spot, for reasons which are not clear, was particularly revered in Greek and Roman times. Today, too, at the bottom of the slope, a crude shrine, distinguishable on account of the votive cakes and some large stones, shows that it is still a hallowed spot.'[2]

So lived Pachomius, in this place inhabited at all times by gods, demons and spirits, and he would perhaps have stayed all his life with Palemon if one day when he was alone in the desert he had not met an angel.

THE MEETING WITH THE ANGEL

The meeting with the angel is one of the most famous incidents in the life of Pachomius, although there is no reference to it in any of the older versions. The Sahidic version merely states that he 'heard a voice coming out of the sky' and the Bohairic *Life*, written at a much later date, speaks of 'a bright figure'. Obviously, it is a question of a belated addition intended to justify and—by giving it divine significance—to consecrate one of the most disputed aspects of the Pachomian undertaking: the founding of the first monasteries. But first the 'facts' must be reviewed: 'One day it happened that, as was his custom, young Pachomius set out across the desert, through the large, dense forest of acacia-trees. Moved by the Holy Spirit, he went on for about ten miles until he reached a deserted village called Tabennisi, on the river-bank. It occurred to him to enter this village and offer a prayer. While he was praying, a voice spoke to him out of the sky, saying 'Pachomius, make this your dwelling-place and build your home here. Many men will come to you and it will be good for their souls.' In later versions, the event is more precise in detail: an angel appeared to Pachomius, gave him his instructions and held out to him a tablet of bronze containing the Rule for his future monasteries.

This desert of the Revelation, as it might be called, was situated near the village of Tabennisi, on the west bank of the Nile, and not far from

[1] Jean Doresse, *Les Livres secrets du Gnostique d'Egypte* (Plon), p. 148.
[2] *Ibid*, p. 150.

the ancient town of Denderah. It was here that Pachomius settled in order to follow out the angelic instructions. It was here that he founded his first monastery some time later.

This episode of the angel is a direct illustration of the remarks made at the beginning of the preceding chapter. Every time that some discovery or some example of human initiative was fraught with consequences to mankind, people immediately attributed its origin to a god, a spirit or a hero. To the cases already indicated (writing, fire and language) must now be added that of the laws. The responsibility for the laws was almost always attributed to gods and this tendency is also to be found in Hebrew and Christian traditions. The Ten Commandments and the Rule of Pachomius were of divine inspiration. Moses on Mount Sinai and Pachomius in the heart of the Tabennisi desert received from the hands of God or the angel the stone or bronze tablets, on which were engraved the Destiny of man and the Law by which he must live. As far as Pachomius is concerned, the biblical influence was all the clearer just because the episode of the angel was added later. It was introduced at a time when the number of Pachomian monasteries along the Nile had multiplied and when Pachomius was venerated as the Coptic Moses. The legend of the angelic tablet very quickly confirmed that the destinies of these two men were parallel. In any case, the essential fact is that at a certain moment in his life Pachomius received the revelation—or the idea—of his vocation: to lead men from the world by his own example, group them around him and institute in the desert communities dependent upon absolutely new social rules and principles. The stupendous originality of the Pachomian enterprise was the important thing: to found a society of men 'starting from scratch' and to organize their lives and relations according to an original system was so unusual that Pachomius's contemporaries and disciples considered it to be the inspiration of an angel.

What did Pachomius do after his encounter with the angel, that is to say after the revelation of that strange notion hidden within him? He hesitated. Very naturally, such an idea caused him some anxiety. The tendency of the times was towards solitary asceticism, anchoritism: any candidate for the ascetic life first placed himself in the hands of an elder and then, after a time, continued his experiment alone until he became an elder in his turn. If it happened that rumours of his miracles or ascetic exploits attracted people to him in excessive number, he retired a little further into the desert as if *permanent contact with others was a hindrance to his asceticism and his salvation.* And now Pachomius felt within himself the need to live with others, to draw others to him and to leave the 'beaten tracks' necessary to anchoritism! Could salvation really be achieved collectively? Was not the presence of other people a permanent obstacle to asceticism and meditation? The idea caused him such anxiety that he hesitated a long time before coming to a decision. One day when he was alone cutting reeds by the Nile, he received a second 'reminder' to set out along the path to monasticism. This time there could be no more hesitation and he obeyed the angel. In other words, his idea had ripened; he now knew where he was going.

In the meantime Palemon had died, and Pachomius was able to establish himself in the Tabennisi desert, where his brother, his first disciple, joined him. In company of this brother, and while receiving his first candidates for asceticism, he gave himself up to terrifying mortifications: praying in a standing position and spending long periods in the full heat of the sun while wearing cloaks. Yes, they

. . . 'would put on fur cloaks and seek out the hottest places, would spend whole nights in prayer, indulging in mortification while at these devotions. They moved neither hand nor foot, but held their arms outstretched to prevent their being overcome by sleep. In order to combat sleep they never knelt down, so that their feet swelled through fatigue, and their hands were covered in blood because they did not lower them even when they were attacked and bitten by a horde of mosquitoes. If a little sleep became necessary, they would sit down where they prayed, but without leaning against any of the walls.'

From that time, the life of Pachomius underwent a complete transformation. To be brief, the number of his disciples increased to such an extent that the temporary building constructed at Tabennisi became inadequate. Another had to be built and Pachomius chose for the purpose a spot near Diospolis Parva, where he had undergone his early anchoritic experiences. This second monastery was established near the village of Pabau which gave it its name. It was a few hours' walk from Tabennisi.

There is no need to state that the demons looked unfavourably upon this strange man's undertaking. Were they to allow Pachomius to defy them and raise up celestial cities in the open desert, their own territory? On the day when he laid the first stone of his monastery, his temptations began, and they never left him. While he lived alone with his brother, the demons had sought to tempt him, but the Devil had evinced unwonted poverty of imagination: for instance, when Pachomius was about to kneel down to pray, 'the demon created beneath his feet a sort of pit so that he might feel afraid and refrain from praying to the Lord' or, when he sat down to eat, the demons 'came to him in the guise of naked women who sat down to eat with him. Then the holy man would close his eyes and his heart until they vanished.'

When Pachomius, giving up his solitary life, attempted the difficult task of gathering disciples around him, his temptations appeared in another form. It was not only the Ascetic that was to be tempted, but also the leader of men. Did it ever cross his mind, even for a moment, that he was a Leader? Just as he entered his monastery, the demons, in mockery, began to march before him as if ushering in a magistrate, saying, 'Make way for the man of God!'

Did discouragement lead him to think that so remarkable an under-taking might serve neither God nor man and risk being exposed as useless? Immediately

... 'a crowd of demons assembled and, forming into groups on all sides, pulled at a growing leaf with a show of effort and encouraged one another to make the attempt, as if it were a question of moving a stone of tremendous weight. This the wretched spirits did with the sole purpose of making him laugh and giving cause for reproach.'

For, in the desert, a laugh (or even a smile) was sufficient to destroy the benefit accruing from long periods of asceticism and mortification. To laugh, if only for an instant, was to become associated with the questionable delights of the profane world, to fall into the snare of the 'age' and be unmindful of one's salvation. To the demon, the ascetic's laugh was an indication that the man was no longer on guard against himself and that it was possible, by means of this relaxation, to get into him. On this earth, a smile on the face of an ascetic foreshadowed the grotesque grimace of the damned soul. That is why a laugh or any other indication of a lack of seriousness was severely forbidden in the monas-teries and the hermitages, for it is like an open door to the demon. In the desert, everyone had to meet assaults with the stern, *tight* expression of a man on his guard against the pitfalls of laughter. What is more, as for the other 'lapses' of which the ascetic might prove blameworthy, laughter might be a sign of pride, of excessive self-confidence. To what extent might an ascetic be justified in feeling proud of himself or pleased with his asceticism or undertaking? Pachomius himself gives a surprising answer in this episode: 'When Pachomius had completed the building of the Muchonse monastery, which had been fitted with pillars, he felt pride in his work, which he considered beautiful. But the fear

8A. DESERT ANCHORITES

8B. DESERT ANCHORITES

8C. MONASTERIES OF THE WÂDI NATRÛN

9A. DESERT ANCHORITES

9B. MACARIUS THE YOUNGER

came upon him that this feeling might be due to vanity and he hastened to shift the pillars so that they leaned to one side and, as a result, the structure was more misshapen than pleasant to behold.' That is one explanation of Coptic art of which the critics never thought. Who knows, indeed whether certain aspects of this art, the crude and often distorted faces it depicted and the absence of every aesthetic consideration in its architecture, might not be the result of a perfectly conscious suppression of the beautiful? Who knows whether the ugliness, the lack of symmetry in this art and what is thought to be its clumsiness, were not felt by the Coptic 'artists' to be so many means of salvation, a sort of *artistic asceticism* in which the suppression of beauty was of a piece with the rejection of the body in physical asceticism?

THE ANGEL'S RULE

From the founding of the first monastery at Tabennisi until Pachomius died of the plague in 348, he devoted himself wholeheartedly to the organization of cenobitic life. The term 'cenobitic' is here used intentionally. The cenobite (from the Latin *coenobium* (community)) was any man of those times who lived as a member of a community, whereas a monk was a man who lived alone. Later, the term 'monk' was also used to denote a member of a community and became synonymous with 'cenobite'. But in the days of Anthony and Pachomius there was a clear distinction between the two forms of existence. The word 'monastery', as it was almost always used by translators of the Lives of the two men must not be misunderstood: most often it represented a cave or unpretentious hut of branches in which a solitary lived. For the sake of convenience, however, the word will always be used here with the generally accepted meaning of a building which houses a community of monks.

Before his death, Pachomius completed his cenobitic work and founded nine monasteries. They were all situated between Thebes in the south and Akhmim in the north, with the Khenoboskion or Tabennisi region as the centre, the place where Pachomius had undergone his early trials. After those of *Tabennisi* and *Pabau*, he founded in succession the monasteries of *Sheneset* (the Coptic name for Khenoboskion, already mentioned), that called *Muchonse*, near Sheneset on the left bank of the Nile, then, further north, those of *Thbeu* and *Tesmine*, near Akhmim, and, finally, *Phnenum*, in the neighbourhood of Thebes in the south. Near Pabau and Tesmine, he also founded two monasteries for women. If the year 318 is approximately the date of the building of the first monastery, it is clear that for thirty years Pachomius led a purely cenobitic existence. His experience of solitude, tombs and angels was at an end. As Pachomius saw it, a man could henceforth be a saint while living in the heart of a community.

Of what did the Pachomian communities consist? According to what principles was the life of the monks organized? Two things must be remembered first of all: Pachomius was an Egyptian, a child of pagan Egypt; and in spite of his personality and his gifts of innovation he could not have invented a type of society totally foreign to the traditional Egyptian spirit. Many of the aspects of the Pachomian communities come directly from ancient Egypt: for example, the *superiors* or *priors*, who maintained the strictest supervision of the monks' activities and who remind one strangely of the labour-gang masters of the pharaohs' days. For Pachomius's undertaking would never have met with such success if it had not taken into account the peculiar neutrality of the Coptic peasant. Nor must one lose sight of Pachomius's objective: to take Christians from the world and group them into a new society. Pachomian cenobitism could never have taken root in Egypt if he had not been aware of the characteristic partiality for the desert and the renouncement of the world shown in Egypt in those times and adapted it to his purpose. Cenobitism offered no denial of, or opposition to, anchoritism. On the contrary, it implied it. Just as the anchorite, in the desert, became one of God's rebels, so did the Pachomian monasteries become Cities of God. They claimed subjectivity to God's law (whence the legend of the angel, which transmitted God's will directly to Pachomius) and often even constituted centres of opposition to temporal authority.

How did a Pachomian monk live? First of all, one did not become a monk just by wishing to become one. The ascetic discipline imposed by Pachomius demanded proof of the applicant's sincerity and determination before he could be accepted into the community. Some of these tests, with respect to Anthony and Pachomius, have already been noted. Eventually they became a sort of ritual, much the same for all candidates:

1. shutting the monastery door in his face;
2. making him wait for several days (ten days, according to Cassian) without speaking to him on his entry into the monastery;
3. compelling him to prostrate himself and lie down on the ground before each monk who went in or out.

Once he had passed this test, the candidate was admitted and entrusted for a time to the door-keeper and then to a provost. The testing of his strength of purpose and his detachment from the world was continued. He was given the most repugnant tasks to perform, some-times he was even spat upon or he was ignored, or else he was told that his mother, his sister, his son or his brother was dying and was asking for him, so as to see if all fondness for the world was really dead in him. Of course, these tests were varied to meet individual cases. In general, they were left to the discretion of the superior. But as discipline and obedience were obvious principles and a necessary part of communal life, there is no point in discussing them here. On the other hand, the organization of the monasteries was itself much more original: the basis was the *cell* composed of three monks. Twelve cells constituted a *house*, four houses a *tribe* and ten tribes a *monastery*. The grouping of monks therefore operated as follows:

$$3 \text{ monks } = \text{ a cell}$$
$$36 \text{ monks } = \text{ a house}$$
$$144 \text{ monks } = \text{ a tribe}$$
$$1{,}440 \text{ monks } = \text{ a monastery}$$

The Order as a whole (when there were several monasteries) was under the direction of a *chief*. This chief was always Pachomius and, after his death, his disciple Theodore. Each monastery had at its head a superior or *hegumenos*, and each house a *prior* or *provost*. It was the rule to group the monks in the houses according to trades: there were houses of cobblers, weavers, tanners, stewards, joiners, locksmiths, etc. Upon this allocation, established according to fairly simple and logical principles, was superimposed another, which was much more complex and mysterious and which was known as the 'angel's rule'. For that reason, it may be assumed that it was introduced by Pachomius per-sonally: it consisted of dividing the monks into twenty-four groups corresponding to the twenty-four letters in the Greek alphabet (since the Copt used the Greek alphabet in writing). It was long thought that this division duplicated that into houses, but it is not clear why Pachomius should have instituted a double division into houses and letters of the alphabet. The allocation to houses was made in accordance with the physical aptitudes of the monks. The division by letters, on the other hand, was to make it possible to group the monks according to their intellectual or spiritual aptitudes. The proof of this is that it was far from being an arbitrary division. The details are not all known, since most of them were contained in two letters written by Pachomius to his successors in an unknown language called the 'language of the angel' and indecipherable. One merely knows, through St Jerome, that the letter *iota*, the simplest and smallest letter of the alphabet, stood for the simple innocent monk, and that the letter *chi*, of more complex design, applied to the monks of difficult temper. Of course, no monk knew his letter. Only the chief, the superior and the priors were conversant with the code.

The asceticism practised by the Pachomian monks was also subjected to very strict rules, for it was soon acknowledged that a collective asceticism presented problems very different from those of an individual asceticism. The only danger from an ascetic life led in the solitude of the desert was pride: the pride of being able to have greater mastery than was necessary over one's body, to abolish completely the bondage of the flesh and to wish to live as an unsubstantial being while on this earth. That is why the elders so often counselled prudence, advised the novices against too great fasting, telling them not to believe themselves to be free of the demands of the flesh and always to take a very little food even against their inclination, so as to avoid pride. In the Pachomian monasteries, it appeared that another danger lay in wait for the monk: that was ostentation, resulting from fasting and self-mortification for the benefit of others, since everything was done publicly. The *Lives* of Pachomius and his disciple Theodore abound in anecdotes in which the chief is seen always to check this ostentation in asceticism. Here is one significant example: meals were taken once a day in a refectory, when the monks were served with cooked herbs, fruit, bread and water. If a monk wished to fast, he could do so only in the refectory, and a monk was frequently seen to rise from the table without having touched his food. The situation soon became intolerable, for it was enough that a monk should ostensibly refrain from eating for the others to feel guilty and accuse themselves of being too lukewarm in their asceticism. In the end, nobody dared to eat. To overcome this difficulty, Pachomius devised the plan of making the monks wear capacious hoods so that they could cover their plates and hide from inquisitive glances when eating and also be prevented from seeing what other monks were eating. Thus, in the course of the communal meals, all those lowered hoods became, literally and figuratively, a sign of humility.

Moreover, as a general rule, Pachomius was not in favour of extreme or too-frequent fasts. In a situation where it was so difficult to draw a line between pride and humility, the mere fact of refusing a mouthful of bread was ambiguous; was it done through pride or on account of asceticism? And Pachomius soon reached the point of requiring each monk to eat at each meal '*four or five mouthfuls of bread in order to avoid vanity*'.

The rules for asceticism also applied to work. Every monk was required to work and, in addition to house duties, to make a rush mat every day. This mat he placed before his cell door. One day, out of vanity, a monk put two such mats by his door. Whereupon, Pachomius shut him up in his cell for five months and compelled him to make two mats a day while he was there.

Naturally, these oppressive measures in regard to food, sleep and work were intended to facilitate the monk's mental asceticism, so that he might master the inner man and, as the anchorites had it, 'kill the worldly man'. Corresponding to these physical measures were others of a different kind intended to work upon the monk's sensitivity, his affective reactions and his individuality. For instance, laughter was formally forbidden and silence was the rule at meals, during work and throughout the day. 'Learn to keep silent' was one of the essential rules of the Pachomian communities. But nobody 'was proof against language', against the ill-timed word or the unfortunate phrase betraying profane interests. One day, Theodore, Pachomius's chief disciple, observed a monk returning from a journey. 'Where have you been?' he asked him. Pachomius was present at the time. He called to Theodore. 'Theodore,' he said, 'make haste to control your heart. Accustom yourself to never asking anyone, "Where have you been?" or "Where are you going?", except to discover where his soul is going.'

The temperament of the Coptic monks clearly found it difficult to conform to this iron discipline. Quarrels, disputes and tussles often occurred and Pachomius had constantly to repress these outbursts of pride or anger, inseparable from the Coptic temperament:

'Why is it, holy father,' asked a monk one day, 'that when I am spoken to harshly, I immediately become angry?'

'Because,' answered Pachomius, 'when an acacia is struck with an axe, it immediately pours out gum.'

When Pachomius died, at sixty years of age during an epidemic of plague, 'a great awe reigned in his cell, which shook three times. Many elders told how they saw bands of angels, grouped one above another, gaze upon him, then walk singing before him, and so it was that the cell in which he died gave forth a sweet smell for many days.'

In other words, Pachomius was 'saved' and his experiment had been successful. At the time of his death, according to an approximate estimate, the nine monasteries which he had founded must have contained between six and eight thousand monks. Cenobitism had been born and it was to make rapid progress through Egypt and then, in different forms, in Syria, Palestine, Cappadocia, Greece and the West. Born of the will to renounce the world, the Pachomian monasteries 'went back' to the world in so far as, by their importance, they came to play a great part in the religious, economic and political life of Christian Egypt. That is the most paradoxical aspect of this experiment: the decision to assume a position beyond time and History, and then finally to become a religious force whose material power in fact exerted an influence upon History. But already a clear fact was emerging, viz. that it is possible to bring about changes in a man, provided care is taken to make him live in artificial conditions (and the 'angel's rule' is, by definition, an artificial rule). At all events, the positive fact is that, when Pachomius died, there were eight thousand men outside the world, living according to the 'angel's rule'. Contemporaries were quite sure about it: the desolate places of Upper Egypt were peopled by monks, for 'something' had come to light there, a new way of life, a new order of things, which transformed the desert of Tabennisi into a 'field of saints', as one author of those days put it.

CHAPTER 5

CONTESTANTS IN EXILE—I

'When athletes of this world get ready for the contest, they obtain sustenance from profane foods and go forth to combat. In the same way, athletes of the spirit must strengthen themselves against demons by fasting and prayer.'

NESTORIUS: (*Homilies on the Temptations of Our Lord*)

THE EMPIRE BECOMES CHRISTIAN

Anthony and Pachomius both died about the middle of the fourth century. Their lives seem to have been, as it were, a continuous meditation on man and God, and were led beyond the reach of time, broken only by short-lived interruptions on the part of demons or visitors in search of miracles. Anthony and Pachomius lived, one in his 'inner desert' of Colzim, the other behind the wall of his monastery, screened from the influences of the secular world and history.

But history, all through the fourth century, knew great upheaval, the echoes of which were heard in the furthest corners of Egypt. This upheaval was the official recognition of Christianity by the emperor Constantine, the final victory of a religion attacked for three centuries: the empire became Christian, the Church became imperial. Of course, such an upheaval did not strictly coincide with the proclamation of the famous Edict of Milan. It may even be said that the phenomenon worked in reverse and that by officially proclaiming the freedom of Christian worship, Constantine merely confirmed an actual fact: the final establishment of Christianity in the *orbis romanus*. The Edict of Milan could change nothing in the Christian's spiritual convictions but it profoundly modified the material lot of the Church. It enabled the body of the faithful to feel aware of a reality not yet clearly apparent: namely, the importance of the Church as a temporal power and its historical vocation.

A thousand details, a thousand changes in the daily life of the Christians, helped moreover to bring about this awareness. One of these was the end of persecutions. The Christians ceased to be the enemies of

87

the Roman Empire, they no longer pursued their activities in secret, nor were they treated as rebels; they became officials or allies of the new Empire. There was henceforth no incompatibility between being a Christian and being a Roman citizen. Christians were seen to become 'aediles, praetors or even—although it did not involve them very seriously—flamens of Jupiter. The supreme authorities, commencing with a pagan like Aurelian (in the affair of Paul of Samosata), began to treat bishops not as robber chiefs but as highly respectable dignitaries.'[1] Almost from one day to the next, the latter became official personages whose travelling and residence expenses incurred on account of council meetings were met by the Emperor himself, so that some bishop 'who had lost a leg, an arm or an eye in the last persecution was to be found lording it in the *plaustra* of *divus Augustus*. And the whole Church went the same way.'[2] Throughout the Roman world, the spiritual and the temporal were reconciled, so that the Roman Empire, which was considered to be the incarnation of Antichrist, became the 'new Kingdom of God on earth' (Eusebius of Caesarea).

Yet, just when the 'resistant' elders of the era of persecutions accepted the gratification of collaboration with authority, there was a move in the opposite direction, towards the deserts and the ascetic existence by a great number of Christians in all walks of life: first peasants, outlaws, slaves and workmen, and then wealthy townsmen, 'men of the world' and even highly-placed dignitaries of the Empire. In other words, while one part of the Church acceded to history, another part was violent in its rejection and took refuge in the timeless life of the desert. That was not a mere coincidence. Between the two there was a cause and effect relationship which has been emphasized by all historians—from Ferdinand Lot to Louis Bouyer. 'The Church, now immensely enlarged,' writes Ferdinand Lot in *La Fin du Monde antique*, 'could no longer remain in the Society of the pure in heart, the saints who were awaiting the end of the world. Identified, or almost so, with the 'world', the Church suffered greatly from the degrading influence of life. To escape it there was only one thing to do: to live beyond the reach of the world, artificially, by seeking the desert or solitude, by leading a separate existence, either alone or in the company of others. It was not by mere chance that eremitical and monachal asceticism appeared in Eastern lands at the moment when the Church was triumphant. For monachism, as Louis Bouyer states, was undoubtedly 'the instructive Christian

[1] Louis Bouyer, *Saint Antoine et la spiritualité du monachisme primitif.* (Editions de Fontenelle, 1950.)
[2] *Ibid.*

reaction against a misleading reconciliation with the times which the imperial conversion might seem to justify', a reaction which, if it is to be understood, must be put back into the context of the Constantinian Church making peace with the world'.[1] Why? Because, before the Emperor Constantine's conversion, to remain a Christian meant to risk losing everything: life, possessions, employment. After his conversion, one could be a Christian and lose nothing. The movement to the desert was therefore a response to this new allurement, the temptation of the world and temporal authority.

Within the scope of this book, this phenomenon has also another significance: to Christian society the end of the persecutions meant the end of the ideal model, the Martyr-Saint. The need for a new 'model' was felt, so that this society might pursue its antisocial dream. The end of secret activities, together with official recognition of the Church, did not, for many Christians, mean an end to struggles against the world. These struggles went on as before, but in another form, through the agency of the desert anchorites. The latter continued in body and spirit to battle against the world which had once persecuted them but which now adopted a 'coaxing' attitude. And so the 'semblances' of lions and other wild creatures which beset the ascetics during their nightly vigils were, for the members of Christendom, basically only the *sublimated equivalent* of the beasts which had attacked martyrs in the arena. It was the same kind of combat, demanding the same physical strength and moral courage, with the same veil of secrecy to the setting for the struggle: the Anchorite-Saint took the place of the Martyr-Saint and, in the deserts, continued the combats already begun in the arenas: he was undoubtedly a *contestant in exile*.

But was this phenomenon, which was real at the individual level of the Anchorite, equally real at the collective monastic level? Was there not the risk that, with the change in the size of its scale, there might also be a change in its character and meaning? By no means. As the Christians left in increasing numbers for the deserts, an identical phenomenon was observable, the constitution of large communities to battle with the world in their own fashion: by the setting up of *artificial societies, governed by original systems which stood as the negation of those of the secular world.* It is a very interesting phenomenon, and one to be found in other periods of history wherever a society makes a sudden break with its past. The quite recent constitutions of the people's Communes in Mao-Tse-tung's China is perhaps a historic phenomenon of this order. In both cases, the break with the past amounted to a break with the

[1] Louis Bouyer, *L'Ascèse chrétienne et le Monde contemporain.* (Ed. du Cerf.)

former social systems, through the formation of communities built round a nucleus which was no longer that of the family, for instance, (Pachomian monasteries and Chinese communes). And it is clear to see to what end such a sudden break with the traditional social structures tends: the creation of a new human type, whose value and place in society are to be judged by completely new criteria. The hierarchy of the Pachomian monasteries, for example, systematically took the opposite view to the other, and vice versa. The principles which were to govern the celestial city were already being applied *on this earth*. Whereas secular society extolled the merits of individuality and favoured everything which was an expression of the Ego, the rule of the Pachomian monasteries was intended to break down that individuality, and 'reconstruct' man on new bases which implied the negation of the Ego. In the Coptic *Life* of Bgoul, one of Pachomius's disciples, who founded a monastery in the region of Sohag near Akhmim, we read: 'It happened that he gathered his disciples together and obliged them to give an undertaking in writing that they would all live in the same way, with regard to their food and clothing, and that there would be no difference between them or discord in anything they did, whether it originated in the mind or the heart.' In short, it was a quest for what might be called a *collective soul*. This was clearly seen by Louis Bouyer when he wrote, in his essay on the spirituality of early monasticism, that monachism 'developed, like a series of planned activities, the practical equivalents of the conditions which previously obtained' in the persecutions.

In other words, the Christian monk reconstructed around him, in the form of ascetic and collective restraint, the aggressive world of the old persecutions. And it was by the way he met this aggression (in which demons played the part that formerly fell to idols or lions) that he progressively built up within himself a new personality. To new social and cultural conditions there was a corresponding new Being, and it may be said that, fundamentally, monachism as it was conceived in the Pachomian communities of Upper Egypt was an unconscious method of hastening man's spiritual and biological evolution.

It should be pointed out that, in fourth-century Egypt, economic conditions favoured in the highest degree the introduction and success of this experiment in 'artificial societies'. There was nothing in the daily life of a Coptic fellah of the fourth century that could prompt him to attach himself to the institutions of the past or to a social system of which he was the chief victim. The land did not belong to him, of course, and he was practically no more than a slave in the service of the ground landlord (often a foreigner, Greek or Roman). The life he led as a peasant hardly had advantages over that which he could have as an anchorite. Many passages from the Lives of the desert saints supplied information on that subject. What, for instance, did the *Life of St Arsenius* have to say? Arsenius was a Roman of noble birth, who was for a time a high dignitary at the court of Theodosius the Great (at the end of the fourth century) and who, eventually, at the age of forty, decided to devote himself to asceticism and set out for Egypt. One day, when he was ill, his disciple laid him on a bed and placed a pillow under his head. An anchorite came to call upon him and was shocked at this 'luxury'. Then Arsenius's disciple asked him: 'What did you do before becoming a hermit?' 'I was a peasant,' was the reply.—'And how did you live?'—'As I do now: I slept on the ground, and each day I ate a few lentils, with bread and oil. But my soul was not at peace.'—'Well,' said the disciple, 'Arsenius, here, was once tutor to the Emperor's children, he had a thousand servants at his command and slept in a sumptuous bed. What a difference between his former state and yours! You had a worse life than you have now! In leaving the world, you exchanged a hard life for an easier one, whereas Arsenius gave up opulence for poverty.' Naturally, there again was an example of those edifying episodes often to be found in the *Lives* of the desert saints. But it is a good indication of the awful conditions under which a Coptic peasant lived in the fourth century: he was a slave working without respite, sleeping on the ground, sometimes without a roof over his head, feeding from one year's end to the next on beans or lentils, cooked herbs and dry bread.

It is therefore understandable why, in the early days of monachism—and with the exception of the 'founders', who were all from well-to-do families—the monks were recruited almost exclusively from the peasants, the lesser artisans and the village folk on the banks of the Nile. In general, they came from the rural and working classes. The life in the desert offered a 'solution' to the problem of everyday existence and at the same time conferred upon the former fellah *a prestige and a dignity which he could never have enjoyed as a peasant, a shepherd or a waterman.*[1]

And it is also understandable why so many slaves sought refuge in the monasteries and finally became monks or hermits. This flight to the

[1] This explains that it is always the unfortunate classes which are particularly suited to the reception of new social experiments. In the fourth century, belonging to the cultured urban society meant not only being privileged to enjoy a certain luxury but being conditioned by a way of life and an upbringing that resulted in permanent social distinction. On the other hand, each generation of peasants was just as ready to embrace radical social changes, whence their wholesale conversion to Christianity in the third century and their equally great enthusiasm for monasticism in the fourth.

desert was the cause of serious social disturbances and, consequently, of reaction by the Church in the fourth century. The Council of Gangra, for example (which took place in 342), excommunicated Bishop Eustathius and his followers for having advised the slaves to leave their masters and become ascetics. The Church, moreover, very quickly assumed the defence of the social order, the interests of the masters and the powerful. 'We shall never,' said a Canon of the Holy Apostles of the fourth century, 'allow such a thing, which brings sorrow to the masters to whom the slaves belong and which is a disrupting influence.' Later, an edict from the emperor Valens even provided for the 'forcible return of slaves in hiding among the monks'. These arrangements finally influenced hagiography itself, since Theodore, a fourth-century saint, 'possessed the miraculous power of binding the slaves with invisible ties which made flight impossible. If, despite this precaution, the master lost his slave, he could spend the night sleeping on the saint's tomb. The saint would indicate to him in a dream the place where his slave had taken refuge. It seems obvious that St Theodore preferred the masters to the slaves.'[1]

Thus, having created the model of the Anchorite-Saint, the contestant in exile and new desert martyr, and having created and developed in the Nile valley the amazing 'artificial societies', or Pachomian monasteries, Egypt, at the beginning of the fourth century, soon became a 'Second Holy Land' where 'Christian equality, based on the New Testament, the celestial City and the idealized example of the first Christian communities, were given extraordinarily vigorous expression.'[2]

But the name 'Holy Land' implies pilgrimage. From the second half of the fourth century, indeed, a host of travellers came to Egypt to visit the most famous anchorites and the principal monasteries; some out of curiosity and attracted by Christian wonders, others, on the other hand, to follow the instruction of the great ascetics, to become their disciples and bear witness to their exemplary existence.

The former merely tarried in Egypt and hardly ventured beyond the neighbourhood of Alexandria, the Wâdi Natrûn deserts or Lower Egypt. Among them were many ordinary visitors, travelling alone with a guide on camel or mule, but also many 'people of the world', wealthy Roman ladies, senators and important dignitaries of the Empire with a considerable escort. One such was that great Roman lady, Paula, the friend of St Jerome, who, with her attendants, visited the anchorites' cells in

---

[1] Anne Hadjinicolaou, *Recherches sur la vie des esclaves dans le monde byzantin.* (Institut Francais d'Athènes, 1950.)

[2] Raymond Ruyer, *L'Utopia.* (P.U.F.)

the desert of Nitria, and another was that mysterious Gaulish lady known as Etheria or Egeria, the author of a *Peregrinatio ad sancta loca,* who paid a visit to Egypt at the end of the fourth century, after her journey to Jerusalem. Yet another was the Roman noble Postumianus, who passed through Egypt in the fifth century and brought back with him many anecdotes which Sulpicius Severus put to use in his *Dialogues* and his *Life of St Martin.*

The second group, those who went to Egypt to share the anchorites' life, brought back from their visits the main evidence used in this chapter to describe the desert life of the 'God-possessed'. We are chiefly concerned here with Palladius, Rufinus of Aquileia and Cassian.

Palladius was a Greek from Galatia who went to Egypt about 388 to 390 and lived for twelve years in the desert before repairing to the Desert of Cells as a disciple of Macarius and Evagrius Ponticus. Eventually, he left Egypt, stayed for a time in Constantinople and Rome, was appointed Bishop of Helenopolis in Bithynia and returned to Egypt, where he remained until his death. In the early years of the fifth century (about 420), he wrote his famous *Lausiac History* (so called because it was dedicated to the chamberlain Lausius) which tells the life, the ascetic feats, the miracles, temptations and utterances of the principal anchorites of Egypt.

Rufinus of Aquileia is remembered for his differences with St Jerome on the subject of Origen. About 371 he went to Egypt with a great Roman lady, Melania the Elder, and stayed for six years with the anchorites of the deserts of Nitria and Skete. He wrote no personal account of his stay in Egypt, but translated from Greek to Latin the *History of the Monks of Egypt,* generally attributed to Timotheus, Archdeacon of Alexandria. (It was long believed that Rufinus himself was the author, and for convenience we shall always refer to Rufinus as the author of this famous *History.*[1]) In part, this work duplicates that of Palladius, but on certain points shows very interesting differences. It should be noted, moreover, that St Jerome himself, as a consequence of the disturbances caused by his presence in Rome and the premature death of his disciple Blesilla, made his way to Egypt in 385 and spent some time in the ascetic centres of the deserts of Nitria and Skete.

The last of the three, Cassian, in his youth lived for more than ten years with the monks of Egypt. Later, he stayed in Constantinople, Rome and Marseilles, where he became a bishop and founded two

---

[1] In the opinion of A. J. Festugière (*Les Moines d'Orient,* Editions du Cerf, 1961), the *Historia Monachorum in Aegypta* was not written by Timotheus but was the anonymous work of a group of Palestinian monks.

monasteries, one for men and the other for women, about the year 415. It was at this time, more than twenty years after his stay in Egypt, that he produced his *Institutions of the Monks* and his *Talks with the Fathers*, works which abound in solid details of the lives of the Egyptian monks and anchorites but which are of very doubtful historical accuracy. Written essentially for the monks of Provence, whose ascetic methods and spiritual directives differed appreciably from those of the monks of Egypt, Cassian's two works are much more informative about the monastic centres of fifth-century Provence than the Egyptian monasteries.

The same is true also of the texts referred to above. The *Lausiac History* and the *History of the Monks of Egypt* contain many concrete details and first-hand accounts of the anchorites of Egypt, yet they are far from being historical documents in the modern sense. The accounts by Palladius, Rufinus and Cassian bear to a very high degree the stamp of the aretological tendencies so dear to the age. The aim of these pilgrim monks was not to carry out any sort of 'report' or to investigate the exoticism of the desert. What they were seeking in the second Holy Land was above all a moral instruction, an exemplary asceticism, the sight of a miracle or of some remarkable fact which might strengthen their own faith and their own ardour. From the very first, they saw the anchorites whom they visited and whose sayings they recorded as actors in a gigantic drama, a drama enacted between the forces of Evil and the forces of Good in the solitude of the desert. And when they wrote up the episodes in this fabulous struggle they produced works which were more akin to the 'romance' or the epic than to historical record. There again, historical fact must be sought 'between the lines', from the hidden or sporadic truths to which the works testify in spite of themselves.

IN THE DESERTS OF UPPER EGYPT

When Pachomius and Anthony died, at an interval of a few years, there were already some thousands in the communities founded by these two innovators. During the fourth century their development continued along the Nile from the Delta to Syene, in Upper Egypt, originating from the two chief centres: Pispir and Mount Colzim for the Anthonian monasteries and Tabennisi for the Pachomian institutions. It is strange that there does not seem to have been much connexion between these two great sources of monasticism. The isolated Pachomian communities, in the heart of Upper Egypt and over three hundred and fifty miles south of the Delta, stayed remote from the tourist 'routes' and were even unknown to many travellers. St Athanasius, the author of the *Life of Anthony*, was one of the few people to venture as far as Tabennisi, which he did during one of his enforced exiles to the desert, and of the authors mentioned above Palladius was likewise the only one to visit the monasteries and the ascetic centres of Upper Egypt. If men like Rufinus and Cassian had got to Tabennisi, it is interesting to speculate whether their stay in the Pachomian monasteries would have supplied much information about their rules and history and the monks' daily life. What has Palladius to say on this subject?

'We also saw many other solitaries in Egypt. A great deal could be said about these admirable men and the countless numbers in the neighbourhood of Syene in Upper Thebaid, whose virtue is so far superior to that of other men that it may appear unbelievable. They still raise the dead and walk upon the waters, as did St Peter.'

The remoteness of these monasteries seems to have contributed to their legendary fame. The deserts of Upper Egypt, practically inaccessible to travellers, were reputed to contain anchorites still more amazing than those of other regions, and stories of these ascetics which began to circulate in the fifth century are among the most striking in Coptic literature. In these texts the Anchorite becomes a barely human character whose life is most often spent among animals and who flees at the very 'smell of a man'. One of these texts, discovered and translated by Robert Amelineau, is entitled *Le voyage d'un moine égyptien dans le désert* and may be considered as a model of its kind.

'There was one anchorite whose name was Paphnutius. He spoke to the fathers who loved God, saying: "I am Paphnutius and, one day, I felt moved in my heart to go into the depths of the desert to see if there was a monk there. I walked for four days and nights without food or drink. On the fourth day I came to a cave and, before going inside, I knocked on the door in the manner of the brethren so that the friar might come out and permit me to embrace him. I waited. I continued to knock until the middle of the night, but there was no reply." '

A typical scene from desert life. It was a very common habit among the anchorites not to open their doors to visitors or disciples but to let them knock for as long as possible in order to test their patience. Some texts mention disciples who kept knocking for two or three days in succession.

' "I said in my heart: 'Perhaps there is no friar in this place.' I went into the cave crying: 'Your blessing upon me father!' When I was inside, I looked around me: I saw a friar sitting there in silence. I immediately stretched forth my hand and took him by the arm. It fell to dust in my grasp. I felt over his body and I saw that he had remained in that state since his death. I looked around, and I saw a cloak. When I took hold of it, that too fell to dust. So I rose to my feet and offered up a prayer, took my cloak, covered the body and buried it. Then I went out." '

This is a theme frequently to be met with in the literature of the desert. Naturally, it was not entirely imaginary: the dry, torrid climate of Upper Egypt had the effect of desiccating and preserving the body. But the literary usage of this anecdote nevertheless reveals a typically Egyptian preoccupation: the physical preservation of the dead. What is more, it made its appearance in Coptic literature at a time when the Christians finally discontinued the practice of embalming. It was not mere coincidence.

' "I resumed my walk in the desert, until the setting of the sun. I looked around me and espied a herd of buffalo. A friar was walking with them. When he had drawn nearer to me, I saw that he wore no clothes: his hair covered his nakedness, enveloping him like a garment. When he was close to me, he became very much afraid, for he thought that I was an apparition. He stopped to pray, for he had suffered very many temptations. I observed that he was filled with dread and I went up to him: 'Why are you afraid?' I asked. 'See, I too am flesh and blood.' But he lifted up his eyes to heaven, recited his prayer and pronounced the amen." '

Again, a very typical anecdote. The desert was the realm of the unseen and the supernatural; hence the instinctive hesitation shown by the anchorites towards any approaching visitor—especially if he came at twilight, as here. It was either an angel, to be treated with consideration, or a demon, to be shunned, or else it was a man, in which case he had to be dealt with in one of these two ways. The journey continues:

' "I went on my way again and walked for seven days. At the end of that time I looked behind me. There was a man, also walking. His hair hung down over his body like a leopard's mane, for he was naked. Darnel-leaves covered his secret parts.
' "As he came towards me, I was seized with fear and climbed on to

10. THE DESERTS OF THEBAID AND SKETE

11. ST. MARY THE EGYPTIAN

a corner of rock. He came close to the rock and flung himself down in its shade, overcome by suffering caused by hunger and thirst and the scorching heat of the desert. He had suffered greatly. He looked up and saw me. He spoke to me: 'Come down, you man of God, for I also am a man. It is because of God that I am here in the desert'.

' "He went on: 'I am Benofer (Onuphrio). For seven years I have been in this desert, sleeping in the mountains as do the wild beasts. I eat darnel and leaves from the trees. In all that time I have never seen a single man'." '

A similar episode—but one even more definite—is to be found in the *Coptic Life of Paul of Tamweh*, another anchorite of Upper Egypt who passed through the desert and met a man surrounded by a herd of buffalo:

'Paul asked: "What is your name?" The man answered: "Aphu is my name." Paul said: "How many years have you been in this place?" He said: "Fifty-four years." Paul went on: "Who gave you the coat you are wearing?" "Father Anthony, from Shiît," was the reply. And Paul asked: "On what do you live among the buffalo?" He answered: "I live as they do. I eat the grass of the fields." Paul said: "Are you not cold in winter or hot in summer?" He said: "In winter I sleep among the buffalo, and they warm me with their breath. In summer they stand close together and provide shade for me." Paul said: "In truth, you are worthy to be called Aphu the Buffalo." '

The theme of the anchorite who had never seen men and lived among buffalo here becomes almost a religious variant of that of the wild child brought up in the care of animals. But in Egypt there was an additional meaning to this, because of the importance animals always had as a medium for the reception of divinity or as divinities themselves. When it passed into Christianity, this conception gave birth to the typically Egyptian theme of the 'saintly buffalo-man', and comparing a man to an animal or giving him an animal nickname (like Aphu the Buffalo) was always, in Christian Egypt, a sign of great spiritual distinction.

It is easy to conclude from this, as Amelineau does, that all these stories 'are nothing but the old Egyptian romances adapted to other ideas' and that Onuphrio, Paphnutius and Aphu never existed.

It is not the case, however, with the anchorites now to be studied, such as they are described by Palladius, Rufinus and Cassian; they belong to the real old world. They have faces, and names. They built hermitages or monasteries which may still be seen. They lived in a district the name of which is historically famous: Thebaid.

THEBAID

When, in the seventeenth century, Jansenism attracted to Port-Royal-des-Champs a certain number of men anxious to leave the world and the 'age', these new solitaries quite naturally turned to their Egyptian ancestors—St Anthony, St Macarius and others—in search of both confirmation and example. That appeared fairly logical, since the departure for the Port-Royal 'desert' reproduced as a whole the phenomenon which had taken place in Egypt thirteen centuries earlier. It was from this time, indeed, that dated the chief studies on the desert Fathers and that one suddenly 're-discovered' the saints of Egypt and Syria popularized in the Middle Ages by the *Golden Legend* of Jacopo de Voragine. They included, among others, St Anthony and St Mary the Egyptian. At intervals of a few years appeared the admirable translations by Arnauld d'Andilly under the title of *Vies des saints Pères des déserts d'Egypte et de Syrie* (1654). They include the *Lives* of St Anthony, St Paul of Thebes and St Pachomius, the *History of the Monks of Egypt*, the *Lausiac History*, the *Institutions* and the *Conversations* of Cassian, the *Spiritual Meadow* of John Moschus, the *Ladder to Paradise* of John Climacus, and many others. These were followed in turn by the *Histoire des moines d'Orient* by Bulteau (1678), the *Monuments de l'Eglise grecque* by Cotelier (1677-1688) and the *Mémoires pour servir à l'histoire des six premiers siècles de l'Eglise* by Tillemont at the end of the seventeenth century.

But after a space of thirteen centuries and in a society as different from Egyptian society as that of the *abbés* of Port-Royal, such a return to source could not but involve misunderstanding. The Jansenists of the *Grand Siècle* treated the heroic saints of the desert as the tragic writers of the age treated pagan heroes: by expressing through them the morals, the ideas and the preoccupations of the seventeenth century. In Arnauld d'Antilly's translations, St Anthony, St Paul of Thebes and St Macarius converse in a courtly style of language which is one of the great charms of these texts but which is a little surprising in a setting beneath the Egyptian sun, in deserts which are the home of wild beasts. The *Grand Siècle* pictured the wastes of Nitria or Thebaid as a sort of Ile-de-France miraculously transported to a spot amid the sands, and accompanied by its ponds, its foliage, its green hillsides and its ploughmen.

The famous deserts of Thebaid, which the Jansenists made a peaceful oasis of meditation, were, however, very different from this. In the strict sense of the term, Thebaid was the region around Thebes in Upper Egypt (where the first Pachomian monasteries were established) but, in fact, all the fourth-century writers and the travellers who followed them gave the name Thebaid to the secluded districts bordering the Nile from Memphis to Syene, the whole of Middle and Upper Egypt. It is in this wider sense that the term is taken here, so as not to add greater confusion to geographical details which are already very vague.

What were these deserts of Middle and Upper Egypt where so many anchorites settled in the fourth century? They were stony expanses where only a few palms and a little grass grew, where water-holes were few and far between, expanses broken by hillocks at the bottom of which the ascetics built huts of branches or just dug holes to shield themselves from the sun, where no deserted underground tombs existed. Those who settled near the Nile lived like troglodytes in the great rocks and escarpments which, in places, overhung the river, or in caves which can still be seen today. An eighteenth-century traveller writes:

'From Cairo to Upper Egypt, thousands of cells are to be seen, contrived in the rock in the most inaccessible places. Only by means of the narrowest paths could the anchorite saints reach these caves, and they were often cut by precipices which they crossed by small wooden bridges. These bridges they drew in and so made their retreats inaccessible. That is the district called Thebaid, once famous on account of the huge number of hermits it accommodated. Many of the caves can be seen from the boats which sail along the Nile. From some of them, with the aid of long ropes water was drawn from the Nile itself when it was in flood. At such times the waters washed the base of the steep rock-face.

'But there is more to Thebaid than these caves. There are also the lonely, barren hills which extend for a distance of three or four days' walk in the direction of the Red Sea. There, properly speaking, are the deserts of Thebaid which were so famous in the ecclesiastical history of the early centuries. There, between Suez and Mount Colzim, six or seven leagues from the sea, are the famous monastery of St Anthony, St Paul's cave and various other similar retreats hallowed by the penitence of the old anchorites.'[1]

It was there, indeed, in the caves of Mount Colzim where St Anthony

[1] Maillet, *Description de l'Egypte* (1735).

died, and at the foot of the mountain, that the first anchorite centre developed. Although St Athanasius hardly alludes to the fact, St Anthony did not spend the last years of his life entirely alone. Apart from the many pilgrims who visited him, he had around him several disciples, some of whom, like Macarius, founded centres of anchorites on his example. The first monastery founded at Pispir—which was much more a building where the anchorites, scattered about the neighbouring wilderness, used to meet once a week than a monastery in the modern sense—also very soon became a centre from which anchoritism spread northwards along the Nile to Memphis and southwards as far as Thebes. Rufinus and Palladius, who travelled through the whole of this region of Lower Thebaid at the end of the fourth century, hardly half a century after Anthony's death, speak of anchorite cells and 'holes' all along the Nile. According to Rufinus, the anchorites installed in Lower Thebaid (that is between Memphis and the present town of Asyût) numbered some ten thousand. As for the monastic centres, the chief of these, apart from Pispir and Colzim which were founded in Anthony's lifetime, were at Faiyûm, Arsinoe, Oxyrhynchus, Aphroditopolis, Babylon and Memphis. Rufinus writes that at Oxyrhynchus 'the encircling walls are full of solitaries and surrounded by them outside. Everywhere in the town there are more monasteries than houses to be seen. There is not a door, a tower or a corner which does not house a solitary.' He adds: 'the town contains twenty thousand virgins and ten thousand solitaries.' In short, a celestial city, whose inhabitants were already wholly dedicated to the beyond and which had lost all touch with this earthly world!

Palladius writes that at Antinoe, a little further south, 'there are two thousand solitaries in the monasteries surrounding the town'.

The same impression was obtained by Sulpicius Severus, or rather by his informant Postumianus, who visited Egypt at the beginning of the fifth century: 'When I left Mount Sinai I went back towards the Nile and I visited the great number of monasteries on both banks of the river. I saw that in most of these places the monks lived together in groups of a hundred. But frequently there are in some villages as many as two or three thousand monks.'

We do not take much account of these figures, which are most certainly exaggerated. But the prevailing impression—which testifies to the reality of the phenomenon—was everywhere the same: all along the Nile, for reasons already seen, there was a multitude of hermitages and monasteries, in such great numbers that the 'solitaries' sometimes gave the impression of being more numerous than the laity.

Among Anthony's principal disciples are two who claim attention: Paul the Simple and St Sisoes. Paul, who was named *the Simple* by Anthony because he 'had no trace of malice in him', came to the desert at the age of sixty. He was a peasant endowed with never-failing steadfastness and obedience. To begin with, he spent three days and nights knocking at Anthony's door, waiting for the saint to admit him. Afterwards, Anthony took him into his company to instruct and test him, giving him the most irksome tasks and the most extravagant orders: he had to weave mats in the full heat of the sun for a whole day, make a basket, unmake it, make it up again and once more take it apart, break a pot of honey and pick up the honey from the ground with a shell, taking care not to collect any dust, etc. Paul the Simple obeyed. He obeyed all orders, even those which were not given to him. One day, when Anthony was speaking with visitors in his cell, Paul asked Anthony a very innocent question and Anthony, a little put out, told him to be silent. Paul held his tongue—for one day, two days, a week. He spoke to nobody, and Anthony asked him why. 'Did you not tell me to be silent the other day?' answered Paul. And Anthony exclaimed: 'He puts us all to shame.' This anecdote—one of those which were not invented—makes clear what the principle of 'instruction' in the desert was: to stamp out any personal or affective reaction in the disciple, to stifle all judgement or criticism, to exact pure and simple obedience so as to abolish the ever baneful expression of the Ego. Paul, continually making and unmaking the same basket for several days, reached the very limit of obedience just when it bordered on the ridiculous.

St Sisoes also lived on Mount Colzim with Anthony. Paul had made much of the virtue of obedience. Sisoes made much of the virtue of humility. If the practice of obedience sometimes borders on the ridiculous, that of humility tends to abjection. Admittedly, these extremes were not often reached in Egypt, except by St Sisoes who, Palladius says, put into practice all his life 'a love of holy abjection' and whose dearest wish was 'to be held in contempt by everybody', who 'so dreaded the praises of men that, when he prayed in the desert with his hands upraised to heaven, he would lower them as soon as he thought he was observed, for fear that it might be made an occasion to enhance his reputation'.

A possible exception may be made of St Isidora, mentioned in the Coptic *Life* of Theodore, who lived in the first convent for women founded in the time of Pachomius near Tabennisi and who, from a love of humility, feigned insanity. The *Life* of Theodore states that her sole concern was 'always to be despised'. She therefore spent her days in the monastery kitchen, barefooted and with her head wrapped in rags, feeding on *'bread-crumbs, which she picked up from the ground with a sponge, and swill'*. Such behaviour was fairly frequent in the lives of the saints, from the fourth century, especially in Syria. There is in it a sort of transferred asceticism, in the sense that by mortifying the body one aims, in fact, at the mortification of one's social being, at cutting oneself off from society *while living in the bosom of the society itself*. Obviously, this is something the anchorite could not do. That is why, in the succeeding centuries, when this idea was more clearly understood, the 'simulator saints' as they might be called were no longer located in the desert or even in monasteries but right in the towns (like Mark the Mad in Alexandria or Simeon Slos in Antioch), or with their own familes (like St Alexis).

The anchorites scattered among the desert caves and holes situated near the Nile long remained anonymous; by reason of their remoteness, in the first place, since none of them retired to inaccessible places or underground tombs, and also because, more often than not, the anchorites shunned rather than sought visitors. That is a fairly logical phenomenon; the greatest anchorites were not necessarily the best-known. It is even certain that among the multitudes of ascetics of the Egyptian deserts were some who attained to a degree of perfection sufficient to 'complete the circle', that is to *renounce saintliness itself*.[1] As for the rest, those whose names and ascetic achievements have come down to us, it is evident that the most famous were not necessarily the most saintly. The very peculiar spiritual atmosphere of the Christian East in the fourth century led certain anchorites into a sort of ascetic rivalry, into a heedless display of mortifications and macerations, in which discipline and sincerity did not always count for much. But it must be remembered that, after an interval of twenty centuries, it is extremely difficult to judge of the experiences of men who lived forty or fifty years in solitude. Therefore, so that the reader is not misled, in all the examples he has already been shown and in those yet to come, the criteria by which the ascetics' behaviour must be examined are contrary to the usual criteria: he who withdraws from the world generally takes care to confuse the tracks leading to his retreat. This is equally true in the spiritual realm: absurdity, stupidity, degradation, simulated madness and other 'abnormal' forms of behaviour are ascetic techniques, 'false tracks' intended to mislead the disciple or visitor too greatly influenced by profane criteria. The limit of these techniques was reached in Syria by the

---

[1] A description of these anchorites is given later on page 122, in connection with the Life of Macarius the Elder.

'browsers', those ascetics who spent their lives on all fours feeding on grasses and roots: here, the saint went to the utmost limit in order to 'obscure the track', since he apparently exchanged his human state for that of an animal. The criteria by which an ascetic may be judged a saint, an exhibitionist or a half-wit, are therefore complex and delicate. There was, for instance, nothing *a priori* to distinguish a saint feigning madness from a village idiot who might happen to be in his company. Nor could the 'true' saint be of the slightest help in removing the difficulty; on the contrary, he was pleased to make the situation still more confusing. Sometimes authentic saints were momentarily seized with doubts or amazement to see a 'colleague' in saintliness behaving strangely. Who would venture to attempt to distinguish the real madmen from the false, or true saints from false saints, if he himself had no experience of madness, asceticism and solitude? Behind an anchorite's every gesture and word, there were in reality a hidden logic and a secret language, the words and laws of which must first be discovered. The movement into the deserts of Egypt, in the wake of Rufinus and Palladius, was more than a journey undertaken in the face of danger from sun, sand and wild beasts; it was also an undertaking from which one had to learn to distinguish the Real from the Illusory, and even the false-Real from the false-Illusory. The desert was full of illusions, the most dangerous of which were not so much the demons and temptations as those which consisted of a false conception of man's true nature and identity.

'Are you the great Macarius?' asked a visitor of Macarius the Elder, one day. 'The great Macarius? Who is he?' answered Macarius. And the visitor, not understanding, visited all the other holes in the desert, when the anchorites—quite rightly—invariably answered: 'No, I am not the great Macarius'. And he went back to Alexandria without ever meeting Macarius. Thus, in this journey which we are about to undertake into the land of the Real and Illusory, let us in our turn beware of passing by the 'great Macarius' without seeing him, of being mistaken about the true nature of anchoritism and of failing to discriminate among the saintly, the insane and the simple-minded.

Saintly, insane or simple-minded? The life of John of Egypt offers an excellent opportunity for us to reach a decision. John of Egypt was one of those innumerable anchorites who established themselves in the caves of Thebaid and instituted a form of asceticism which became the model for generations of anchorites. Let us leave Mount Colzim, near which lies the body of St Anthony in an unknown spot. As we go on our way we shall greet Paul the Simple, busy making and unmaking the same basket, day and night, looking thoughtfully down at his work. We shall wave encouragement to St Sisoes who, with outstretched arms, is praying in the distance, and who will lower his arms at the sight of us. And, in order to please him, we shall let him know how much we despise him. Those two have found their paths, the 'paths' of the basket and the lowered arms. And what of the others?

Let us make our way towards the Nile. Let us follow the river bank southwards to a place called Lycopolis (the town with the wolves), the present Asyût. Near this town is a mountain with a grotto, in this grotto is a hut and in the hut is a man: John of Egypt. He has been living there for fifty years. 'He had moved to the high land in the neighbourhood of Asyût where the monks of the monastery of Hanadah built him a large hut, in which they made a sort of prison. John lived there, and every day he was brought the seeds on which he fed.' People came to visit him but did not stay long in this prison. Only Palladius, after eighteen days' travelling through the desert from Nitria to Lycopolis, managed to spend some time with him and persuaded him to speak of his 'life'. But can that be called a life? Solitude, darkness, silence, prison: what name can be given to that voluntary seclusion in the hills, that conceal-ment in the depths of night? St Anthony had stayed but a few years in his tomb at Coma. John of Egypt stayed for fifty years in his hut, living on seeds and water like a bird. A bird which had no further use for its wings and had changed into a statue. Later, in Syria, other anchorites undertook the experiment of complete seclusion in tombs, caves or dark holes, sometimes even in *hollow tree-trunks* or on top of pillars where for years they lived an almost vegetal existence, reminding one of 'human flowers' strewn about the field of the saints.

Let us accustom ourselves to these pictures of the saint crouching in the shadows like a beast in its lair, the sightless holy-man hidden in the bowels of the earth, the 'mole-saint' as he might be called. He will often be found within the covers of this book since, through such pictures and visions of sanctity, the men of the fourth and fifth centuries gave expression to their amazing dream: of hiding themselves in the depths, far from the world, of remaining for years in darkness and silence, living on seeds and water.

Let us leave John of Egypt to continue with his asceticism in the darkness of the cave. And now we are in the full light of the desert by the Nile. Let us follow the west bank of the river, through Hermopolis Magna and Oxyrhynchus, to Heracleopolis, a little to the south of Faiyûm. All these regions abound in hermitages and monasteries. The anchorites—or at least those of them who were not perturbed by the 'publicity' of their ascetic achievements—performed miracles in increasing number, and certain of them, like St Apollo—according to Rufinus, who visited him—had a following of more than five hundred disciples. St Apollo is famous in the annals of anchoritism because, one day, he brought to a standstill a whole crowd of pagans who were celebrating a sacrifice, 'so that, after suffering the effects of excessive heat, they became burnt by the sun's rays, without understanding the cause of such a strange occurrence'. Without dwelling upon the nature of this 'miracle', let us recall that at the time of St Apollo (who lived in the desert in the days of Julian the Apostate) the pagans were still very numerous in the rural areas of Egypt. Rufinus states that around Hermopolis Magna (in the desert where Apollo lived) there were 'nine or ten towns full of pagans, where devils were worshipped with ungodly superstition and a strange passion (no doubt it was a question of Dionysus-Osiris), for they had a temple of wonderful size in the middle of which was an idol which the priests—in the presence of the whole multitude—took out and carried about the towns like Bacchantes and celebrated sacrilegious ceremonies to conjure rain from the skies'. In fact, the 'miracle' performed by Apollo was nothing but a detail in the increasingly violent struggle in the second half of the fourth century between the Christians and the pagans. A generation later, when paganism was officially forbidden throughout the Empire, Christian monks under the guidance of Shenute or Macarius of Tkôou pillaged the heathen temples, set fire to them, smashed the idols and sometimes killed the temple personnel. In Apollo's day, instead of indulging in such violence, one merely massacred the pagans or symbolically 'neutralized' them, but the 'miracle' here bears too great a resemblance to what was later to be real history for it not to be purely and simply the literary expression of the Christians' unconscious desires. The analysis of this aretological 'miracle' must not be carried too far, but it should also be noted that it is clearly a matter of a 'solar' miracle (heathen crowds brought to a standstill and burnt by the sun) which was perhaps attributed to St Apollo because of the homonymy with the ancient Greek sun-god.

A little further north, near Heracleopolis, lived a certain Paphnutius whose life, according to Rufinus, was so saintly 'that he was considered to be less man than angel'. But let us beware! There again, appearances are deceptive. Paphnutius an angel? After years spent in the desert, he was hardly higher in the scale of virtue than a musician of Heracleopolis (as was revealed to him by an angel of whom he was rash enough to ask the question). And Paphnutius redoubled his fasting and praying.

'Where do I stand now?' he asked the angel a few years later. 'Level with a citizen of the nearest town', was the reply. And again Paphnutius intensified his fasts and prayers. A third time he asked the angel, 'What is my position now?' 'Equal to that of a tradesman in the town,' answered the angel. Such was Paphnutius: a man who had formed a wrong estimate of himself. He was more the equal of a musician or a trader than of a saint, and the confusion about him was further expressed, more literally, in a famous episode at a later date: the conversion of Thaïs, a courtesan of Heracleopolis. One day, Paphnutius, the false desert angel, 'dresses in conventional clothes, provides himself with money, and going into the town calls upon a well-known courtesan named Thaïs', with no other intention, of course, than to convert her. And convert her he did, for, not long afterwards, she was known to be in a women's monastery, 'shut in a cell the door of which Paphnutius sealed with lead'. For three years Thaïs stayed in this cell, living on bread and water, and she ended her days there. The story might well stop here, but it is necessary to refer again to this conversion, which Anatole France helped to make famous by his novel *Thaïs* and which was the source of the popular *Méditation* by Massenet. Everything is apparently simple and logical in this story: on the one hand a saint who was almost an angel, and on the other a prostitute seemingly possessed of the Devil. In short, opposite extremes of life; but, in fact, each of these characters hid a double personality. The saint only appeared to be an angel and was, in reality, no more angelic than an undistinguished musician or tradesman, or an ordinary member of society. As for the prostitute, she must have had a secret inclination to virtue, since she so easily passed from a life of immorality to one of solitary confinement. Now, the striking feature of this story is the meeting of two beings, apparently of widely differing characters, who were, so to speak, 'complementary to each other', since the saint assumed the guise of a libertine and the courtesan changed into a saint. Everything suggests *an exchange of sanctity* between Paphnutius and Thaïs, as if Paphnutius must have renounced his own sanctity (expressed in the legend as 'assuming the guise of a libertine') so that the courtesan might become a saint. Naturally, Rufinus makes no mention of such an 'exchange', since Paphnutius returned to his desert after the conversion of Thaïs. But Anatole France, fifteen hundred years later, gave clear expression to the meaning of the myth (for such it certainly is—one of the very earliest Christian myths), by picturing Paphnutius, after the conversion, yielding to the temptations of the flesh, denying his God and giving himself up to lustful living. Here is revealed the basic structure of the myth: the acquisition of sanctity cannot occur *ex nihilo*, but is possible only through an exchange, at the price of another's sanctity. The Christian myth of Thaïs belongs fundamentally and typically to a pre-Christian era.

CHAPTER 6

CONTESTANTS IN EXILE—II

'As I begged him to take a little rest after he had stayed awake so long, he answered: "First persuade the angels to sleep".'

LIFE OF ST DOROTHEUS

THE DESERTS OF THE WÂDI NATRÛN

Some sixty miles south of Alexandria and about fifty miles north-west of Cairo lie the desert wastes of the Wâdi Natrûn, which the Greeks call Nitria. This name is derived from the soda lakes with which the region is dotted—the soda or natron which the ancient Egyptians used for embalming their dead. The level of these lakes, which number about fifteen, rises in winter and spring and falls again in May, depositing on the banks incrustations of nitre which is still used for various purposes in present-day Egypt. For centuries these soda deposits have given the region a strange appearance which has impressed all visitors or pilgrims that have passed through it: fossilized vegetation lies heaped up, giving the appearance of forests of stone in weird shapes in which every traveller, according to his imagination, fancied he could see the remains of mummified giants or great sailing-ships turned to stone in the depths of the sea. Says Coppin:

'There, may be found pieces of human bones which have changed into rocks. They can be identified only from their shape, but such great quantities of them are encountered that there can be no doubt that they were once real bones.'

A hundred years later, Maillet in his turn passed through the Wâdi Natrûn, and he writes:

'It is on this canal route (the Faiyûm canal) that the desert of St Macarius lies and the valley known as Baharbalaama, an Arabic term

108

meaning *waterless sea* because the sea once filled this valley. It can be further recognized from the large number of masted ships to be found there in a petrified state, ships which had probably sunk in those times when the gulf was covered by sea-water. Further incontestable proof of its origin is provided by the sea-shells which litter its rocky sides. In the middle of this frightful, barren expanse is still to be seen today the monastery of St Zacharias and two or three others occupied by a few Coptic monks. To such small proportions have now been reduced the famous monasteries which peopled those wildernesses in the days when Egypt was a Christian land.'[1]

Human bones, sunken ships—the imagination of seventeenth and eighteenth century travellers was haunted by such human disasters. Rufinus, who travelled these deserts in the fourth century, at the time when the number of anchorites there was beginning to increase, put a very different construction upon the strange atmosphere of the place:

'We came next to Nitria, about forty miles from Alexandria and the most famous of all the monastic localities. It gets its name from a nearby township where there are great resources of saltpetre, and I believe that divine Providence has enabled this state of things to be so, for in due course the sins of men were to be washed away there just as spots are removed from clothing by the use of saltpetre'.

Now we are back again amid the familiar surroundings of the fourth century, where the need for symbols is so great that even saltpetre becomes synonymous with a purifying constituent.

It may be supposed that these deserts were not easy of access. Those petrified areas, where the sun's rays, reflected by the milk-white soda deposits, were unbearable, where wells were few and far between and vegetation limited to a few palms and reeds, presented no landmark that could be of use to the traveller. '*One had to make one's way,*' says Rufinus, '*by observation of the stars*', by night, having slept all day in some hole, in the shade of a palm-tree. It was an exhausting, even dangerous, journey, a very picturesque description of which has been given by Rufinus. No doubt, the many hazards of the desert, such as they are set out in the following account, have a symbolical meaning. It is not by chance that dragons, quagmires, thieves and crocodiles lie in the traveller's path. How could it be so, since the very minerals, the stones, the nitre, the rocks in human shape, are there by the will of God?

[1] Maillet, *Description of Egypt.* (1735)

Throughout Rufinus's romantic narrative—and it is very clearly a symbolical narrative—one can discern real hardships and dangers, which show that this 'pilgrimage to the source' was a very fatiguing enterprise. In the latter part of his *History of the Monks of Egypt*, Rufinus writes:

'The first danger we encountered was death from hunger and thirst after our journey of five days and nights in the desert.

'The second danger occurred in a valley, the atmosphere of which was so heavily saline that as soon as the heat of the sun became effective the air was changed to salt, as fog is seen in winter to change into ice. These deposits formed spikes of salt and the way became so rough that our feet were pierced and lacerated. Not only did those who walked barefoot suffer in this way, but even those who were well shod.

'The third danger we met as we were walking in the desert and came to another valley, which, like the first, produced a certain humidity. When we made up our minds to cross it, we found the bottom to be full of stones and putrid, stinking mud, into which we plunged breast-high. Therefore, being near to death, we cried unto our God: "Save us, O Lord; for the waters are come in unto our souls. We sink in deep mire, where there is no standing: we are come into deep waters, where the floods overflow us and our strength fails us!" (Fortunate are those who can always find an apt quotation from the Psalms, even at the point of death!)

'The fourth danger came when, walking by the sea, we met robbers. They followed us for ten miles and, unable to bring about our death by violence, they nearly killed us with fatigue, so long did they pursue us.

'The fifth danger was provided by certain waters left over from the Nile floods, where we remained for three days, extricating ourselves only with the greatest difficulty.

'The sixth danger came from the Nile itself, when the boat in which we were sailing nearly foundered.

'The seventh danger threatened us on the lake called St Mary, where we were battered by a most violent storm and blown on to an island in the depths of winter.

'The eighth and last danger we encountered when we were nearing the monasteries of Nitria and discovered that the Nile had been in flood and later subsided, leaving a kind of lake in which there were several creatures, particularly crocodiles. These creatures had left the water after sunrise and were lying on the banks, seemingly dead, with the result that we went close to them to observe their extraordinary size. As soon as they heard a sound they awoke, as from a deep sleep, then rushed upon us and pursued us with the utmost vigour. With loud cries and lamentations we called upon the Lord God. His goodness did not fail us, for, as if repulsed by some angel, those huge beasts plunged back into the pool, while we ran with all our might to reach the safety of the monasteries. There we gave thanks to God for having delivered us from so many dangers and shown us so many miracles.'

In spite of the many dangers which they concealed, or perhaps because of them, these hostile places were to become, from the second half of the fourth century, an anchoritic and monastic centre of the greatest importance; anchoritic in the first place, since the anchorites of those times always preceded the cenobites according to a process which was to recur fairly generally throughout the Christian East: an anchorite lights upon an ideal spot (that is to say an unlivable spot, a parched wilderness, possibly infested by wild beasts and fiends), its reputation attracts followers who make their abode at a reasonable distance from that of their leader, spend the week in isolation and come together again on Sunday for a religious service in some structure—a hut or a cave—which is dubbed a church and which will subsequently be enlarged to become the nucleus of a future monastery. Such were the events which took place in Nitria. About the year 325, a certain Ammon, after eighteen years of apotactical marriage (his father had obliged him to marry), left his wife and set out for the desert. He discovered the seclusion of Nitria and settled there. Disciples very quickly thronged about him.

Life in the Wâdi Natrûn was even more arduous than in Thebaid. The Nile was far distant—more than twenty miles away—and, in this nitre-encrusted soil, water was scarce. Where it existed it was deep down and of unpleasant taste. Most of the anchorites lived in ordinary huts or in caves hollowed out of the mounds which surrounded the lakes. In the main, they were dressed in skins, which gave them the 'advantage' of suffering more harshly from the heat when they prayed in the sun and of making them look like large animals in human shape which frightened away visitors. In spite, or rather because, of these ideal conditions, the anchorites flocked there in large numbers. Palladius, who spent twelve years there at the end of the fourth century, mentions '*five thousand hermits living in this desert*'.

From the multitude of ascetics it is difficult to choose the most typical. The anonymity under which they lived and their concern to attain the impersonal made it an arbitrary matter to distinguish between them: fasts, nightly vigils, prayers in the full heat of the sun or meditations in the gloom of a cave, the expressions of asceticism are the same for all. In the desert day follows day without change. Some of the hermits, however, gave a particular character to their asceticism. Such a one was St Pior, who lived for fifty years on a daily ration of a little bread and

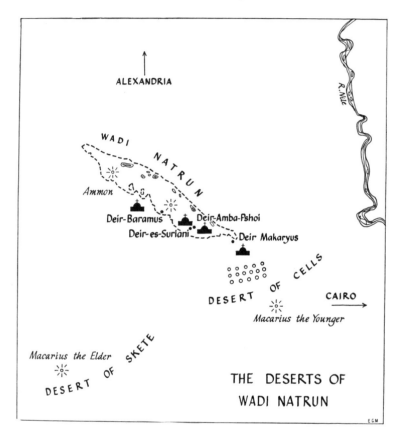

THE DESERTS OF
WADI NATRUN

five olives, eating them '*as he walked about*, because,' he said, '*eating must be a transitory occupation*'. In that there can be discerned a state of mind quite common among these desert-dwellers: the literal interpretation of the meaning of symbols. The smallest events of daily life, the least significant of natural phenomena, are interpreted in terms of their symbolical meaning. They are always considered as forces, values and impulses emanating from the unseen world and intruding upon human existence. But since most of these anchorites were illiterate and often simple-minded men, they frequently misunderstood the symbolical

12A. ST. SIMEON STYLITES   12B. ST. ALIPIUS

13A. ST. DANIEL

13B. AN UNKNOWN STYLITE

meaning of an elder's particular utterance or action and took everything quite literally. Thus, St Pior, who was told that 'eating must be a transitory occupation', understood that it should always be done 'in transit', that is while he was walking. But occasionally St Pior was much less naïve in his understanding of symbolism, as witness the following anecdote: One day when he was going to the 'church' in Nitria, he overheard anchorites speaking ill of other ascetics in the neighbourhood. He therefore took a large bag of sand, which he put on his back, and a small basket of sand, which he carried in front of him. Equipped in this way and without saying a word, he began to walk about in front of the anchorites. Puzzled by his action, the latter asked him what he was doing, to which he replied, 'This large bag of sand represents my sins. I put them behind me so as not to see them. This small basket contains the sins of others. I keep it before me so that I may see nothing else.' The anchorites changed their conversation.

'LIKE HYENA-HOLES . . .'

At the eastern end of the Wâdi Natrûn and ten miles further south, the nitre gradually disappears and the ground becomes softer. It can be more easily dug, so that many ascetics made holes for themselves there and covered them with palm-fronds or reeds as protection from the sun. Or else they made their quarters *underground*, in hollows which were so confining that there was hardly room to turn round in them. It was in the famous *Desert of Cells* (from the Greek: *Kellia*) that Palladius stayed for three years as a follower of Macarius the Younger. 'Some of these cells,' he writes, 'had no opening but a hole through which one could creep, for they were made in the inner desert to which no visitors were admitted. It was in these that Macarius lived during Lent. They consisted of dark, underground caves, like hyena-holes, in which space was so restricted that it was impossible even to straighten out one's legs in them.' It was to this retreat that Macarius the Younger (so called to distinguish him from his namesake Macarius the Elder) went for forty days every year to keep Lent and practise self-mortification; after which he would return to one of his more spacious cells in the Wâdi Natrûn, where he received pilgrims who had come to see him from all corners of the Roman world.

This Macarius, unlike the other anchorites who most often looked like wild animals in human shape, was 'a little man, very weak and delicate. The only hair on his face was around his mouth and there was very little on his upper lip, the extremes of austerity to which he had subjected himself inhibiting the growth of beard on his chin'. 'Extremes of austerity', in the words of Palladius. One wonders whether the word *extreme* is not itself a euphemism when it is known, for instance, that in order to overcome sleep Macarius spent twenty days and nights in the open desert, exposed to the scorching rays of the sun by day and perished with cold by night, with the result that by the end of that time 'I had', as he later told Palladius, 'to fling myself immediately into my cell, or I should have fallen in a faint, so dried-up was my brain'. He went even further than this.

'One day when Macarius was sitting in his cell, a mosquito chanced to sting him. He was hurt, and crushed the insect. Immediately, he became contrite for having acted out of vengeance and made up his mind to stay for six whole months, naked and motionless, in one place in a swamp of Skete, situated in a dreary waste, where there are mosquitoes the size of wasps and with stings capable of piercing even the hide of wild boars. He thus reduced his body to such a state that when he returned to his cell everyone thought he was a leper, and it was only by his voice that he was identified as St Macarius.'

Admittedly, certain of these anchorites must be considered insane, but of an insanity which in reality reveals a mentality both archaic and arresting. For killing a mosquito, Macarius permits all the rest to avenge his 'victim'. Such action may be interpreted as a penance which Macarius inflicts upon himself by way of expiation and particularly as a balance restored, an exchange effected between the world of men and that of animals. Life in the desert is comprised of a continual interplay between man and the living world around him, both seen and unseen. In heaven, on earth, in the company of humans, angels and devils record each man's faults in their ledgers and everything has its due place in these meticulously kept records, every comforting deed and each everyday thought.

Objects, plants, animals, all go into the making of a sacred universe, where nothing is left to chance and where everything, from the vision of a cherub to the sting of a mosquito is a *sign* from the unseen world. If, then, Macarius lets himself be stung by mosquitoes, it is because mosquitoes, just as much as men, have their rightful place in the immense, unfathomable Divine Plan.

Near the end of his life (Macarius came to the desert at the age of forty and remained there for sixty years), it was rumoured in the Wâdi Natrûn that there existed in Upper Egypt monasteries where men lived according to rules very different from those of St Anthony. The news must have seemed strange to the hermits of Nitria: was it possible to be a saint and yet live in the company of others, without being able to indulge freely in self-mortification? Macarius decided to clear the matter up and he set out for Tabennisi. Pachomius was still in control of the community there, which fixes the date of the journey as between 330 and 350. Macarius arrived at the monastery gate 'incognito', presenting himself as a novice, and had the greatest difficulty in obtaining admittance by reason of his age. But in the end Pachomius allocated him to a cell and Macarius began to practise his 'extreme austerity'. The fasts undertaken at Tabennisi were mere child's play to him. Thus, being aware that for the whole of Lent the Tabennisi hermits ate nothing that had been cooked, he decided to do likewise for seven years. He kept strictly to this abstinence, eating nothing but raw herbs, sometimes dry and sometimes soaked in water, as he came upon them; and he experienced no great hardship in doing so.

He even introduced into Tabennisi a rather strange form of asceticism, concerning the manner of eating bread:

'Learning also that a hermit ate only one pound of bread in a day, he crumbled the pieces of bread which he had and put them into a jar, resolved to take out only as much as he could extract with his fingers. Which is great austerity, for, as he very readily explained to us, he could take hold of quite a few pieces but could not get them out, since the neck of the jar was so narrow. For three years he observed this strict abstinence, eating no more than four or five ounces of bread a day and drinking an equivalent quantity of water, and consuming during the whole of the year only a tiny pitcher of oil.'

So much for the usual fasts. But on special occasions, such as Lent, Macarius practised a more thoroughgoing denial of food and drink:

'When Lent came, he took palm-leaves and dipped them in water; then he stood in a corner of his cell for the whole of Lent until Easter Day, without kneeling, sitting or leaning against anything whatever, without eating a crumb of bread or drinking a drop of water, contenting himself with taking on Sundays a few raw cabbage-leaves and eating them in the presence of the monks to show that he was taking food.'

The result of all this was that the monks of Tabennisi were frightened of this man's presence and some wondered whether he was a demon come to provoke them. They complained to Pachomius who then questioned Macarius, learned who he was (after a seven years' sojourn at Tabennisi!) and, being convinced that he was indeed a man, rendered homage to his virtue. Only then, at the age of ninety, did Macarius return to his cell in the Wâdi Natrûn, where he died.

Naturally, a crowd of anchorites had already established themselves around Macarius in the Desert of Cells, vying with one another in asceticism.

St Benjamin, for instance, put into his hut a little pitcher of oil and made a small hole in it *so as to drink no more than a drop of it every day*. But a few months later, when he went to visit another anchorite, he observed that the latter's oil had not been touched. He was 'beaten' in asceticism.

St Dorotheus used to choose 'the greatest heat of the noonday sun for gathering stones in the desert and building cells for those who could not build them. He made one in this way every year. And when I asked him: "What can you be thinking of, father, in your old age, to kill your body in this way in such intolerable heat?" he answered, "I mean to kill it, since it is killing me."

'Each day he ate no more than six ounces of bread with a handful of herbs and drank only a little water. I call God to witness that I have never seen him stretch out his legs or get into a bed in order to sleep. He spent all his nights in a sitting position, making ropes from palm-bark. As he worked or ate, he would doze a little, so that I often saw bread fall from his lips, so sleepy was he.'

These ascetic refinements obviously constituted all the 'charm' (if it may so be called) of life in the desert. But the concern with outdoing others in asceticism had its own limits. If fasting were carried to excess, it would result in the sin of pride and the notion that one can exist apart from the common human state and live like an angel; a presumptiuous and even 'heretical' notion, since it would create the belief that asceticism and mortifications could, in the effects produced, be a substitute for Grace.

The thin dividing line between extreme humility and extreme pride therefore led the ascetics to attempt to mark its limits with the help of arbitrary but definite criteria. These criteria were to enable the anchorite to avoid the two pitfalls which always lay in his path in the desert: following his inclination or giving way to pride by suffering excessive privation, in either case falling a prey to demons. Certain ascetic rules therefore quickly became necessary. The rules were specific and gave confidence, enabling the ascetic to distinguish the good from the bad, and if he respected them, while still surrounded by this uncertain world through which he groped rather like a blind man, he was sure of being on the right road to the angels and to heaven.

It was evidently in relation to food and fasts that the rules were first established. We learn from Cassian that most anchorites restricted themselves, for instance, to eating seven olives a day. One should know, 'even in the matter of the number of olives', where sin begins and ends. Thus, the ascetic knew his position: if he ate six olives instead of seven, he would sin through pride; if he ate eight, he would sin through gluttony.

It may appear to be exaggeration to attach such symbolical importance to food, but failure to give it consideration would mean failure to understand the vital part it has played in most religions and societies as a symbol of spiritual states, social relations, even of the highest mystical experiences. This symbol is clearly to be seen in primitive or ancient religions and it certainly has not been unknown to Christianity. When Richards, the British ethnologist, writes for instance that in archaic societies 'food is the source of the most intense emotions, and supplies the basis for some of the most abstract notions and metaphors of religious thought. To the primitives, food may become the symbol of the most lofty spiritual experiences, the expression of essential social relationships',[1] he puts forward evidence and a principle which are valid also in respect of the ascetics of the Egyptian deserts. Bread, to the ascetic, could represent the 'reflection' of the soul, and a striking illustration of the fact is found in an episode from the life of an anchorite as told by John of Egypt to Palladius. This anchorite was in fact so perfect that God relieved him of 'responsibility concerning his food and met his needs by his own Providence. When hunger caused him to go back into his cave, he always found on the table a loaf of exquisite flavour and unequalled whiteness. But, since his progress, great and gratifying as it was, gave him a feeling of vanity and attributed to his good behaviour benefits which came from the liberal hand of God alone, he immediately began to show a certain lessening of spiritual zeal.' He gave less time to prayer and more to sleep, and no longer recited the Psalms with the same concentration. At first, this relaxation passed unnoticed, for 'just as the current of a stream is aided by the action of oars in the water and carries the boat on even if the rowing stops, so this man, from habit, carried on with his usual exercises and seemed no different

[1] Richards, *Hunger and Work*.

from before'. But his slackness increased, until, 'goaded by the impor-
tunities of the flesh, he was one day filled with a desire to return to the
world. When he went into his cave, he indeed found a loaf on the table,
but it was less white than usual.' Then, one day, his unchaste desires
caused him actually to see a woman standing before him and he longed
to possess her. 'Returning to his cave he found on the table a loaf which
was very dirty and dry, and apparently eaten all over by ants and
gnawed by dogs'. That was the situation when, suddenly, his soul
appeared to him, and 'like a horde of barbarians his thoughts came
crowding in upon him from all sides, raining down as it were a shower
of arrows, and set about taking him back, bound hand and foot, into
the world'.

'THE HUMBLEST MEN IN THE WORLD'

Places are themselves sometimes symbols. In the deserts of Egypt,
where there was a sameness in the appearance of things, there were yet
some places of greater symbolical meaning than others. For Rufinus,
the Wâdi Natrûn was already a place of purification, but two days' walk
from it in a southerly direction there was another desert, which
sheltered the most austere and most inaccessible ascetics: the desert of
Skete. It was there that Macarius the Elder lived, the first to make it his
dwelling-place, Macarius, called by his biographer Serapion 'the great
luminary, the great pneumatophore, chief of the monks of the holy
mountain of Skete'. The words themselves are fascinating: Macarius
(from the Greek *makarios*: blessed), luminary and pneumatophore
(literally: *pneuma*-bearing—inspired by God). The man also was a
fascinating character, combining all that was implied in the term
anchorite, the symbol of everything that Egypt had come to seek in the
desert. Consider the striking fourteenth century portrait—or rather
image—of him by Theophanos the Greek, in the Church of the Transfiguration in Novgorod. On the face of the ascetic, burnt by the sun and
weathered by the wind, with a veil of long hair, there is no distress, no
joy, nothing to remind one of the man of flesh and desires, but on the
contrary that *hesychia*, or tranquillity of the soul, that 'silence of the
heart and mind' which is sometimes achieved by the anchorite after
years of praying and fasting. It is neither Macarius the man nor Macarius
the ascetic that Theophanos has painted, but a projection of the inner
man, the 'awakened' man hidden within the 'sleeping' man, in the terms
of the great anchorites. This image the contemporaries of Macarius, his
disciples and his visitors perceived at once, when after several years of

seclusion he founded the first colony of ascetics at Skete. His *Life*, written in Coptic by his disciple Serapion, the *Apophthegms* or sayings attributed to him and the information supplied by Palladius and Rufinus are all in agreement that Macarius the Elder was an 'awakened' personality.

And how could one sleep—in any sense—in such a desert? Strictly speaking, it was an unlivable spot, even more terrible than the others, where only the most seasoned ascetics would venture. It was, says Rufinus, 'as far distant from Nitria as could be walked in a day and a night. There was no trace of a path leading to it, nor was there any possibility of a landmark for reaching it. But it was found by observation of the stars. Water was rarely found there, and when it was it had a most offensive smell, like tar, but its taste was not too unpleasant. There were solitaries there of immeasurable perfection; the place was so frightening that nobody could live there but men who adopted a perfect life and whose courage and confidence could withstand any test.'

Macarius did not settle in this desert until he was forty years old. Before that, in accordance with the almost classical plan for many of the saints' lives in those days, his parents compelled him to marry a girl from his own village and he lived with her on an apotactical basis. Soon afterwards, he lost both parents and wife, and was then able '*to leave his village, occupy a cell at the approaches to another village and live there alone for some time*'. It was at this time, while he was living in retirement near this village, that he was accused of having caused a young woman's pregnancy. Macarius did not deny it and came near to being stoned by the villagers. It was only incidentally that, after the girl's confinement, she confessed that she had lied and had falsely accused the anchorite in order to protect her lover by diverting suspicion from him. When Macarius heard of this, he again had nothing to say, thereby already giving evidence of indifference (by worldly standards) which soon became legendary. He had occasion to give further proof of this indifference a few years later, when he was installed at Skete. One day, on returning to his cave, he found thieves rifling his cell and loading the booty on to their camel. He therefore made haste to assist them in their task, and even ran after them with a pair of sandals which they had forgotten!

While he was awaiting, then, the summons to the desert, Macarius lived in his cell near the village, to which his asceticism attracted many visitors, some of whom were strange indeed. 'One day, when Macarius was in his cell, he looked to the right and saw—a cherub nearby, with six wings and a large number of eyes. And when Macarius had begun to look at him, saying: "What is it? What can it be?" he was overcome by the splendid presence of his visitor, by his brightness and glory, and he fell upon his face and lay as if dead.' The restrained style of this Coptic text of the *Life of Macarius* makes the passage almost unique in the Christian literature of Egypt. Neither the visions of Anthony, which are very literary and no doubt invented by Athanasius, nor those of Pachomius, many of which were added at a later date, have this conciseness and directness, this quality of surprising sincerity. It is difficult for a man to endure the vision of angels and cherubs, which is really the lightning manifestation of a certain mental condition induced by fasting, a condition which the ascetic finds it hard to believe originates deep down within himself. That is why the anchorite is gripped by fear and anguish when he sees and hears this 'thing' that is suddenly 'there' and begins to speak: 'The following night the whole place became bright as a summer noonday and Macarius knew that it was the cherub returning. First of all, the Virtue stayed for some time without speaking, so that he should not be frightened'; then, as Macarius became more accustomed to the brightness of the angel's presence, the cherub showed him in a trance the desert of Skete and bade him make his dwelling there.

Macarius set out for Skete, found the places which he had seen with the cherub, espied a hill and carved for himself a cave in it, took reeds to make a bed, dug a well for his supply of water and settled there. But there were things to worry him in this desert. It was the demons first, who arrived 'above his cave like a troop of horsemen and made a show of attacking one another', while others 'stood near the door making fireballs, which burst when they threw them into the cave'. (Is it not an excellent demoniacal description of storm in the desert?) Then, he was troubled by the many disciples who were already attaching themselves to him and whom 'he put to hewing caves from the rock. These they covered with palm-leaves and reeds from the wâdi, before making them their abodes.' Macarius did not feel that he was ready to assume the position of a master or elder and, after this first stay at Skete, he decided to go to Anthony on Mount Colzim and become his disciple first. There he spent some years with his friend Serapion (who was later to become his biographer), was present at Anthony's last moments (Macarius's stay at Colzim therefore took place between 340 and 360) and then went back to Skete, where he remained until his death in 390.

'I have spent twenty years in this desert, suffering from hunger, thirst and lack of sleep,' he confides to his follower Evagrius, 'for I took but a little bread each day; I measured out my drinking-water and, with my back resting against the wall, I took as if by stealth the little sleep I had to have.'

Fresh temptations were added, for the demons, 'seeing how great was the number of souls helped by the saint, became extremely angry and visited him at noon, when he was sitting alone. Then they all stood around him like so many dogs, spat in his face and tore at his flesh, so that his whole body was black and blue.'

Macarius therefore often went far from Skete, away from the crowd of visitors and disciples, in search of *apatheia*, that bodily and mental detachment in which *'one is at peace with oneself'*. Alone, he ventured well into the desert, praying day and night. Yet he was not always alone. The desert had its own secret life which was gradually revealed to whoever was strong enough to wait in patience. There was the secret life of the tombs, in the first place, those deserted pagan tombs of which there was such an abundance as one drew near to the Nile. Not all of them had been looted by robbers and some still had their idols and their mummies. Which was not the sort of thing to frighten Macarius. One day, he went inside one of these tombs to rest, found a corpse there and used it as a pillow. And while the anchorite lay there with his eyes closed, there began a strange dialogue in the darkness.

'Now, get up and come with us!' whispered a demon to the corpse.

'Impossible,' was the reply. 'There is a man on top of me.'

'Who is the man?' asked the demon.

'Great Macarius,' answered the body.

'Will you leave me in peace,' said Macarius, losing patience. He made the sign of the cross, the demon fled, the corpse fell silent and Macarius went to sleep again.

But living creatures also were encountered in the desert, nameless anchorites who, unbeknown to all, had left the world, shunned all visitors and refused disciples. Perhaps they were the true saints referred to earlier, who had given up everything, even their saintliness. Beyond the more usual texts of the literature of the desert which always present the anchorite saint as a character as famous as the emperors themselves, one can sometimes imagine the nostalgia felt by the perfect saint who is unknown to everybody, even to the other saints. The men of the desert had their 'heroes': Anthony, Pachomius and Macarius, but they also had their Unknown Anchorite, in the sense in which one speaks of the Unknown Soldier.

One day, Macarius left for the desert in the neighbourhood of Skete. He walked for four days and came to a lake with an island in it. He made his way to this island and this is what he saw there:

'There were two men whose skin had turned black and rough by exposure and whose hair and nails had grown long. They were so changed in appearance that when Macarius saw them he became afraid and thought, "They are spirits!" But when they saw that he was so frightened that he almost fell to the ground, they called to him in the Lord's name. Macarius went up to them and touched them, so as to see whether, after all, they were not spirits. When he saw that they were indeed real men, he fell to worshipping them.'

Macarius the Elder had just discovered on this unknown island the perfect type of man which he himself dreamed of becoming and of which he talked to his disciples, such a man as had succeeded in 'vanishing from the sight of men', had found hesychia and had become 'like to a stone'.

On the death of Macarius, his followers continued with his teaching and in their turn handed it on to the neophytes. While Serapion, Macarius's chief disciple, was writing the life of 'the great luminary and great pneumatophore', the words of Macarius, heard by the anchorites, were going round the deserts of Egypt. It was from these words, or Apophthegms, some of which were certainly authentic, that the fifty *Spiritual Homilies* were formulated. These *homilies*, traditionally attributed to Macarius the Elder but, in fact, posterior to him, must have been written by a Syrian ascetic of the fifth century. To tell the truth, Macarius spoke but little, and he taught mostly by example. If he wished to teach humility, he never answered when he was addressed as 'Great Macarius', but always replied whenever he was affronted.

This teaching may be said to have borne fruit and, in the fourth and fifth centuries, the desert of Skete brought together those who might today be called the 'humblest men in the world'. St Elladius, for instance, who lived twelve years in a reed hut and who told Rufinus, when the latter pointed out that his roof was damaged, that 'he could not have seen it, because, from modesty, he had never looked upwards for twelve years'. The humility of some anchorites was such that they did not even answer to their names (does it not, in fact, require a certain measure of boldness and pride to believe that one is actually Mr So-and-So on this earth?), which caused inexperienced visitors serious misunderstanding. But more circumspect visitors like Palladius and Rufinus knew quite well what to believe. When they were looking for a certain Poemen in the desert and met an anchorite who told them, 'No, I am not Poemen', they calmly concluded from this statement 'that it was certainly he and that he was keeping his name secret from motives of modesty.' Here, the logic of the desert reclaims its rights.

Anyone, in those times, who had followed Palladius and Rufinus on their journey to the desert of Skete, would have found some strange men in their train. A sort of drama extraordinary was being enacted in these deserted spots, a drama in which everyone seemed to be interpreting an endless role with attention to the smallest details, punctiliously and earnestly.

A coal-black anchorite was seen walking in the distance (there were negroes from Nubia and Ethiopia who became anchorites) with four suspicious-looking characters tied to his back. We were not mistaken; it was Moses the Ethiopian, a former brigand, hooligan and robber, who one day turned hermit and brought to the service of God the same brutality that he had formerly employed in the service of the Devil. The shifty characters he was carrying were four of his old 'colleagues' in robbery and brigandage, whom he had taken prisoner and was hauling to the 'church' of Skete in order to convert them. His *Life* supplies the additional information that in this way he 'converted as many as seventy-five thieves, who became his most ardent disciples'.

And now, for a change, was an anchorite who was gentleness itself, too gentle even. He spent his days and nights in tears as he passed through the desert. For what was he weeping? For the world, or on his own account? No. Palladius says, 'He weeps because of original sin, bewailing the faults of the first men in the world.' This was Bessarion, the wandering hermit, 'who never entered an inhabited dwelling'. He slept in the open desert, where he performed the most incredible miracles: he stopped the sun in its course, he raised up the dead (mistakenly, as it happened, believing them to be merely ill, or otherwise he would never have been sufficiently lacking in modesty to do so) and he crossed the Nile by walking on the waters, 'feeling the water come up to his ankles but remain quite firm below'. When, for the only time in his life, he went to a village, he saw so many poor people there that he gave his cloak to one, half his jacket to another, the other half to a third and then, finding that he was stark-naked in the village square, he had to run and sit in a porch, crossing his legs and covering himself with his hands, having nothing left but the Gospel under his arm'!

Further on, we came to an old heathen sanctuary taken over by an anchorite who was engaged in a strange occupation: he picked up stones, stood in front of an idol and flung the stones at it one at a time while begging the statue's forgiveness. If you questioned him he would answer: 'I am trying to be like that idol, for man must be as statues are, insensitive to blows and praise alike.' His name was Poemen.

What was that other anchorite doing still further off? He was watering a dry stick in the open desert with water which he brought from a well two miles away. He was called John the Small (his own modest name for himself), famous on account of his miracle of obedience and perseverance: for two years, on the order of an elder, he watered a dry stick in the desert until it turned green again! And the stick, Palladius tells us, did indeed turn green. When Jean Coppin visited the monasteries of the Wâdi Natrûn, he noticed 'among all those hovels a small dome forming part of a church dedicated to John the Small and, nearby, one is still shown the tree produced by the stick which he watered for two years on his superior's order. It has been given the name of Shajaret el Tâ, which means the Tree of Obedience!'

With the passage of years the number of hermits in the desert of Skete continued to increase. The fame of those amazing anchorites— who spent whole days without food, made dry sticks turn green and walked on the waters—attracted to Skete a number of distinguished visitors. They did not always meet Bessarion or Poemen, who had withdrawn to the heart of the desert, but they visited John the Small, Moses the Ethiopian, Paphnutius the Buffalo and many others.

Among these last there was one, already mentioned, whose fate was most extraordinary: Arsenius the Roman. Unlike the other anchorites, who were Coptic peasants, Arsenius was a very wealthy, cultured Roman of noble birth, who became tutor to the children of Theodosius the Great about the year 383, when he was thirty years old. After ten years at the court of Theodosius he decided to take to the desert and set out for Egypt. There, he heard of Skete and John the Small and went in search of him with the intention of becoming his disciple. John the Small, who knew who Arsenius was and what position he held in the 'world', treated him more harshly than all the other visitors, according to the logic of the desert which required that the anchorites should immediately and eagerly welcome the poor, the beggars and the cameldrivers, and should keep waiting for several hours and, if possible, in full sunlight the officers, the magistrates, the senior officials and even the emperors.

John the Small, therefore, as soon as he saw Arsenius, let him wait for a whole day and, in the evening, threw him a piece of bread, which Arsenius immediately devoured on all fours on the ground. In that way he spent some time in the service of John the Small, carrying out all his orders without argument and eating his food from the ground. When visitors and anchorites expressed astonishment on seeing Arsenius eating in that manner, John the Small replied: 'It is Arsenius, the tutor to the Emperor's children.' Whereupon, everyone showed his approval. When Arsenius had received his training in obedience, he left his master and set out in his turn for a desert cave. In this cave he led a remarkable ascetic existence, which surprised even Rufinus himself:

'When St Arsenius made baskets from palm-leaves and the water in which he soaked them became tainted, he was never willing that it should be renewed but added clean water to the stagnant water so that it should continue to smell bad. Whereupon, the other anchorites said: "Why will you not accept clean water instead of that stagnant liquid which makes your whole cell stink?" He answered: "Once I used the most wonderful perfumes and it is only right that I should endure this bad smell, so that on the Judgement Day God may deliver me from the unimaginable stench of Hell".'

As for his meals, they consisted of two plums and a fig per day, with a little bread, but he did not eat the fruit *until it was overripe*.

About the year 395, an invasion by nomads from the South put the hermits of Skete to flight. Arsenius left for the nearby desert of Memphis, where his reputation brought him many visitors. True to the tradition of the desert, he received them all the more grudgingly because they were of the upper classes, and—perhaps because of his birth—in doing so he brought to bear an extraordinary enthusiasm. One day, a great Roman lady, who had come purposely from Byzantium, knocked at the saint's door. Arsenius opened to her, 'thinking that it was his disciple Daniel. Seeing that it was not Daniel, he threw himself face downwards on the ground and, as the lady asked him to stand up, he answered: "I shall not move from here until you have left." The lady waited for some hours but as the saint still remained where he was she finally went away.'

The case of Arsenius is most certainly a very special one, but that of the other Egyptian anchorites is quite remarkable. When one thinks of what they were before taking to the desert, one can see the extent to which the condition of anchorite or cenobite added to a man's stature by increasing his prestige to an extraordinary degree: a former peasant— who was merely a slave, a victim of his master or the landowner—could, once he had become a hermit, allow himself the 'luxury' of keeping nobles or magistrates waiting and teaching them a few lessons! Many anecdotes even quote instances of masters who came to beg 'instruction' from their former fellah or slave: this radical change in social status certainly explains many aspects of the sudden call of the desert felt by peasants: those are factors which play a decisive part in a man's life, be he Copt or not. The desert restored dignity to the peasant or fellah, it made him what he had never been before: a man.

END OF THE IDOLS

In accepting this description of the deserts of Skete and the Wâdi Natrûn one might think that Christian Egypt, during the fourth century, lived in a kind of waking dream: John the Small untiringly watering the same stick, Poemen wishing to become like the statues and stones, Bessarion parading through the desert his inconsolable regret for original sin, were they not to the limits of probability living through the extraordinary dream of the society of their day: to lead, in those barren wastes, an existence like that in the beginning of the world and to regain the innocence which had been lost? The asceticism of the desert, in short, restored the original dream of Christianity and the very first Christian communities. But this dream was at the same time a nightmare: the first days of man's existence in a world regenerated by the blood of Christ were also the last; everyone awaited—in hope or in agony—the end of the world. To put it briefly, the anchorite in his desert lived both before and after history, in a world both inarticulate and senile; which may explain why his hauntings and visions were so contradictory: the angels and the demons lived side by side in the desert, to the point of intermingling, for, in an instinctive and violent way, each ascetic felt within him the combined influence of innocence and guilt.

Between the cherubim and the demons there is no room in the desert either for man or for history.

Yet, all through the fourth century, history made its presence felt more than ever in Egypt, history which was violent and dramatic: to the disorders already described in the section entitled *The Empire becomes Christian* there were added, at the end of the century, the final bloody convulsions of a paganism in its death-throes. Only through bloodshed and massacre did the gods and idols of Egypt meet their doom.

The fact must be admitted that gods do not always die a violent death. With some surprisingly placid peoples it has come to pass that the outmoded gods have died a natural death, without outrage or bloodshed, and have just been forgotten or incorporated in the new gods. But such peoples were few and, in fact, made little impact on history. In Egypt, at all events, the change from paganism to Christianity was brought about with unusual violence.

Egypt needed some time to assimilate the new religion. Monachism and the flight to the desert were a first consequence of this difficult assimilation and the disturbances in Alexandria which marked the end of idol-worship were another. Allusion is made to it here because, from the end of the fourth century, the history of monasticism is constantly bound up with the blotting out of paganism, since Egypt could not live for long with two such contradictory religions.

The edict of Constantine, proclaimed at Milan, resulted at the outset in the compulsory and difficult co-existence between paganism and Christianity. This co-existence, in fact, soon gave place to Christian predominance, since all the emperors, with the exception of Julian the Apostate, henceforth were Christians and openly encouraged the new religion, even to the extent of plain prohibition of paganism by Theodosius the Great in 392.

This prohibition did not, of course, prevent paganism from persisting for some time, both in theory and in practice, since, in order to remove the last traces of a religion three thousand years old, the Christians had sometimes to resort to looting and burning the statues and temples.

When this violence began, the Christians—even some of the most intelligent among them—showed their failure to understand the values and the nature of paganism. To the Christians, the pagans were not merely beings who lived in error and sin, but were also the devotees of a religion which was beyond their comprehension because it was irrational. At best, they appeared simple or childish, at worst—and that is how they saw the Egyptians—they seemed mentally deranged. In the third century, Clement of Alexandria wrote in his *Protreptic*: 'Those who are concerned with the care and feeding of monkeys have recorded with amazement that these animals are not deceived by images of wax or clay, even when the statues wear girls' clothes. Will you then be worse than monkeys by giving consideration to idols of wood or stone?' And he added: 'How can insensible objects like statues ever have been deified? I do not understand and I pity the wretches who, in their madness, have gone astray. Some creatures, like worms and caterpillars, are lacking in certain senses, others are blind or weak like moles and shrew-mice, "creatures frightening to behold", says Nicander. And yet these inadequate animals are of greater worth than stupid statues. The oyster has neither sight nor hearing, and is voiceless, but it lives and grows and is influenced by the Moon. Statues are helpless things, inert and insensible.' A century later St Athanasius, the author of the *Life of Anthony*, wrote in his treatise *Against the Pagans*: 'The thoughts of some have become so debased and their minds so clouded that they have invented non-existent beings, unknown to creation, and made gods of them. They mix the rational with the irrational, they combine dissimilar natures and honour them as divinities; such are these gods with the heads of dogs, serpents or asses.'

It was, then, the apparent irrationality of Egyptian worship, the incredible combination of the human with the animal in creating the divine, that particularly offended Christian reason.[1] It was judging Egyptian paganism superficially, of course, and confusing the divinity with its liturgical form. Pagan writers of the times did not fail to point out that fact. But that is not the question at the moment. Reading Christian authors like Clement of Alexandria or St Athanasius, who were very well informed on religious matters, rather gives one the impression that they were unwilling to try to understand certain aspects of paganism and that they objected to the compromise which so many other Christian authors, such as Origen, had agreed to make with certain fundamentals of pagan thought and religion. Such a state of mind, a violence done to their intelligence, was inevitably to lead to the physical violence that was wrought a century later upon the pagan gods and philosophers.

Already, indeed, when the first heathen temples were forced and pillaged in the reign of Constantius (that is, after 330), the Christians flung themselves upon the idols, smashed then and (in the words of Eusebius of Caesarea) discovered to their horror, under the image of the god, 'bones, skulls, soiled fabrics, straw and hay'. (There again was the readiness to confuse the divinity with its figurative expression; one might as well say that an ikon of Christ is nothing but a combination of wood, wax and white of egg!)

The whole history of the last years of paganism consists in Egypt, of this continual amazement felt by the Christians in the face of gods, cults and objects, the meaning of which is lost to them and whose forbidding and odious elements they seem to uncover. With each outbreak against the heathen gods there is the same picture, with the same horrific scenes, crowd movements and choruses of hatred, against a background of idols dragged through the streets, defaced and broken, of temples in flames and pagans hunted down even in the innermost

[1] For the very simple reason that, as God had created man from clay, there could be no possible link, in the eyes of a Christian, between the human domain and the animal ('they combine dissimilar natures'). In the pagan view, however, there was nothing fundamentally to divide the human from the animal. This was the *natural* conception of man, as the height of animal evolution, which obtained verification in the nineteenth century. Today, one can no longer be shocked by such expression of the organic unity of living species.

14. THE BASILICA OF ST. SIMEON STYLITES

15A. ST. BARADATES

15B. ST. THALELAEUS

15C. ST. MARON

15D. A DENDRITE (tree-dweller

sanctuaries. A bishop, at the head of an excited crowd, bursts into a heathen temple, throws down the statues and exhibits the objects of worship, the sight of which causes widespread indignation. Then, convinced of the rightness of their action, the Christians go about the streets harrying the pagans. So it was in Alexandria in 361, when George, the bishop of that town, looted the temple of Mithra and showed to the crowd gathered in front of the sanctuary the bulls' skulls which were used in worshipping the god; so it was, also in Alexandria, in 391, when the patriarch Theophilus pillaged a temple of Dionysus and threw to the Christian horde the ithyphallic statuettes of the god, upon which the incensed crowd rushed upon the Serapeum and smashed the great idol of Serapis; in 415, again in Alexandria, a gang of young Christians, urged on by the patriarch Cyril, broke into the house of the philosopher-mathematician Hypatius, one of the greatest pagan thinkers of the fifth century, dragged him into the streets, knocked him senseless, cut up his body and publicly burnt the pieces![1]

What was the more or less avowed object of these acts of violence? In principle, it was to remove the last traces of paganism from the hearts of the Egyptians. But the method does not seem to have borne fruit: paganism continued to offer resistance, precisely because of the violence which it was suffering. Isolated centres of paganism persisted in different parts of the land: first, in Upper Egypt, where Isis was still worshipped at Philae in the sixth century, until the emperor Justinian, in order to abolish the cult, closed the temple, imprisoned the priests and had the statues removed to Constantinople; at Akhmim, pagan temples still flourished in the fifth century (in spite of the prohibition by Theodosius!), and even at the gates of Alexandria in the Delta, at Menuthis for instance, at the end of the century, there were still Isis worshippers and 'the Christians there were so few and so weak in their faith (according to contemporary records) that they accepted the heathens' gold for undertaking not to interfere with the sacrificial rites'.

There is no need to add that all this violence against the temples met with most brutal reactions on the part of the pagans—at least until the edict of Theodosius. Libanius, one of the principal pagan writers of the

---

[1] In fairness it must be stated that a certain number of Christians in Alexandria protested against such violence and refused to be carried away by the patriarch Cyril's fanaticism. Moreover, he could hardly have been held in affection by his flock since, at his death, one of the bishops of Alexandria delivered over his grave the following model of a funeral oration: '*At last this hateful man is dead. His survivors rejoice at his departure, but there is the danger that it may cause distress to the dead themselves. They will soon weary of him and send him back to us. Therefore, place a weighty stone upon his tomb, so that there will be no risk of seeing him again, even in spirit form!*'

fourth century, even addressed to the emperor Theodosius a work entitled *Pro Templis*, in which he called in question the Christians' vandalism. What did the Christians claim to achieve by giving themselves up to pillaging? The conversion of the heathen? Such was not the case, according to Libanius:

'If they tell you, O emperor, that, thanks to these measures, they have converted heathens, do not be deceived. Such converts are so only in appearance. They have in no way changed their faith but are content to say that they have done so. They attend their persecutors' ceremonies, mingle with their number and make a pretence of praying, but in fact they invoke nobody but their own gods. . . . Just as in the tragedies he who plays the tyrant's role is not himself a tyrant, but remains the man he was before putting on the mask, so each of them remains the same and has only apparently changed.'

'*All those altars utterly destroyed*', those priests '*who have to choose between silence and death* and even that imperial army dishonoured *by making war upon stone*', hardly testify (says Libanius) in favour of the Christians' religion. As for the monks, who are the quintessence of that religion, who are the object of general enthusiasm and devotion and are considered almost as saints, do they behave in a manner befitting saints? No. You see them 'rush forward like torrents, devastating the countryside and ruining all the temples. The temples, O emperor, are the soul of the countryside, buildings set among the fields, and have come down to us through many generations. A countryside that has suffered all that devastation is a lost countryside. A peasant's courage vanishes with his hope, when he is deprived of his gods.'

The ineffectual 'dialogue' between Christian and pagan writers, which had been going on for more than three hundred years, continued to the end of the fourth century and beyond. But now violence had taken the the place of speeches and literary invective. One imagines that Libanius, underneath his emotion, was defending not merely the temples but also the life of the priests who lived in them and the faithful who worshipped their gods there. Now that matters had reached such a dramatic pitch, neither Christian nor pagan could see in his adversary's values any more than their most superficial, warped and unreasonable aspects. In *The Pedagogue*, Clement of Alexandria, wrote:

'Would you have me describe for you those who worship idols? Their hair is dirty, they wear filthy rags of clothes and they never wash, their long nails are like the claws of wild beasts. They prove by example that their sanctuaries are merely tombs and prisons. Such people mourn gods more than they worship them.'

This is an excellent description—of the future desert anchorites! What would Clement of Alexandria have said if he had seen Onuphrio, Paphnutius and Aphu the Buffalo, whose only covering was their hair, if he had met John of Egypt, shut in his mountain prison, or Bessarion in tears in the desert because of original sin? And what of all those monks to be seen dressed in black and dismal robes in the village streets of Egypt or in Alexandria itself, to whom the pagan author Zosimus referred when he asked, quite reasonably, 'For whom are they in mourning?'

'COMPEL MEN TO LOVE GOD'

The account of the end of the idols would be incomplete if no mention were made of the monk who, from the fifth century, had the greatest share in it: Shenute of Atripe. Shenute was one of the strangest and most captivating figures of Egyptian Christianity and his *Life*, written by his disciple Visa, was one of the masterpieces of Coptic literature. This work enables one to follow more closely than do the *Lives* of Anthony and Pachomius the incredible adventure of Coptic monachism, the extent of which is clearly shown in the life and work of Shenute.

Shenute was born in Upper Egypt in 333, in the village of Shenalolet (now Geziret Shandanil) to the north of Akhmim. His parents were poor and at an early age he was sent out to watch over the beasts in the fields. But everyone knows that minding animals in one's childhood is the best way of becoming a saint one day; and when those animals are in Upper Egypt, beneath a blazing sun, in heat which continuously offers one a choice between torpor and fever, there is only one alternative: to sink into torpor and remain a leader of beasts all one's life or to fall into the grip of fever and become a leader of men. At eight years of age, Shenute chose the latter course. In the evening, once the animals had been folded, he would set out again alone for the fields, instead of returning home, and spend long hours there. And while he was there he prayed, 'standing neck-deep in an irrigation channel'.

His parents decided to let him do as he wished; and what he wished was to become a monk. At the age of fourteen he was taken to an uncle who was in charge of a monastery not very far from the village and situated on Mount Athribis. Bgoul, the uncle, accepted his nephew Shenute, who was impatient to press on with an asceticism which was insane and fanatical, so as to reach his objective without delay. It was a cruel, impatient asceticism, matching Shenute's character. At sixteen (says Visa) he had already fasted so much 'that he was quite gaunt and his skin hung on his bones'. And not without good reason, for 'often he ate only once a week, on Sunday, when he took vegetables and boiled berries. His body grew very weak and dried-up, and his tears were honey sweet, his eyes became deep-sunk and very dark because of the copious tears he shed.'

At times, he also intensively practised what might be termed the 'brick technique' inaugurated by Pachomius: the ascetic took a brick and stood upon it, praying continuously until its substance was broken down by sweat and tears.

One day, Shenute even found nothing better to do than to tie himself to a cross and remain hanging there for a week. After which, he left for the desert, where he spent five years. When he returned, he had become a man, prepared to face other men, to found a monastery and discipline the monks according to a rule of his own invention.

This rule, in fact, owed much of its inspiration to that of Pachomius, but Shenute, who knew that it was his own work and not an angel's, added a few personal principles such as the systematic use of violence and the rod for the benefit of the monks. In particular, no doubt influenced by Bgoul's rule, he went further than did Pachomius in monastic discipline, the suppression of all individuality and the principle of a collective physical and spiritual existence. In Shenute's monasteries all individual asceticism, mortification and even prayer, were forbidden. Prayers were said collectively, with all the monks prostrated. The latter fasted together, wore the same type of clothing and had, on every occasion, to perform identical movements, whether in the chapel or the refectory or in carrying out the appointed tasks of the monastery. Shenute had the brilliant notion that the achievement of a collective soul first requires the formation of a *collective body*. There can be no other explanation of the care which, all his life, he devoted to shaping the bodies and the souls of his monks by simultaneously imposing both physical and spiritual exercises with the intention of bringing about their 'unification'.

Here are a few examples of both kinds:

Exercises for physical unification: Obedience to any kind of order whatever was obviously an absolute principle and such obedience meant in the first place complete domination of physical reactions. The monk was to be capable—in prayer, the recitation of the psalms or in the performance of some profane exercise—of repeating the same prescribed movements or of remaining motionless for a fixed period of time. For instance, when the bell rang for chapel or for a meal, the monks had immediately to leave their work and remain perfectly still until the second bell, before repairing to the chapel or refectory. Shenute relentlessly punished any monk whom he caught going on with his work or continuing a movement after the bell had rung. Obviously, this sometimes gave rise to difficult situations: one day, a monk in the bakery was surprised by the bell just as he was putting wood in the oven. He remained motionless in this position until the second bell, when he withdrew his hand, completely burnt. Another example of physical unification concerned the making of bread. With dry fruits and cooked herbs, bread was the essential food of the monks and was made in accordance with a definite ritual. The preparation of the flour, the kneading of the dough, the placing in the oven and the baking were carried out within a period of time and according to a fixed technique. In particular, the task was to be performed in complete silence. If a monk needed anything, he would strike according to an agreed plan with a piece of wood, but he would never speak. This rule was carried so far that the mere fact of spattering a little flour through pouring the water too quickly into the kneading-trough was accounted a sin and severely punished.

Exercises for spiritual unification: These were clearly very numerous and cannot be enumerated in detail here. At the most elementary stage, there were first of all some prohibitions: it was forbidden to use the possessive pronoun and to speak of *my* cell, *my* bread, *my* clothes, and laughing was not allowed. The simple fact of laughing or smiling exposed the monk to a beating and none of them cared to be beaten by Shenute, for he sometimes struck the monks so hard 'that they rolled on the ground as if about to die'. It even happened that after one of these beatings a monk would just be taken away to the monastery cemetery, and the incident was regularly recorded in the *Life of Shenute* in admirable euphemistic terms: 'the earth opened and the criminal was swallowed up alive in Hell!' So Shenute came to inspire his monks with real terror, so that everyone ran away as soon as he reached for his cudgel or looked as though he might become angry.

The use of terror and the rod in this training may seem strange, but there again it was a typical Egyptian characteristic of Coptic monachism. By his continual recourse to beating, Shenute, with spiritual objectives in mind, was only making use of a weapon which for three thousand years had proved its value to Egypt in 'facilitating' output by the fellahin in the fields. Shenute continued the tradition of the labour-gang overseers of the pharaohs' days who beat the peasants at every turn, even for leaving just an ear of corn forgotten on the ground; with this difference—and it is a vital difference—that the blows inflicted on the monk at least had the advantage of promoting his salvation, whereas those suffered by the peasant merely benefited the landowner or the pharaoh. The rod, which was already of use to Egypt in all circumstances of life (for the cultivation of the soil, the payment of taxes, the recruitment for war service), naturally came to be used in the attainment of salvation and paradise. Moreover, it would be wrong to think that beating was a humiliation for the peasant or the monk. In 1887, after a long stay in Egypt, Amelineau wrote that 'even today the wife of a fellah despises her husband when he pays taxes of his own accord. But if he pays only as a result of a beating, she immediately feels admiration and respect for his courage'.

The most original contribution made by Shenute in this task of spiritual unification was, therefore, not so much the use of the rod as an instrument of salvation as his success, during the eighty years that he was in control of his monastery (for he probably died in 451 at the age of a hundred and eighteen!), in imposing his own visions upon others, in directing and unifying the aspirations and mystical imagery of the monks.

In order to understand this amazing fact, one must accept that Shenute's peasant monks were incredibly ingenuous. They took everything literally, even the most abstract symbols. One such monk, for instance—no doubt newly converted and having just received an explanation of the mystery of the eucharist—thought that, during Mass, he saw an angel cut up a child at the altar and serve the bleeding morsels during the communion. Another such monk—because he had been told by Shenute that the more pains he took in this world the greater would be his reward in the next—went every day to fetch water from the well and took very short steps in doing so (so that there might be more to his credit), instead of taking his usual two or three strides!

It is understandable that in so fertile a psychic soil the most glaring hoaxes sprouted and multiplied. On his own admission, Shenute showed himself to be as skilful a 'handler' of visions and miracles as he was of the rod. Moreover, he could not do otherwise: no monk, even if he were Coptic and a disciple of Shenute, would have consented to years of flogging unless he had at least a hope of entering the Kingdom of Heaven one day. The use of violence and the rod implied confidence in the future and beyond, and Shenute undertook to see to it that the monks had that confidence. One day, for instance, he summoned a peasant from a distant village, dressed him in costly clothes and made him read the Psalms in church before the full congregation. When the enraptured monks asked Shenute: 'Who was that stranger?' he answered: 'It was David in person come to read the Psalms!'

Another time, the monks were awakened by the bell in the middle of the night. They all ran to the church, where they found three veiled figures going silently round the building before vanishing in the night. Shenute explained: 'They were John the Baptist, Elijah and Elisha, who came from heaven to see how you lived!'

On yet another occasion, when a monk asked him why he had the Apocalypse read every Saturday evening, he replied: 'Because an angel told me recently that in heaven they read the Apocalypse every Saturday evening!'

Thus, all Shenute's authority was invested in the combined use of visions and beatings. But it must not be thought, for all that, that Shenute was just a charlatan. He evidently called rather too often on Heaven, Jesus and his angels whenever it was a matter of punishing or impressing a monk, but it is possible that he himself sometimes believed in such testimony. How often one finds in the *Life of Shenute* incidental phrases or parentheses such as: 'One day, when Shenute was sitting on a stone chatting with Jesus', or: 'One day, when Shenute was walking with Jeremiah in the desert', or even: 'As Shenute's conversation (with the prophet Elijah) showed no sign of coming to an end, I decided to knock on his cell door.' Yes, there comes a time at last when, having every day invoked the testimony, the words or the presence of the angels and the prophets, one comes to believe in them. The more so because these cohorts of angels and prophets were not invoked vainly, for the mere pleasure of causing surprise or of asserting himself, for (as Shenute says in one of his sermons) 'it is not so much on my own account that I chat with the angels as to compel the monks, by such an example, to love God'.

Truth to tell—and it is one of the reasons for his fame—it was not only his monks that Shenute compelled to love God, but many other people as well, including heathens. The name of Shenute is, indeed, bound up with a whole series of undertakings—they might even be called raids—against the pagan temples in the neighbourhood of Akhmim, raids which the *Life* reports innocently and in all good conscience. How could men who chat every day with Ezekiel and St John the Baptist and who take their instructions from Christ personally have the slightest doubt of the great value and saintliness of their under-takings?

At first, Shenute was concerned only with the religious observances and the buildings: he was 'content' to break into the heathen temples with his monks, throw down the idols, smash their faces and throw the pieces into the Nile, while not omitting to remove to the monastery all the vessels, figures and precious objects capable of realizing money! But Shenute and his monks later also attacked the priests of the cult and, in an obviously eulogistic form, the *Life of Shenute* and the *Sermons* have preserved the accounts of some of these 'sallies'. Here is the first of them: 'It came to pass that one day Shenute entered the town of Akhmim to destroy the idols in the house of Gesius, a heathen, while he was away during the night. He and two monks, mounted on asses, came to the river.' They crossed the river, went inside Gesius's house, the doors of which opened of their own accord (a Coptic way of saying that they had accomplices on the spot, probably Christian slaves of the owner), took the idols, broke them up and threw them into the river.

When he returned, Gesius was furious to find his house completely ransacked and went and complained to the governor. He had cause to rue it, for, says the *Life of Shenute*, 'since Jesus took his wealth away nothing has been heard of him'. Clearly, it did not pay to run counter to these monks. Without going to the extent of showing approval, the Byzantine emperors—Theodosius the Great and his successors—did nothing to prevent or stop these acts of banditry carried out under the banner of Christ. The pagans of Akhmim and the surrounding villages began to quake at the very name of Shenute. And with just cause, because, some time later, a much more serious incident took place at Akhmim, which Shenute himself records in one of his *Sermons*. This incident occurred in respect of a statue which pronounced oracles and around which the pagans continued to flock. One day, during such a gathering, Shenute and his monks burst into the town, overturned the statue and shattered it. There followed scuffles which degenerated into massacres, the monks like raving madmen having begun to set fire to the houses, to loot the town and butcher the citizens in the streets. For having opposed the monks (states Shenute), these pagans met the same fate as Gesius: 'They were not heard of again and, after their death, their bones were scattered to the winds. They were burnt because of their insolence in having cursed the servants of God and uttered blasphemies against Christ in person.'

In short, in his struggle against the pagans, Shenute revealed the same temperament and the same violence that met with such great success in his struggle against the ignorance and ingenuousness of his monks, except that in the former case he was both judge and plaintiff, predicting for the pagans catastrophes which he lost no time in bringing about personally in case Heaven's wrath failed to manifest itself! And nothing could stop Shenute, apparently, in this murderous madness, since even in 450, shortly before his death at the age of a hundred and seventeen, he was still sacking a heathen temple with his monks in the middle of Thebaid!

It is true that Shenute was not the only one to hasten the end of paganism. A rather curious text, the *Panegyric of Macarius of Tkôou*, written about 450 and attributed to Dioscurus the patriarch of Alexandria, reveals the uneasy tension which existed at that time between the pagan and Christian communities in the country districts. Thus, in a village of Upper Egypt, where there were heathen Greeks who still worshipped the god Kothos (fifty years after the prohibition by Theodosius the Great!), it was suddenly rumoured and spread about by the Christians that these Greeks 'stole the Christians' children in order to offer them as sacrifices to the god Kothos'. One day, 'they were observed in this wickedness, taking the Christian children and leading them to the altar of their god'. In fact, the Greeks 'confessed': 'We entice the Christians' little children by giving them pieces of bread and other good things to eat, we catch them and hide them in a secret place so that their cries are not heard. After that, we butcher them on the altar and remove their entrails to make strings for our cithers and extol our gods. As for the bodies, they are burnt to ashes. And every time there is treasure hidden somewhere, we take a large quantity of these ashes and scatter them over the hidden places. We sing to the accompaniment of our cithers with the strings made from entrails and the treasure immediately appears.'

Hearing of these 'confessions', Macarius of Tkôou set out with his monks for the temple in question. On seeing them, the pagans 'came out with weapons in their hands, axes and spears, and took their wives with them to the roof in order to stone us'. They even succeeded in laying hands on Macarius and were preparing to sacrifice him when, at that moment, one of his disciples appeared, brought them to a standstill and released Macarius who had been put in irons! The monks took Homer the high priest and, having lit a great fire, 'threw the high priest upon it, together with all the idols they could find in the houses'.

So did paganism come to an end, in the little village of Tkôou!

	HISTORY	CHRISTIANITY
350	BYZANTINE EMPIRE	
	THEODOSIUS	
		391 Sacking of the Serapeum of
	395 Death of Theodosius	Alexandria by the Christians.
	Arcadius, emperor.	
400		
	408-450 THEODOSIUS II	415 Murder of the philosopher Hypatius by the Christians.
		422 Beginning of the Nestorian heresy.
		431 Council of Ephesus condemns *Nestorianism*.
450		
	457-474 Leo I	451 Council of Chalcedon condemns *Monophysism*.
	476 Zeno	Spreading of Monophysism in Egypt, Syria and Armenia.
500		
	518 Justinian dynasties	Persecutions of the Monophysites in the Byzantine Empire.
	527 JUSTINIAN	Justinian closes the temple of Isis at Philae.
550		
	565-578 Justin II	Extension of Nestorianism into Persia, Mesopotamia and
	582-622 Maurice	Central Asia.
600		
	602-610 Phocas	Final schism of the Eastern Churches with Byzantium.
	HERACLIUS	—Creation of the Monophysite Coptic Church.
		—Creation of the Jacobite Syriac Church.

EGYPT AND THE NEAR EAST	LITERATURE
First lauras in Palestine and and first anchorites in Syria.	Works by St Ephraem.
389 Birth of St Simeon Stylites.	389 *Pro Templis* by Libianos.
	390 *Concerning Prayer* by Evagrius Ponticus.
	400
	404 St Jerome translates the *Rules of Pachomius*.
St Simeon installed at Qal'at Sim'ân.	420 *Lausiac History* by Palladius.
	Spiritual Homilies by (the false) Macarius.
	425 *Institutions of the Monks* and *Conversations* by Cassian.
450 Death of Shenute?	450 *Religious History* by Theodoret.
459 Death of St Simeon Stylites.	
	473 Syriac *Life* of St Simeon Stylites. *Ecclesiastical History* by Evagrius the Scholastic.
	500
St Daniel the Stylite.	*Life of St Mary the Egyptian*?
St Alipius the Stylite.	
496 Death of St Simeon the Younger.	
	600
	615 The *Spiritual Meadow* by John Moschus.
	630 The *Ladder to Paradise* by John Climacus.

CHAPTER 7

CLOSER TO HEAVEN

'Simeon lived like an angel in a mortal body and, by harsh treatment of that nature which tends by its own weight to keep man pinned to the earth, he rose up between earth and heaven, spoke with God and offered prayers on behalf of men.'

LIFE OF ST SIMEON STYLITES

The principles underlying anchoritism and monachism were the same in all Christian countries of the Near East: an identical conception of human destiny and an identical manner of regarding the continual struggle on the part of man against the world and Evil drove men into the desert. Throughout the Near East, anchoritism and monachism ought, then, also to be alike *in form*, during the centuries in which they came to light. And yet, the ascetics, monks and saints to be found in Palestine and Syria, differed appreciably from their Egyptian models. The reason is that an undertaking of this sort, however original it may appear to be, had its roots in the past, in the legacy of particular images, symbols and feelings. The ascetic's judgement, objective and methods might be the same in Egypt, Palestine and Syria, but the enduring influence of the past was felt in different ways.

Two Greek writers, Theodoret of Cyrrhus and John Moschus, who travelled in Palestine and Syria in the fifth and sixth centuries are the guides in our further investigation of the realm of asceticism.

Theodoret, who was born at Antioch in 393 and later became the bishop of Cyrrhus, near that city, was the author of an important *Religious History*, written about the middle of the fifth century and incorporating the *History of the Monks of Syria*, which describes the lives and miracles of some thirty Syrian ascetics. The testimony offered by Theodoret of Cyrrhus is personal, because he visited and came to know the saints he describes, including the famous St Simeon Stylites. Additional testimony is supplied by St Ephraem, the great fourth-century Syriac poet who was himself an ascetic of the desert and wrote a *Eulogy of the Solitaries of Syria and Mesopotamia*, as well as by a few fragments of the *Ecclesiastical History* by Evagrius the Scholastic, written in the sixth century with reference to the ascetics of Syria.

John Moschus, born in Damascus about the middle of the sixth century, was the author of the *Spiritual Meadow*, one of the most interesting and wonderful books in Christian literature. It is a collection of three hundred edifying and miraculous stories 'gathered' in the deserts of Syria, Palestine, Sinai and Egypt and describing the daily lives of eastern ascetics, most of them the author's contemporaries. They abound in miracles and demoniac scenes, but the 'fault' does not lie with Moschus, for his informants believed in such things as much as he did, and he merely reported what he was told. Moreover, Moschus was himself a monk, an itinerant monk who travelled through all the deserts, interviewing the ascetics even in the most inaccessible places. It was not circumstances or actions that interested him, but men, and this interest in humanity gives the *Spiritual Meadow* the free and living quality that was to be found again, centuries later, in the *Stories of a Russian Pilgrim*.

ON TO SYRIA

A traveller making his way on foot from Egypt to Syria about the middle of the fourth century would have observed a strange contrast in these two lands. On leaving the Nile valley, with its caves and desert places already peopled by anchorites, he would have found before him, at the foot of the Sinai peninsula and in the deserts of Palestine, nothing but a vast wilderness. The anchorites had not yet come so far, or were just beginning to do so. A youth of fifteen, 'dressed only in sacking and a hair tunic', who had left Gaza in search of a suitable place for meditation, stopped 'between the sea and the swamps of that vast and terrifying wilderness which lies to the left, seven miles from Maiyûm, as one goes along the coast from Palestine to Egypt'. This youth was the future St Hilarion, the first of the Palestinian anchorites, whose life was described by St Jerome with the same, rather questionable, enthusiasm as that of Paul of Thebes. St Hilarion, it is true, has never quite been accepted by history—at any rate with the characteristics given him by St Jerome—and, there again, the author is alone with his model; an admirable and impressive model, it is true. The devil himself, accustomed to tempting anchorites of venerable age in Egypt, was taken unawares by this fifteen-year-old ascetic who 'ate only fifteen figs a day after the sun had set', and, 'being powerless to do more, was reduced to causing him sensual excitement by striving to create in a body which was experiencing its first youthful promptings the urge to indulge in pleasures so far unknown to it'. This temptation explains the harsh, rigidly methodical asceticism practised by St Hilarion: between the ages of twenty-one and twenty-seven he lived entirely on lentils soaked in cold water, bread, salt and water. From twenty-seven to thirty years,

roots and wild herbs. From thirty-one to thirty-five years, half a pound of barley bread a day and a few cooked herbs. But, St Jerome adds, 'he felt his sight becoming dimmed and his skin as rough as pumice-stone. He therefore added a little oil to all that I have just mentioned, and he practised this extreme abstinence until he was sixty years old'.

On venturing further into the Sinai peninsula, the traveller would have found a more broken landscape, with barren mountains, gorges and wâdis, but as empty as St Hilarion's desert. The monastery of St

Catherine—established near the top of Mt Sinai—and first called the Monastery of the Confabulation, to commemorate the dialogue between Moses and Jehovah, was not built until the time of Justinian, two centuries later. In the middle of the fourth century, Sinai was as yet just a bare peninsula, peopled by a few anchorites who lived in caves or at the bottom of the wâdis in almost unbelievable solitude and privation; such a one was the anonymous ascetic whom St Simeon the Elder encountered and who was installed in a mere hole in the desert. 'After walking for two days along the road to Sinai', says Theodoret, 'St Simeon the Elder and his disciple noticed in the desert a man's hands in a raised position protruding from a hollow.' They thought they were the victims of a mirage (the mirage being always a device of the devil), offered up a prayer and went near. 'They saw a small pit like a fox-hole but observed nobody in it, for the man with the raised hands had withdrawn into hiding when he heard their footsteps. The saint leaned forward to look into the hole and entreated the occupant to be good enough to show himself and to say whether he was man or demon. So the man who had hidden in the hole made his appearance, a wild look in his eye, his hair matted with filth, his face covered in wrinkles, the rest of his body dried up and wearing a poor, tattered coat of palm-leaves.'

Still more strange was the anchorite described by Sulpicius Severus in his book on *The Virtues of the Eastern Solitaries* and mentioned to Postumianus when he visited Sinai towards the end of the fourth century:

'It is said that in the most secluded places on Mount Sinai there lives an anchorite whom I sought for a long time without success, and I am told that it is nearly fifty years since he gave up all conversation with his fellow men. For clothing he had only his hair, which covered his entire body, God thereby granting him a particular favour in affording the means of hiding his nakedness. When pious men made an attempt to meet him he removed himself to inaccessible places so as to avoid them. About five years ago, by the power of his faith, one man gained the extraordinary favour of making his acquaintance. In the course of several talks with him, he asked the reason why he took such pains to avoid men's conversation. The anchorite replied that those who are visited by men could hardly receive visits from the angels at the same time; which created the general impression that the angels did visit him.'

The appearance presented by Palestine is not obviously very different.

As the traveller passed through the desert of Judah, there too he might have seen a few anchorites installed in the wâdis that run into the Dead Sea. At the beginning of the fourth century, the very first anchorites settled in the caves of the Calamon desert, to the south of Jericho, where they replaced the Essenes. (It was in this desert that the Dead Sea scrolls were discovered.) Such an anchorite was St Chariton, who founded the laura of Pharan about the year 330, and another, of later date, was St Gerasimus, who became famous for having looked after a lion which stayed with him until he died. The whole of this region, the deserts of Judah, Cedron and Calamon, later became the chief eremitic and monastic centre of the country at the beginning of the fifth century, thanks to St Euthymius and St Sabas who, in the religious history of Palestine, played a part similar to that of Anthony and Pachomius in Egypt. The anchorites, scattered among the caves which overhung the wâdis, spent the weeks in solitude and met together on Saturdays and Sundays in some church (as in Skete and Nitria) where they sang the Psalms and performed the office without interruption. These communities, which lasted for a very long time in Palestine side by side with the monasteries properly so-called, were known as *lauras*.

Leaving the Dead Sea and the desert of Calamon, and continuing on his way northwards along the right bank of the Jordan River, the traveller would have seen no living creature in the eastern desert, unless it was a figure in the far distance running away at his approach. This figure could only have been that of the woman who was the sole inhabitant of this desert: Mary the Egyptian.

St Mary the Egyptian was not the first woman to take to the desert. Already, in Egypt, in addition to the nuns living in the convents founded by Pachomius, Theodore and Shenute, there were women anchorites. But there were few of these women, and their existence in the desert very soon gave rise to a certain number of narratives in which it is difficult to distinguish between history and legend. In the view of the anchorites of Egypt, the desert was not the place for women and whenever they saw one they considered her as a demon rather than a human being. The reason is that the devil very often took the form of a woman, usually poor and hungry and lost in the desert, who begged the anchorite to grant her hospitality for the night. This explains that the few women who lived as anchorites in the desert preferred to pass for men. So it was with St Apollinaris Syncletica, who lived for several years in the desert of Skete as a follower of Macarius the Elder under the name of Dorotheus, and whose true identity was unknown to him until the time of her death, when he buried her. Another such woman was

16A. LIFE OF ST. EPHRAEM

16B. ST. JAMES OF NISIBIS

17. THE TEMPTATION OF ST. ANTHONY
(detail of painting by Grünewald)

Athanasia, who lived at Skete some time afterwards, in the sixth century, and whose very beautiful story is briefly as follows:

At first, Athanasia was a woman of the age, beautiful, simple and happy. She had a husband, Andronicus, and two children whom she loved. But the children died and she and her husband decided that they should dedicate their lives to God and set out for the desert. When they arrived at the Wâdi Natrûn they bade each other farewell and went each one to a different place. They lived separate lives in this way for twelve years. Athanasia had cut off her hair, put on a man's coat and taken the name of Athanasia. It so happened that, after twelve years, her husband Andronicus asked to be sheltered in her cell, but he failed to recognize his wife 'whose beauty had so faded because of macerations that her face had become as black as an Ethiopian's'. Moved by the asceticism and the kindness of 'brother Athanasius', Andronicus suggested that he should stay with him and that they should practise self-mortification together. They lived in this way for twelve years and Andronicus never suspected his companion's identity. It was only when she was about to die that Athanasia disclosed her sex and her name to her husband.

This tale of the desert—for such it is, even if it has some basis of truth—is built around a central theme frequently to be found in Mediterranean stories: that of the hero who assumes a false identity and lives unrecognized in the bosom of his own family. The theme dates from pre-Christian times and already appears in the *Odyssey*. When Ulysses returned, nobody (except his dog) recognized him and he lived for some time as a beggar in his palace of Ithaca. With Christianity, the theme produced, for example, the very beautiful legend of St Alexis, the 'man of God' who left his home for the desert. He later returned to his family and, until his death, lived with them as a servant without being recognized by his mother or his wife.

The meaning underlying this kind of story is readily understood: they are tales of 'initiation', in which the hero, after a series of trials (consisting of long sea-voyages or sojourning in the desert), comes back as a victor, inwardly transformed. The new man has completely replaced the old one and the story symbolically illustrates this metamorphosis with a change in the hero's appearance: he becomes so different that even his wife or mother fails to recognize him. But, in its passage from paganism to Christianity, the content of the story underwent appreciable modification: in the pagan versions the initiatory theme was most often combined with that of an *avenger's return*. It was in order to be avenged upon Penelope's suitors that Ulysses did not allow himself to be recognized; it was to avenge his father Agamemnon that Orestes, after twenty years' absence, returned to his mother Clytemnestra in the guise of a foreign traveller. The change in appearance, whether it is due to time or disguise, means above all that the hero acquires a new power, a new physical strength that ensures victory over his enemies. In the Christian context, the legend was given moral significance. The enemies to be fought by Alexis and Athanasia became 'inward' enemies: they were no longer suitors or usurpers but the temptations of this life, the thousand familiar images which life set up around them and within them: a wife, a husband, beings once the objects of tender affection. The strength they acquired in solitude was a new strength which enabled them to be so 'dead' to the world that Alexis could live for years with his former wife and Athanasia with her former husband as if they were both unaware of everything, including their own sex.

This predominantly Christian theme of *dissociation from the world* is to be found in conjunction with other legendary and aretological elements in the *Life of St Mary the Egyptian*. There one finds the theme of the sinner turned saint (Thaïs), that of the woman so unaware of her sex that she is mistaken for a man (Athanasia) and, finally, that of the saint who, on the example of Paul of Thebes, lives on by God's goodness and shortly before her death receives a visitor who makes her incredible existence known to posterity; after which she dies and is buried by lions.

The first two of these instances might well belong as much to history as to story. There have certainly existed courtesans or prostitutes who were converted and some of whom even became saints. Certain details of the life of Mary the Egyptian (such as the account of her struggles against the temptations of the flesh and the world) have the ring of truth and were not invented, but originated from stories concerning some unknown woman anchorite. But the appeal which the *Life of St Mary the Egyptian* made for such a long time to Eastern and Western readers shows that it was less its historical aspect than its fictitious quality that was so fascinating to the Christians and later generations. Furthermore, the theme of the repentant sinner—as historical as it could be—made a late appearance in Christian literature and coincided approximately with the ascendancy of Christianity. It is probable that the Christians of the early centuries—obsessed with virginity, chastity and the encratic or apotactical life—would have found it difficult to admit that a profligate woman might become a saint. On the other hand, later, when Christians ceased to be persecuted and their *struggles with the world became inner struggles*, a new type of saint made his appearance: the repentant libertine or criminal, chosen by God to become a saint by reason of his very sins, whose struggle is in the first place a continual battle fought *against his own past* and the temptations of the world; such was the pattern of the new conflicts facing Christendom. But, in fact, within the scope of religious history these two themes are identical; whether she is virgin or martyr on the one hand or profligate on the other, the future saint is particularly endowed with religious powers and values. It is a fact that in ancient societies there were only two ways in which a woman could serve the gods and draw near to them: by sacred virginity or by sacred prostitution. In either case, whether it was a question of preserving sexual energy (virginity) or of expending it (prostitution), the path led away from human society, towards the gods and, eventually, towards God. In brief, Mary the Egyptian was a fairly clear case of the sacred prostitute in Christianity. Therefore, the author of her *Life* (written probably about the beginning of the sixth century and for a long time wrongly attributed to Sophronius, the patriarch of Jerusalem) perfectly applied the secret logic peculiar to religious thinking by attributing to Mary the Egyptian every imaginable sin. The greater the sinner, the greater the repentance or, in other words, the further one is from God in one sense, the closer one may be to him in another. But let the reader be reassured: all the sexual exploits laid at Mary's door were probably as legendary as her ascetic exploits in the desert. For the seventeen years she lived in Alexandria, she did indeed put herself at the disposal of all comers, through her addiction to vice and for her own pleasure. 'It was not for rewards that I ceased to be a virgin. No. I refused the money that was offered to me and the passion that raged within me made me think that there would be many more men ready to come to me if I desired no further reward for my sinning than the sin itself.'

But giving herself to all and sundry, even in Alexandria, was not enough for Mary the Egyptian. She therefore decided to accompany some pilgrims on their voyage to Jerusalem for the Exaltation of the Cross, because, as there were more than three hundred of them, 'I should have had many to share my passion'!

When they came to Jerusalem, she wanted to go inside the church of St John the Baptist, but an unknown force prevented her from doing so. Terrified, she bethought herself of her past life and decided to be converted and dedicate herself to God.[1] She therefore left Jerusalem, passed through the valley of the Jordan and plunged into the eastern desert, far from men and her former associates.

---

[1] It is noteworthy that, as for Thaïs and Athanasia, it was a sudden conversion, the immediate inversion of values, impurity suddenly became transformed to purity.

One morning, forty-seven years later, a monk of the name of Zosimus
was at prayer in the desert to which he had withdrawn for a few days,
and just as he was raising his eyes to Heaven while singing the Psalms,
he observed to his right hand 'a vague human shape. At first, he was
filled with fear and astonishment, thinking that it was one of the Devil's
illusions, but, having strengthened himself by making the sign of the
Cross and dispelled his apprehension, he looked round and saw indeed
that there was somebody walking very quickly in a westward direction.
What he saw was a woman whose body had been blackened by exposure
to the fierce heat of the sun and whose hair was as white as wool but so
short that it came down only to her neck.'

Zosimus followed 'the shape that was running ahead of him', not yet
quite sure that it was a human being, and they both came to a dry river-
bed, which the 'shape' crossed. Zosimus stopped at the near bank and
the 'shape' said: 'I ask your forgiveness, father Zosimus. I cannot turn
round to speak to you, for I am a woman and, as you see, quite naked,
but, if you will help a poor sinner, throw me your cloak, so that I may
cover myself with it and turn towards you to receive your blessing.'

And Mary the Egyptian, wrapped in Zosimus's cloak, told him the
story of her life, of her profligate existence in Alexandria, her strange
pilgrimage to Jerusalem, her miraculous conversion and her leaving for
the desert forty-seven years before. On what did she feed during all that
time? 'When I crossed the Jordan river, I had in my possession two and
a half loaves of bread which soon became dry and as hard as stones. I
ate only a little and they lasted me seventeen years'! Seventeen years of
a difficult existence in which the acquisition of virtue and the conflict
with the temptations of the world were a daily struggle against the
memories of the flesh, the pleasures, the glitter and the music of a world
left behind:

'Yes. I spent seventeen years of ceaseless struggle against violent,
insistent and preposterous longings: I yearned for meat, I missed the
fish I had to eat in Egypt, and I should so much have liked some of that
wine which I enjoyed in the days when I was of the world and which I
drank to such excess that I became unconscious. Here, I had not even a
drop of water, which created in me a thirst so burning that I thought I
should die. And I also had a longing to sing ribald songs, which are the
work of the Devil and which, since I had learnt them in the world,
memory brought back to fill my troubled mind.'

But, thanks to fasting and prayer, Mary overcame her desires and acquired such great virtue that the desert became for her a place of miracles: she walked on the waters of the Jordan, rose up into the air as she prayed, talked with animals and lived on bread sent from Heaven. Zosimus left her but returned the next year to the meeting-place which had been agreed between them, the banks of the same stream. He found the body of the saint lying on the ground, her hands folded and her face turned towards the East and, while he was wondering whether he should bury the body on the spot or take it back to the monastery, he saw these words being written in the sand: 'Father Zosimus, bury the body of wretched Mary, give back to the earth what is the earth's, add dust to dust!' It was the saint's last miracle, posthumous in this case, since, in her lifetime, 'she had told him that she could not write'!

The history of Christian Syria was not unlike that of Egypt. Like Egypt, Syria had a river (the Orontes), a cosmopolitan capital (Antioch), some mountains such as the Amanus group and large expanses of desert. But, unlike Egypt, which faced the sea and was open to all external influences, Syria was a country which faced inland, towards the eastern deserts that linked it with Mesopotamia and Persia. This continental aspect of Syria should be noted: it explains why, at the time of the great schism in the sixth century, when (on the example of the Coptic Church) the Syriac Church broke away from Byzantium and became Monophysite, it led all eastern Christendom into heresy and schism. Although Antioch was for a long time a great centre of Hellenism and Syria itself was occupied for centuries by the Greeks and Romans, the country was never a Roman or Byzantine 'bridge-head' to the East but rather the opposite: the furthest advance-post towards the West and the Mediterranean for the various lands of the Middle East, that whole spiritual continent of which Edessa, Nisibis, Mosul, Seleucia and Ctesiphon were the religious and cultural capitals.

There was another essential difference between Syria and Egypt: Syria never had a religious past like that of Egypt, with gods, customs and creeds deep-rooted in a people and a soil for thousands of years. When Christianity made its appearance, Syria was in fact, religiously speaking, virgin ground, occupied by a paganism which was much less virulent than that of Egypt and which, in particular, was not in any sense intermingled with precise national feeling. Syria never had Egypt's ethnical unity and was much more what might be called a mosaic of peoples: Syrians speaking the Syriac tongue, Syrian Jews speaking Aramaic, Greek and then Roman occupants.

In short, lacking such roots and cultural unity, Syria was able to embark on the Christian adventure much more freely than Egypt, to create, without any compromise with a dominating past, its own religious forms and creeds and engage in anchoritic experiment which would result in the complete reformation of its culture, its literature, its art and its architecture.

This reformation began at the end of the fourth century. At that time the great names of Egyptian asceticism were known in Syria, thanks to Evagrius of Antioch, who translated the *Life of Anthony* into Latin, and to the works of St Jerome. But, from the outset, in Syria anchoritism and asceticism followed paths which were very different from those of Egypt and much more extreme, so much so that the influence of Egyptian asceticism may be considered to have been negligible.

The country lent itself very readily to the many forms of asceticism. Whereas Egypt offered only deserts as places of retreat for the practice of asceticism, a barren land which compelled one to live in the open or to burrow in the earth, Syria, on the other hand, offered the anchorites a great variety of landscape and climate: the mountainous or forested region of Amanus, between Antioch and the sea (which was rather suited to the *recluses* living in hollow tree-trunks and the *browsers* living on herbs, roots and fruit), the plain of Dana, between Antioch and Aleppo (more favourable to the *stylites* who lived motionless on top of pillars and could not settle too far from the towns or villages), the desert of the Apameia region to the south which supplied ascetic conditions similar to those of Egypt. It therefore seems that there existed in Syria a close bond between the different types of asceticism that were created there and the natural setting in which they were practised. It was evidently a bond in a double sense, for the choice of a certain setting by any particular ascetic undoubtedly corresponded to an inner selection, according as he was seeking a barren spot (the desert) or one of prolific growth (the forest). In either case, the choice indicated a fundamental attitude with regard to Creation and the outside world, corresponding to each of the two types of asceticism mentioned above which might be called *asceticism in a restricted setting* (the recluse living in the forests) and *asceticism in an open setting* (the stylite on his pillar, set among crowds of people). In the first case the anchorite was obliged to lead an existence which was the negation of a 'natural' life: living under restriction, as a *recluse*, confined to a cave, a tomb, even a hole made in the ground, the inside of a hollow tree or a cage. Such a life, in the depths of silence and darkness, in a place where the influences of the outside world were almost entirely abolished (and in any case distorted), led the ascetic to retire within himself and to suppress the outer world by a sort of return to pre-natal existence. It certainly seems as if this was the basic meaning of that seclusion, of that hiding in the darkness: to act as though the living world no longer existed, by creating around oneself an *artificial world* and by abolishing all *social acquirement*.

The second choice—asceticism in an open setting—was obviously more difficult to attain, since it meant living in the world and preserving contacts with society: the ascetic had disciples, received visitors, gave advice and harangued the crowds of pilgrims. In brief, *he endeavoured to obliterate the Ego without abolishing the social relations*. In order to be effective such asceticism required extremely rigorous methods in practice, because of the continual temptations to which the ascetic was exposed; methods which, again, consisted in adopting an artificial attitude *as different as possible from that of the human state*, precisely because he continued to live among men. Such was undoubtedly the meaning underlying the asceticism practised by the *browsers* (consisting in feeding on herbs and roots, even in moving about on all fours and living 'like an animal'), the *stylites* and the *dendrites* (who lived on top of pillars or in the branches of trees and 'regressed' to the vegetal stage) and the *statics* who remained motionless amid the crowd, without uttering a word or even raising their eyes; the ascetic then became a sort of human statue, 'regressing' to the mineral stage. In each of these cases it was one of the essential attributes of man—speech, movement or posture—that was repudiated and repressed.

THE RECLUSES

Reclusion was not a form of asceticism peculiar to Syria. John of Egypt in Thebaid and the anchorites of the Desert of Cells lived as recluses in caves like 'hyena-holes'. But the Syrians intensified this type of asceticism and, what is particularly important, practised it continually. In the *Life of Macarius the Younger*, it is stated that Macarius used to retire once a year for forty days to his hole in the Desert of Cells. In Syria, on the contrary, Theodoret and John Moschus mention ascetics who lived as recluses for several years in succession.

Most of the time they shut themselves up in narrow huts which they built for themselves and they saw nobody. A disciple brought them food and drink once or twice a week.

Thus, St Marcianus's cabin was 'so tiny that it was not large enough for him alone. Whether he was standing or lying down he was always in great discomfort. He could not stand up without his head touching the roof and could not stretch out his legs when lying down, since the hut was shorter than he was.'

Another, St Acepsimas, 'whose reputation was widespread throughout the East, shut himself in a small house, saw nobody and spoke to nobody. When he was brought food, he took it through a hole made obliquely in the wall so that one could not see through it into the inside. This food consisted of soaked lentils and was brought to him once a week. As for water, he came out at night and took as much as he needed from a nearby spring.'

This seclusion was evidently accompanied by the deepest silence. The recluses lived in darkness, saw nobody and spoke to nobody. It was *par excellence* asceticism in a restricted setting, implying a complete withdrawal into oneself and particularly strict in the case of St Salaman, referred to by Theodoret, who 'was confined to a cottage in a settlement on the banks of the Euphrates. He blocked up all the doors and windows and through a hole made underground he received, on one single occasion, enough food to last him for a year. He never spoke to anyone at all.' This was almost regression to the animal stage with storage of food and annual hibernation!

Others, for their seclusion, preferred hollow trees. Certain trees, like cedars and plane-trees, had trunks large enough to hold a man standing, sitting or squatting, and became an ideal place for reclusion. The two ascetics, David and Adolas, mentioned by John Moschus, both lived near a town on the banks of the Euphrates. They were 'confined in the hollow trunks of plane-trees' and Adolas 'had a small window made, through which he communicated with those who came to see him'.

St Maron also 'spent eleven years in a hollow tree-trunk' and, later, in the ninth century, near Mount Olympus in Asia Minor, 'a certain Luke lived inside a tree-trunk'.

There were also, of course, recluses installed in tombs: St James, for instance, described by Theodoret, who stayed for several years in a sepulchre before he became a static, and St Sisinnius, who spent three years in a tomb 'without sitting, lying down or walking a single step'.

The sixth century writer, Evagrius the Scholastic, mentions in his *Ecclesiastical History* others who 'shut themselves up in cells so low-built and confining that they can neither stand nor lie down without difficulty. Thus, they retire into the caves and caverns of the earth or spend their lives in holes with the animals'.

But the strangest recluse in the whole of Syria was undoubtedly St Thalelaeus whom Theodoret visited and found reading the Gospels in a sort of cage on a hill covered with olive-trees and fig-trees. This cage was made 'from two wheels, each two cubits in diameter, nailed or pegged to battens some distance apart, and slung from three stout poles.

I found him sitting in it. It was only two cubits high and one cubit wide and he had already spent ten whole years in it, although he could not straighten his back and had to rest his head on his knees.'

To spend one's life cooped up in a tree-trunk or in a cage with one's head down and one's body bent double was apparently not enough, for some ascetics, to ensure their salvation, and to these unbelievable reclusions they added a few 'refinements'! Let us pass on to consider the fasts, which were clearly most austere and sometimes amounted to plain masochism. St Sabinus, for example, not content with staying motionless in his hut, 'punished his body with extraordinary austerities. He ate neither bread nor anything that is eaten with bread, living entirely on flour which he left soaking in water for a month so that it should smell bad and taste worse.'

One of the commonest refinements consisted in wearing iron chains, sometimes very heavy, which made it extremely difficult to stand. St Acepsimas, for instance, was weighed down with so many chains that 'he was obliged, when he went out to drink, to walk on all fours'! One evening, a shepherd mistook him for a wolf and very nearly threw a stone at him. The next morning, when he went in search of the saint to ask his forgiveness, 'he knew that he had been pardoned, not from anything the saint said to him, but because he heard his hands move in the darkness of his hut'.

Another saint, Eusebius, usually wore 'iron chains weighing twenty pounds and added the fifty carried by the godly Agapius as well as the eighty worn by the great Macarius. He wore these chains for three years in the middle of a dried-up lake'.

Even women anchorites (and there were many more of them in Syria than in Egypt) did not hesitate to put on chains. St Marana and St Cyriaca, for example, wore so many of them that they always walked bent double. 'With my own eyes,' states Theodoret, 'I saw these chains, so heavy that the strongest men could not carry them. After many prayers I was able to persuade them to leave them aside but as soon as I left they took them up again. They put them round their necks like collars and wore them like girdles round their loins, in addition to those on their hands and feet. That is how they spent, not five, ten or fifteen years, but forty-two.'

But there is a disadvantage about chains: they are conspicuous and can be heard from a distance when one walks. For those who, like St Polychronius, 'banished from their minds all desire to be honoured by men', such asceticism was capable of two interpretations and, when all is said, was a little too spectacular. St Polychronius therefore had brought to him 'a very large oak-root on the pretence of needing it for some other purpose. He would put it on his shoulders at night when about to pray and by day when he was alone. But as soon as he heard anyone coming he would hide it at once.'

Very silent also—although not entirely free of ostentation—was the incredible asceticism devised by St Maron, who had installed himself inside a tree-trunk lined with huge thorns to prevent him from moving and also arranged a complicated system of stones to press down on him so as to make it impossible for him to move his head. An objection to this asceticism could be made on the score that if one really intends not to move there is no need for such artificial devices. The inevitable limits and pitfalls of these experiments can be seen: endowing ordinary objects, such as nails, thorns or chains, with a purpose and a virtue that the ascetic ought himself to have by reason of his courage and his will.

BROWSERS AND STATICS

In his *Spiritual Meadow*, John Moschus on several occasions makes use of the term *browser* to indicate ascetics who fed on growing plants and roots. According to Rouet de Journel,[1] John Moschus's translator and commentator, the word appears to be used exclusively in respect of anchorites who lived (like animals) on dried greenstuffs. In fact, its application may be extended to include all whose food consisted of produce from the soil, for, all things considered, that is the purpose of this form of asceticism: to live, as the animals do, on what God has abundantly provided on the earth.

The oldest testimony concerning the browsers is that supplied by St Ephraem, the great Syriac poet known as 'the Harp of the Holy Spirit'. He was born at Nisibis about 306 and all that is known of him is that he was ordained in 338. It is not at all certain that he spent any time in the desert, as eremitism had not developed very far in Syria at that time, but tradition early made an anchorite of him and a whole literary and pictorial cycle was produced around St Ephraem's sojourn in the desert. This cycle was enriched by the rapid progress made in Byzantine literature and art and gave rise to the many *Dormitions of St Ephraem*, like that which is reproduced in this book and which comes from the monastery of Docheiarion on Mount Athos. The form and content of these Dormitions also occur in Byzantine art, supplied in exactly the same way to other saints: the *Dormition of St Athanasius*

[1] Jean Moschos, *Le Pré spirituel*. Introduction et traduction de Rouet de Journel, S.J. (Editions du Cerf, Sources chrétiennes, 1946.)

(in the monastery of the Great Laura on Mount Athos) and the *Dormition of St Onuphrio* (in the Byzantine Museum, Athens).

These frescoes or ikons were always made on the same pictorial plan, borrowed no doubt from the Dormitions of the Virgin: at the bottom, in the middle, the dead saint and, leaning over him in an attitude of devotion and adoration, a character with his face close to that of the dead man and expressive also of the agony of the final moment, a sort of silent question posed in the presence of the mystery of holiness and death—silent, and vain also, since the saint will never reply to that anxious questioning look. Then, around this necroscopic group, the episodes of the saint's life, depicted in a fixed order: 'sojourn in the desert, meditation in the caves and caverns of the earth', making of reed mats, reading of the Scriptures, then life on the top of the pillar as a stylite (but St Ephraem was never a stylite) with a disciple at the base filling a basket and, lastly, the miracle of the saint borne away by a wild animal.

No doubt, St Ephraem never knew life in the desert but, in the end, the matter has no great importance. What was the life of a desert saint? First and foremost, a succession of episodes, which were always the same whoever the saint might be, which surrounded the dying saint like a final 'film' of his impersonality and showed *that he might just as well have led another person's life without anything being changed at his death*. St Ephraem, St Athanasius and St Onuphrio can sleep in peace: their days spent in the desert were wonderfully alike and, fundamentally, there was nothing to distinguish them from each other, either in their lives or in their deaths. That is why the Byzantine artists could paint as many Dormitions as they wished and merely change the name of the Sleeper right at the top of their work. Through the agency of this pictorial convention and without realizing it, they thus expressed the underlying meaning to ascetic experience: the attainment of the Impersonal.

At all events, even if he did not really live there, St Ephraem wrote a great deal about the desert and composed, in Syriac, a *Eulogy of the Solitaries of Mesopotamia* which showed that, in the second half of the fourth century, the deserts of Eastern Syria contained browsers and anchorites living under the most terrifying conditions.

'Let us visit their abodes, the places where they live like dead men in their graves.

'Let us gaze upon their bodies and ponder the fact that the only clothing or ornament they wear is their own hair.

'Let us see their drink, always mingled with their tears,
'And their tables with the wild herbs.
'Behold the stones they place beneath their heads.
'If a robber should see them, he throws himself to the ground in their honour,
'And if wild beasts glimpse their sackcloth, they take flight at once as if from some amazing, prodigious thing.
'They tread underfoot all kinds of snakes.
'They live in caves and in hollow rocks as if in beautiful rooms.
'They shut themselves up in the mountains and hills as if between inaccessible walls and ramparts.
'The ground serves as their table.
'The plants of the earth are their usual fare.'

A little further on, he adds:

'They go wandering about the deserts with the wild beasts as if they themselves were animals.
'Like birds they fly about the hills.
'They graze like stags with creatures of the wild.
'Their tables are always prepared, always set, for they feed upon roots and plants, the natural produce of the earth.'

Theodoret, in his turn, described the life of the browsers of Syria, but with less intensity. Concerning James, the future bishop of Nisibis, for example, he states:

'He spent the spring, summer and autumn in the forests, with nothing but the sky over his head, and with the coming of winter he found some little covering by retiring to a cave. He lived only on the natural produce of the soil, on fruit which he gathered from a few wild trees and on plants not unlike our own vegetables. Of these he ate only enough for his bodily needs, in order to keep alive.'

Evagrius the Scholastic, too, in his *Ecclesiastical History*, mentions among other ascetics men

'who have chosen to live in a desert exposed to the scorching rays of the sun. There are men and women who were almost naked when they began their life in the desert and who are disdainful of the seasons, of the bitter cold and the sweltering heat alike. They despise the kind of food eaten by other humans and are content to graze like cattle. They have even much of the outward appearance of animals, for as soon as they see a man they run away and, if they are pursued they make off with incredible speed and hide in inaccessible places.'

As for John Moschus, he wrote in the sixth century, the browsers' 'golden age', when the fact of spending one's life cropping grass seemed so natural that he merely referred to it casually, much as one would speak of vegetarians today!

From certain passages in the *Spiritual Meadow* it would appear that the browsers were particularly numerous in the Dead Sea region and in the deserts of Judah, Cedron and Calamon. An anchorite whom he met on his travels told him: 'There were three of us browsers beyond the Dead Sea, in the neighbourhood of Bessimon, and we were walking in the hills when we saw down below us another browser walking on the shore.'

Further on, he mentions a certain 'Sophronius, a browser, who lived for seventy years in a state of complete nakedness near the Dead Sea, eating nothing but herbs'. It was, then, a common form of asceticism, so common that any anchorite might introduce himself to Moschus with the simple statement, as if he were handing him a visiting-card: 'I am Peter, a browser from the sacred Jordan.'[1]

If certain ascetics spent their lives wandering in the deserts by the Dead Sea, sometimes even on all fours, feeding on greenstuff, others adopted in their asceticism a more human attitude, or at least one apparently so: they were the statics, those who practised *stasis*, remaining upright and motionless for hours and even for whole days. The standing position is one of the privileges enjoyed by *homo sapiens*, but the way in which the anchorites of Syria made use of it soon robbed it of all human meaning. Remaining in an upright position (for several days in succession), without moving, with his arms folded or raised to the heavens, in the wind, the rain or the sweltering heat of the sun, made the static a sort of automaton in human shape, whose body was nothing more than a statue caught in an attitude of eternal prayer or adoration.

Here may be seen the essential difference between him and the recluse. The latter did not move either, but he lived in a restricted setting, in trees, in closed huts or in caves, in circumstances both *artificial* and

---

[1] This form of asceticism extended even beyond Egypt, Palestine and Syria. Jean Doresse, in his book *L'Empire du prêtre-Jean* (Plon), mentions Ethiopian hermits of the Chimezana region who cropped the grass so thoroughly that there was none left for the cattle, and the peasants drove them back to their caves, where they starved to death!

unchanging, whereas the static lived in the open air, exposed to all weathers, in a setting that was *natural* and *unstable*. Thus, St Adolus, 'from evening to early dawn, remained in a standing position, without food, singing and praying on the Mount of Olives, and rain and hail could not drive him away. He was sometimes so wet that the garments which were taken from him to be replaced by dry clothing were dripping with water as if they had been dipped in the river'.

St Marazius, for thirty-eight years, 'walked barefoot'. And, as if it was not enough for him to remain on his feet morning and evening, 'he stood in the shade in winter and in full sunlight in summer, and the most oppressive heat was for him like a pleasant breeze'. What is more, 'he girded himself with a heavy iron chain, rarely sat down and spent the greater part of the day and night in prayer. He was never seen to lie down'.

As for James, the future bishop of Nisibis, he 'had nothing above his head but the sky. He was by turns soaked by the rain, chilled by snow and frost or baked and burnt by the sun's rays'.

It was precisely because he lived exposed to all changes in his surroundings that the static had, in mind and body, to remain unaffected by these changes and follow the example of James of Nisibis who, 'under the weight of his body strove to live as if he had no body'; in which respect he was perfectly successful since, one day when he was standing at prayer during the winter season, he became completely buried by snow without being aware of it!

But the static was exposed, not only to variations of the weather, but also to men—visitors, pilgrims and sighteers—who came to admire his endurance and observe his practice of *stasis*. The ascetics referred to above, and others besides, mentioned by Theodoret, such as Moyses, Antiochus, Zabinas, Baradates and that of John of Sardes who remained motionless all day and slept at night with a rope under his arms to support him, lived permanently with the world looking on. It was a spectacular, dramatic asceticism, and doubly arduous, with an additional self-imposed trial to undergo, since the anchorite sought solitude and had to attain 'silence of the heart and thought' amid the tumult and the shouting of the world. St Domnina, for instance, a woman static described by Theodoret, was 'exposed to everybody's gaze, men and women alike, but looked nobody in the face and allowed nobody to see hers, as she was completely enveloped in her mantle. Her voice was weak and muffled and she never spoke without weeping, a fact for which I can vouch since she often took my hand and put it to her eyes, and it came away quite wet.'

Stasis consisted, briefly, in increasing the number of temptations the better to overcome them, in taking up a position in the heart of human society the better to reject it and in closing the eyes and the mind to its most readily available attractions. Thus, St Elpidius, installed on Mount Luca near Jericho, 'never turned towards the west, although the entrance to his cave was at the summit. Nor did he ever look at the sun or at the stars which came out at its setting. In twenty years he did not see a single star'.

The least distraction, the slightest glance at the world so close at hand and so tempting, was mercilessly repressed. One day, when St Eusebius, the founder of the famous monastery of Teleda near Aleppo, was sitting with Ammian on a rock, reading and commenting on the Gospel, his attention was caught for an instant 'by some peasants ploughing in a field below them', with the result that he could not reply to a question put by Ammian. Because of this one lapse, from that day 'he would not allow his eyes ever to look upon that countryside or to delight in the beauty of the sky and the stars, nor would he permit them to range beyond a small track the width of a palm-branch which he borrowed when repairing to his devotions. He lived in that way for more than forty years'. And to make even more sure of never looking at the sky 'he put on a girdle and a large collar of iron and linked them together with another piece of iron to force himself always to look down at the ground and so punish himself for once having glanced at the ploughmen'!

CLOSER TO HEAVEN

In spite of its statics, recluses and browers, Syria would never have held its unusual place in the history of Christianity if it had not created a still more amazing form of asceticism: stylitism.

The stylites (from the Greek *stylos*: pillar) were ascetics who lived on top of tall pillars and spent whole years there, absolutely motionless. It was extreme asceticism, combining all the foregoing forms. The stylite was a static (since he stayed motionless on his pillar) and a recluse (because of his restriction to a confined space). Moreover, he lived both removed from men (at the top of the pillar) and in the midst of men (each stylite becoming the object of fanatical veneration). The symbolical meaning of this asceticism was therefore very clear and writers of the age did not mistake it: by taking up a position on a pillar and staying at a distance from the earth and men, the stylite attained a higher spiritual perfection and lived midway between earth and sky, so that he could talk with God. That is certainly the sense of the passage quoted at the beginning of this chapter and taken from the *Ecclesiastical History* of Evagrius the Scholastic.

No doubt, some will find the explanation ingenuous, but to the writers and Christians of the age spending whole years at the top of a pillar was concrete proof of the ascetic's spiritual elevation. They interpreted literally a symbol to which John Climacus, an ascetic author of the seventh century (who lived as an anchorite on Mount Sinai), gave a figurative meaning in his *Climax* or *Ladder to Paradise*.

The honour of being the first to think of staying on top of a pillar belongs to St Simeon. His life is known to us because of testimony which has the advantage of being nearly contemporaneous with the saint: first, that of Theodoret of Cyrrhus, who visited the ascetic, spoke with him on several occasions and composed in Simeon's own lifetime a *Life of St Simeon Stylites* as part of his *Religious History*; next, that of a certain Anthony, one of Simeon's disciples, who also wrote a *Life* of the saint, unfortunately very fanciful and unreliable; and, finally, the Syriac *Life of Mar Sim'ân of the Pillar* (*Mar* meaning 'saint' in Syriac) written about 473, some fifteen years after the saint's death, and, historically speaking, probably the most accurate of the three.

The question of sources is of some importance as regards stylites, for their form of asceticism seemed so extraordinary to the historians of Christianity that some of them absolutely denied its reality. Theodoret himself, who was astonished at nothing in matters of asceticism, could not help being impressed by so strange a way of living and took precautions against the incredulity of his future readers. 'All who come under the dominion of the Roman Empire,' he wrote at the beginning of his *Life of St Simeon Stylites*, 'know of the illustrious Simeon, who may rightly be called the great miracle of this world. The Persians, the Medes and the Ethiopians also know of him, and the reputation of his countless works and his quite divine virtues has reached even the Scythians and Nomads. But, although he had as witnesses of his amazing struggles as many as there are men on this earth, I hesitate to write of them, because the truth is so unbelievable that it may be accounted fable.'

But the life of Simeon Stylites is not fable. He was born in 389 at Sisan, a village near Nicopolis on the borders of Syria and Cilicia and (like Shenute) having spent some time tending flocks he decided to dedicate himself to God. He became a novice in the monastery of Teleda, one of the most important in Christian Syria, situated twenty-five miles north-west of Aleppo, and came under the spiritual guidance of an old man named Heliodorus, 'an admirable man who, during his sixty-five

18A. THE TEMPTATION OF JOHN OF EGYPT

18B. THE TEMPTATION OF
ST. ANTHONY

19A. AN ANCHORITE'S TEMPTATION

19B. THE TEMPTATION OF
ST. ANTHONY

years of life, had spent sixty-two of them in this monastery, having been admitted at the age of three' and who, naturally, had no knowledge of the world, which caused him to say that 'he had no idea how even a cockerel or a pig was made'!

There, St Simeon very soon showed himself to be so different from the other monks by reason of his incredible austerity that he was asked, politely but firmly, to leave the monastery. He immediately acceded to the request and, 'going to the most deserted mountainous spot he could find, he discovered a dry well which was not very deep and down which he went to sing God's praises'. He did not stay there long, five days at the most, for the monks of Teleda, stricken with remorse, went out to look for him and found him at the bottom of the well 'from which they had much trouble in pulling him, seeing that it was more difficult to get out of it than to get in'. From that day, Simeon gave up cenobitic life in order to become an anchorite and, in all calmness, to give himself up to fasting and terrible mortification. For this purpose he first settled at the foot of a mountain near Tell-Neschin, a village to the north-west of Antioch. He had himself shut inside a hut for Lent and stayed there for forty days without touching the bread which had been provided for him, so that when the door was broken open at the end of that time 'the saint was found lying on the ground, speechless and motionless, as if deprived of life'. Three years later, he settled at the top of the mountain, in a spot now known as Qal'at Sim'ân (the Castle of Simeon) where he built a dry-wall enclosure of stones and had made for him 'an iron chain twenty cubits long, one end of which he fixed to his right leg and the other to a heavy stone so that he could not move beyong the limits of this tether, even if he wished'. And there, 'since the chain which held him could not prevent his thoughts from soaring upwards', he spent his time in end-less 'contemplation, with the inward eye of faith and spirit, of those things which lie beyond the heavens'. This earned for him a reputation for perfection which brought to his boundary-wall a host of worshipful pilgrims eager to look upon the chained saint. But he soon gave up this spectacular asceticism, when Melecius, the patriarch of Antioch, pointed out that if one wished to remain motionless one could quite well do so by the application of the will, without recourse to walls and chains.

In this episode there can be seen one of the clearest features of Syrian Christianity. Simeon interpreted in a literal sense ascetic prohibitions and injunctions which obviously had only figurative meaning: he had been taught that it was necessary, through asceticism and by the applica-tion of the will, to keep the body captive, and he therefore put his body in chains and walled himself up in a hut or an enclosure. When, therefore, some time later, he wished to be 'raised up' to a still higher level of spiritual perfection, he quite naturally climbed to the top of a pillar so as to be nearer to heaven. His asceticism and his actions were both concrete and symbolical. It seems quite pointless and even mistaken to want at any price to find antecedents to stylitic asceticism and, for instance, to look for its origin in some ancient pagan ceremony in Syria, as certain historians have done. In a passage of his book *The Syrian Goddess*, Lucian of Samosata indeed mentions a rite celebrated in his day at Hierapolis in Syria in honour of the goddess Atargatis, during which a celebrant had to climb a huge stone phallus, a hundred and seventy feet high, and stay for a whole week at the top of it. The only point in common that can be found between this rite and stylitism is the meaning which the Syrian crowds attached to the time spent at the top of the phallus. Lucian of Samosata writes, 'the crowd is convinced that the man, in this lofty place, speaks with the gods, asks them to grant prosperity to the whole of Syria and that the gods are in a position to hear his request more clearly'. These are almost the identical terms employed by Theodoret of Cyrrhus and Evagrius the Scholastic in defining the sense of St Simeon's asceticism. Lucian's text thus helps one to understand that the belief in the value and power of material elevation is of pagan, not Christian, origin and also why stylitism met with such success in Syria. It is because (in pagan Syria), it appealed to widespread sentiment and belief, according to which the higher a man was above the ground, the better he might have speech with the gods.

So it happened that when, after his stay inside the walled enclosure, Simeon took to a pillar in order to avoid importunate visitors, some of whom were already quarreling over pieces of his clothing, he earned the reputation throughout the whole of Syria of being a man 'who speaks with God'. His first pillar, however, did not bring him very near to heaven: it was only sixteen feet high. But, later on, he occupied pillars twenty and thirty-six feet in height. The last pillar—the one on which he died in 459 at the age of seventy—at Qal'at Sim'ân, measured eighty feet, 'his desire to climb near to heaven always causing him to get further and further from the earth'.

The base of this pillar may still be seen in Syria, at the very spot where the saint died, near the huge basilica that was built to his memory and important remains of which still exist. This pillar was surmounted by a platform forty square feet in area, which gave the saint just enough room to lie at full length. In fact, he spent his days standing motionless in prayer or worship and slept sitting down, leaning against the low balustrade which had been made for him all round the platform so that he should not fall if he became giddy. A passage in his *Life* (from the pen of his disciple Anthony) states that it sometimes happened that he even spent his days standing on one leg. In such circumstances the ascetic's stiffened limbs became covered in sores and ulcers which quickly festered, as Simeon stayed day and night exposed to all weathers. So, one winter, Simeon's thigh became putrified and 'exuded a mass of maggots which fell from his body to his feet and down the pillar to the ground, where a young man named Anthony, who attended to his needs and who saw and recorded all these things, was ordered by the saint to pick up the maggots from the ground and hand them up to Simeon, who replaced them on the wound with the words, "Eat, then, what God has provided for you".'

When he was not spending his time putting the maggots back on his wounds, by day he 'remained in full sight of everybody and was so novel and wonderful a sight that all minds were filled with amazement. At times he would bow down to worship God, at others he remained standing as long as possible. The number of his adorations was so great that many people found it entertaining to keep count of them. One of those who were with me counted one day as many as one thousand two hundred and forty-four, and then stopped counting.' And Theodoret gives the additional information that during his worship 'Simeon touched his toes with his forehead, for, as he ate only once a week, his abdomen was so flat that he had no difficulty in bending down so far'!

And Simeon certainly did not spend his nights in sleeping, but in prayer, 'with his hands raised to heaven, from sunset until sunrise on the following day, without once closing his eyes or seeking the slightest rest'.

It is understandable that a life of such a kind should attract a great number of visitors and pilgrims. They came to look, to admire, to place in the basket which always hung at the base of the pillar the offering or the food for the saint's sustenance (for he lived only by charity) and, if possible, to obtain from him a word, a piece of advice or a blessing. Theodoret refers to pilgrims who came from the four corners of Europe, so that at the foot of the pillar there was 'such a great crowd of people that it resembled a human sea fed by various roads—like so many rivers —with an endless number of people of all races: Jews, Persians, Armenians, Iberians, Ethiopians and others from still further afield who came from the West'.

There was even, on occasions, a veritable host of people thronging the hill of Tell-Neschin, to such an extent that Theodoret was one day nearly smothered by the crowd of Simeon's admirers. Most of them stayed for hours watching the saint and the stylite's disciple had the greatest difficulty in dispersing them and getting them to return home at nightfall. Moreover, on the death of Simeon, which (according to the Syriac *Life*) took place in 459, such devotion was to cause serious disturbances around his pillar, and six hundred soldiers from Antioch had to intervene to protect the body of the saint from the Saracens who had come to seize it!

In his lifetime and during the centuries which followed, Simeon had imitators. Although it did not become an institution properly so-called, stylitism spread through Syria and the Near East from Byzantium to Mesopotamia. It must be recognized that the mere sight of a stylite—standing motionless on the top of his pillar and surrounded by an admiring crowd—must have been most sensational and resulted in many being called to an ascetic life. Thus, one day, a monk named Daniel, who came with other monks from Antioch, left his companions when he saw St Simeon on top of his pillar and spent two weeks in his service. Later, after the saint's death, Daniel became a stylite near Byzantium, and the highest dignitaries of the Empire, including the emperor Leo I and the empress Eudoxia, came to solicit his counsel and blessing. Titus, an officer of the imperial Palace, even gave up the army when he saw the saint on his pillar, established himself nearby and invented a new form of asceticism: he had himself slung in the air by means of ropes running under his armpits so that his feet were always off the ground. An ordinary board fixed at the level of his chest provided support when he wished to sleep!

In the seventh century, two famous stylites—St Simeon the Younger and St Alipius—became imitators of the elder Simeon. The former set himself up near Seleucia, the port of Antioch, on a height overlooking the sea which was thereafter known as Mount Admirable. His *Life*, written in the seventh century, contains elements so fabulous—quite unlike that of Simeon the Elder, the tone of which is often very authentic—that it gives the impression of being a collection of Eastern stories rather than a historical text. For example, at the age of two, the young—very young—Simeon began to speak as soon as he was baptized and repeated for a week the words: 'I have a father and I have no father. I have a mother and I have no mother.' When he was seven, he retired to the mountainous region near Antioch, among the animals, where, because of his miraculous powers, he played with leopards as if they were ordinary cats. When he ascended his first pillar, he was 'still so young (states the *Life*) that he had not lost his first teeth'. If such was the case, he is the only known instance of a child stylite. Such precocious asceticism dumbounded the Syrians themselves and they immediately came flocking to admire 'the new Simeon', as he was called. From the top of his pillar he harangued the pilgrims, and he gave himself up to such maceration that the superior of a nearby monastery told him one day: 'All that is left for you to do now is to take a sword and kill yourself.'

The crowd became so pressing and numerous that Simeon the Younger decided to remove himself. But how could this be done, since he was a stylite? Wherever he settled, his fanatical admirers would soon have found him again. He therefore had, for a time, to renounce stylitism and let himself be forgotten by withdrawing for ten years to the most inaccessible solitudes of Mount Admirable; after which, at the age of thirty, he returned to the world of men and had a pillar made for himself which was sixty-five feet high. There he spent the rest of his days, until he was seventy-five years old.

The second stylite, St Alipius, a contemporary of St Simeon the Younger, settled near Hadrianopolis in the Pontus, where he occupied a pillar for twenty-nine years. Although his *Life* contains far fewer miraculous elements than those of the two Simeons, St Alipius acquired great renown and he is one of those most frequently found in Byzantine ikons, frescoes and miniatures.

It is difficult to make even an approximate estimate of the total number of stylites living in the Near East from the time of the fourth century. Historically speaking, the phenomenon began in the fifth century and lasted until the twelfth, and even beyond, since stylites were found at this time in Georgia, Armenia, Asia Minor (near Ephesus) and Greece, on Mount Athos (where there were still stylites in the sixteenth century). Mount Athos seems to have been the extreme western limit of the expansion of stylitism, but eastward it extended very far, to Edessa and even to Ctesiphon. It should be noted that the many documents referring to stylitism (*Lives* of stylites, testimonies, references in numerous *Ecclesiastical Histories*) originate from the dramatic character of the asceticism rather than from the numerical importance of its devotees. A single stylite in any region was enough for the crowds to gather at once, for testimony to increase and for some author—usually the stylite's disciple or the bishop of the region—to write his *Life*. In any case, it appears that the total number of stylites in the East never exceeded a few hundreds.

Besides, as stylitism developed, it ceased to be considered as exceptional asceticism and the stylite *ipso facto* a saint. A sixth-century text mentions, for instance, a certain Theodulus—a former prefect of

Byzantium—who had occupied a pillar near Edessa and lived there for forty-eight years. At the end of his time there, Theodulus asked an angel what would be his reward in heaven. The angel answered, 'You will have the same reward as a certain comedian from Damascus'. Theodulus came down from his pillar and left at once for Damascus in search of the comedian in question. He found him at the hippodrome, in the arms of a courtesan, watching the games! But this comedian had once given his entire fortune to a lady who was reduced to penury, which was enough to earn for him the same reward as for forty-eight years' immobility on a pillar! John Moschus who, it will be remembered, wrote in the sixth century, even mentions instances of heretical stylites (Monophysite stylites) and describes a strange quarrel between two of them—one orthodox and the other a Monophysite—who were established close together and hurled insults at each other from the tops of their pillars. This is one of the few instances of stylites found other than singly; but another document, of the tenth century, attributed to a monk named Epiphanius, refers to a strange colony of a hundred stylites at Geth-semane in Palestine. They occupied a veritable forest of pillars, grouped about a superior! As a rule, the stylites always chose a lonely spot, at the top of a mountain or a hill, but near a town or a village. Besides his usual visitors and passing pilgrims, the stylite had a disciple to serve him and see to his food. This disciple was often a very young lad, who stayed at the foot of the pillar. But if, by some mischance, the disciple was not there and no traveller passed that way, the stylite could only entrust himself to Heaven. Thus, St Paul of Latros, whose disciple left for a whole month's harvesting, almost starved to death and was revived *in extremis* by a passing traveller!

All this did not prevent most of the stylites from living to old age: St Simeon the Elder—according to the Syriac *Life*—died at seventy years of age, St Daniel at eighty-four, St Alipius at ninety-nine and St Luke (a stylite installed near Ephesus in the ninth century) at a hundred, after living respectively for thirty, thirty-three, twenty-nine and fifty years on their pillars! Generally, they died a natural death (if one may speak of *natural* death at the end of a life that was so little like life), unless they were struck by lightning like the stylite of Mesopo-tamia, on a pillar of gypsum, who was mentioned by the Syriac chronicler Thomas of Marga, or like St Nicetas, who spent his life standing on top of a pillar, wearing a coat of mail that was so bright that it shone like silver in the sun and resulted in his being murdered by brigands!

Finally, to end this catalogue of Syriac asceticism, mention should be made of an asceticism derived from stylitism, but much less common, which might be called *dendritism*. Dendritism (from the Greek *dendros*: tree) consisted in living in a tree, which possessed certain 'advantages': in the first place, shelter from the weather (it was not until rather later that some stylites had a cabin or a roof built at the top of their pillars); then the ability to speak more easily to disciples or visitors (the stylites' pillars easily rising to a height of seventy feet, so that both stylite and visitor had to shout themselves hoarse in order to be heard, and nobody caring to trust to the rickety ladder linking the stylite with the earth!).

To tell the truth, there are very few documents relating to dendritism, except for an old ikon in the monastery of St Catherine on Mount Sinai representing one of the most famous of the dendrites: David of Thessalonica, who lived in the sixth century and spent three years in an almond-tree in the courtyard of a monastery near Thessalonica, and two later texts. The first of these two dates from the eighth century and is a *Poem on the Monks* attributed to a certain bishop George. In it, it is stated that some monks

'made a shady tree their retreat and fed on its fruit and leaves. Several of them climbed into it to spend all the days of their lives there and were flung about in all directions by the violent winds.'

The second, a Syriac chronicle from the monastery of Mar Maron, near Apameia, states:

'In the district under the administration of the metropolis of Apameia, there is a village called Ir'enin. In this village there was an old cypress in which lived a man of God. The devil, who always hates good actions, did not cease from attacking him openly and in secret, and often he knocked him down from his tree. At last, the saint made provision against such a happening by obtaining an iron chain and fastened himself to the tree by his foot, so that when his enemy Satan threw him down he remained hanging to the tree by the chain and people from the village would come and put him back in his place. In the end, he said: "May God, in whose name I am here, grant that I shall have no more need of the hand of men, and, if it please him that I shall remain in this spot, may he send me divine strength and restore me to my place." And that is what happened. Whenever the Enemy threw him down from the tree, an angel appeared from Heaven and put him back.'

There again, the determination never to touch the ground was achieved in the most literal and absurd fashion, and one could—as in the case of stylitism—be content with explaining dendritism in that way. But such stubbornness in never being willing to touch the ground betrays—in the dendrite's consciousness—some obscure prohibition which may be more clearly understood from the text of Lucian of Samosata, mentioned above. Indeed, Lucian writes, still with reference to the ceremony of the phallus: 'Others think that this rite is practised in memory of Deucalion, to commemorate that terrible event when men fled to the mountains and climbed trees to escape the flood.'

Such might well be, in the end, the underlying meaning of this asceticism: to find refuge in a tree as Noah found it in an ark, so as to avoid contact with a condemned world in its last agony and lead the gentle life of a bird in the branches and the wind, a bird possessed of God and the thought of Heaven.

DYING AMONG THE LIVING

CHAPTER 8

THE FACE OF SATAN

'When men are taken down to Hell, they begin by crying: "Woe is me, for I did not know the God who created me"; then they stop, for they can speak no more, because of the heat and the great darkness of the place. They no longer recognize one another, by reason of the gloom and the agony which grips them.'

DESCRIPTION OF HELL (Coptic text)

It is a paradox of life in the desert, in which the ascetic, according to the precept of Evagrius Ponticus, was to 'cleanse himself of illusion', that he should in reality live in a world of continual illusions. The desert was an abstract, changeless place, a trial, yet much more than a trial: a back-cloth, huge and blank, for the heavenly scenes and combats between angels and devils which were continued even on the earth. To 'cleanse himself of illusion', the ascetic had to make a clean sweep of the values, the sensations and also the *forms* of the outside world. And, in fact, all the forms appearing in the desert: those creatures in human shape which were always at the ascetic's side, the visions which unfolded before his eyes and the monsters which came to pester him, were surely *new* forms, owing nothing to those of the world. That is undoubtedly the reason why a theme like that of the *Temptation of St Anthony* has for centuries continued to make an impression on painters' imaginations; precisely because it offered them the opportunity to invent new forms and to seek within themselves exclusively, and not in the world around them, those extraordinary creatures which attacked Anthony in the darkness. By shutting himself up in his tomb at Coma, Anthony did not merely initiate a certain form of asceticism; he became the explorer of a world hitherto unknown, discovering and liberating for the first time unsuspected spiritual forces the existence of which, after his day, was never forgotten.

If the ascetic in the desert met so many strange shapes and beings, it was first because he carried them within him. Because the desert was so bare, it presented the ascetic with an ambiguous image. It needed only

171

a change of trend (since it was basically a question of a spiritual optical phenomenon) for the desert to become either hell or paradise. The anchorites were well aware of this dual nature of the desert, which they expressed in their own way, since the supernatural creatures which inhabited it assumed the guise of angels or demons indifferently. The desert was certainly the ideal place for *optical illusions*; it taught the necessity for first seeing clearly within oneself before one could see clearly beyond.

But illusions, shadow-theatres and shapes also imply an illusionist, a demonstrator. Who was it that secretly handled and directed these beings and shapes? Who was the Director of the scenes which continually came and went before the ascetic's eyes? To the anchorites of Egypt the answer was plain: it was God or the Devil. It is impossible to assess the value of an ascetic's sojourn in the desert and follow his innermost thoughts without considering the essential preoccupations which conditioned his whole behaviour and without studying the significance of hell and paradise in his heart and mind.

ANGELIC TORTURERS

It is a well-known fact that most religious writings reveal shortcomings when it is a question of depicting paradise, but exhibit a delirious imagination as soon as it is a matter of describing hell and its torments.

In respect of paradise, it appears that there had always been a dilemma to face: paradise was either a mere continuation and embellishment of life on earth (as indicated by the representations of paradise, on the tombs of ancient Egypt, which supply the most exact and valuable records of everyday life in the Egypt of the pharaohs) or it was something quite different. If the latter, its secret has been carefully guarded.

On the other hand, hell had produced no such dilemma, and it is as though all peoples were in spontaneous agreement about what hell had in store for mankind. (Could we possibly have such a clear and comprehensive notion of Sin?) To list the torments of hell and to describe it in great detail—its inhabitants, its animal life and its vegetation—was one of the great concerns and, it seems, one of the delights of the human mind.

It would therefore be wrong to think that hell and paradise, as regards the place they held in the works of human imagination, represented two equally important extremes. In the Coptic texts, at all events, hell was far from being just the 'negative' of paradise; it was a reality very close to man and he believed in it with surprising ardour and ingenuousness.

Moreover, at that time, hell was identified with the world, or rather with man's conception of the world, and by struggling in the desert against the world the monk and the anchorite believed they were combating hell itself. It was to this conflict that they devoted their greatest strength, and so it was necessary to have a sound knowledge of the world beyond, with its devious paths, its torments and its denizens, the better to avoid its snares and pitfalls. No doubt the Copt imagined that by paying on this earth (in imagination) the tribute due to the Devil, he would be free from it in the reality of the next world. In any case, the Copt was attracted by hell in so far as he sometimes made a trial of it on this earth: this was the symbolic sense of those trials by fire, so frequent in Egypt, in which a monk threw himself into the flames (usually taking the Gospels with him) in order to prove that he was not a heretic or destined to damnation; in other words, he made himself secure against the ever-lasting fire.

This frightening preponderance of hell in the psyche of Christian Egypt in no way astonished a race which for centuries had been obsessed by death and the hereafter. The life beyond remained, for the Copt as for his pagan ancestors, the only real life, to which he had to sacrifice everything. Therefore, in the underworld geography of the Copts, one finds numerous points in common with that of ancient Egypt—mixed, of course, with the traditional biblical conceptions.

What happened when a Copt died in a state of mortal sin and was about to enter hell? As soon as he arrived at this critical moment when 'he no longer recognized anybody, two merciless angels came for his soul. One of them stood by his head and the other at his feet, and they belaboured him until his miserable soul was about to rise up. Then they pushed into his mouth a curved instrument not unlike a fish-hook and withdrew his wretched soul from his body. It was observable that this soul was a dark and sinister thing. Then they tied it to the tail of a spirit horse'.

This manner of removing the soul from the body should be noted. The insertion of a hook into the mouth was no doubt analogous, in the mind of a Copt, to the use of an instrument by ancient embalmers for removing the brain from a corpse by way of the nostrils. The Copt believed that the soul did not leave the body of its own accord but had to be extracted. But what is particularly important is the idea that comes to light in another passage of the *Coptic Life of Theodore* (from which the foregoing excerpt is taken), the idea that whoever had not suffered in this world was condemned to suffer in the next and that any suffering endured on this earth resulted in a corresponding purification of a man's soul. But as this balance between suffering and purification was not always very exact, and since not all suffering had the same value, what happened to those who had suffered little and had not the right of immediate entry into paradise? The merciless angels made them suffer on their death-bed, so that the deficiency was made good and they could go straight to heaven, for a man's soul 'was like unto a cooked meal which still needed a little more cooking before being eaten'. The allusion is clear: it was on this earth that the 'cooking' had to be done if one wished to avoid an eternal roasting in hell.

But some approached the threshold of death in such 'sound' condition that there was no appeal in their case and 'they went straight down to hell and its torments'.

What torments were these? It is easy to picture them: an everlasting fire and a heat so intolerable that the damned, terror-stricken and suffocating, lost their voice. Naturally, the punishment varied according to the sinner's offence and the Copts showed remarkable imagination in describing the various infernal punishments, as witness this excerpt from the *Coptic Life of Pachomius*:

'It happened that one day, at the Lord's command, father Pachomius was taken away and shown the punishments and torments with which the children of men are tortured. Was he taken bodily or was his body left behind? Whichever it was, God knows that he was, in fact, taken away.

'He was taken to the northern part of the paradise of delectation, far from this world and the firmament, and he saw rivers, canals and ditches of fire, in which were the souls of sinners. And while father Pachomius was walking with the angel, he saw certain sinners handed over to angelic torturers of terrifying appearance with fiery whips in their hands. If any of the souls they were tormenting raised their heads above the flames, they were soundly whipped and forced back into the fire. They sighed harshly but could not cry out because they were so weak. The souls in torment were, if not countless, at least very numerous.'

Let us note in passing this frequent theme of the damned who lose their voice. Most descriptions of the underworld, as given by other races, represent the damned as shouting, wailing, gnashing their teeth, weeping and prancing about. In the Coptic hell, on the other hand, an impressive silence reigned: the damned were stifled and silenced by the heat, the suffering and the darkness. If one thinks how important were the voice and speech in the beliefs of ancient Egypt, one can understand that, to a Copt, loss of voice must have been the worst of punishments. It was tantamount to a permanent loss of strength.

'And likewise he saw pits and cauldrons of fire, the heat from which was still more overpowering. Pachomius stared into them and saw that there was only one soul in each. The souls, which retained the physical appearance they had on earth, had one foot on each side of the cauldrons: one at a time the fire consumed the limbs by which the souls had been defiled on earth. Pachomius concentrated his attention on a particular cauldron and recognized one of the damned: it was one of those who are marked men in the towns and who are referred to in the Scriptures as "effeminate".'[1]

It must not be supposed that the angels who tortured the damned felt any remorse at carrying out their tasks. On the contrary, the angelic torturers 'were full of joy and gladness, like a steward who delights at the sight of his master's increasing wealth, for the Lord created them merciless. And if the souls they torture beg for mercy, they are filled with anger against them and chastise them even more severely. Whenever souls are brought to them and delivered into their hands, they are exultant.'

To be deprived of one's voice was a terrible punishment, but what can one think of that invented by the anonymous authors of the *Coptic Apophthegms of Macarius the Elder*?

'It is said that, one day when he was walking in the mountains, Macarius saw a skull lying on the ground. He moved his head and the skull moved also.

Macarius: Who art thou?

The Skull: I am a Greek, from the days of the Heathen. I have been permitted to speak with thee.

Macarius: And who am I?

The Skull: Thou art father Macarius, the pneumatophore.

Macarius: Art thou at rest or in suffering?

The Skull: I am in torment.

Macarius: What kind of torment?

The Skull: There is a river of fire bubbling above our heads, as high as the sky, and another such river beneath our feet. We are in between these fires. We are back to back and cannot

[1] This was no doubt a reference to St Paul, First Epistle to the Corinthians, VI, 10, denouncing the 'effeminate', that is homosexuals.

see one another's faces. When a great prayer is offered on our behalf, we are accorded a little repose.

Macarius: What sort of repose?

The Skull: For a very brief moment we see each other's faces.'

Have there ever been such horror and imagination in describing the reality of hell?

THE FACE OF SATAN

There could be no hell without demons, or demons without a Devil. Demons and the Devil played so important a part in the lives of the anchorites of Egypt and Syria that a little must be said of them here. The anchoritic and monachal phenomenon has so far been considered in relation to all that it rejected, namely History and Society, but the place of the Invisible and the Intemporal must be recognized and a proper balance effected. No human phenomenon, particularly if it is collective, is reducible to its purely negative aspects. If the anchorites rejected the historical and the social, it is precisely because they had something else to counteract them, other values to which they geared their lives: their souls' salvation, everlasting bliss, paradise. In fact, it was less the historical than the ephemeral that the anchorites attacked: what they wanted was to live in an intemporal world, in which human expectation was no more, in what may be called the world of *essential beings.* This was the world in which angels and demons lived and it was fatal for the anchorites to encounter them just when they were devoting themselves wholly to the quest of the invisible world: they attached infinitely greater importance to this world, with its angels and demons, than to the so-called real world. There is nothing comprehensible in the attitudes or words of the ascetics of Egypt unless one is convinced that they acted much more *in accordance with the judgement of angels and demons than of men.* This is borne out, for example, by the following anonymous extract from the *Apophthegms of the Desert Fathers*: 'An old man who lived in the desert and had no water nearer than twelve miles from his cell, was so tired when he went one day in search of it that he said to himself: "Why do I give myself so much trouble? Would it not be better if I made my abode nearer the water?" As he said these words, he noticed that a young man was following him and counting his footprints in the sand. "Who art thou?" asked the old man. "I am an angel," was the reply. "The Lord of Lords has sent me to count thy steps so as to

20A. THE BEAR AND THE
ANCHORITE

20B. PARADISE

ΟΙ ΕΧΝΟΙ

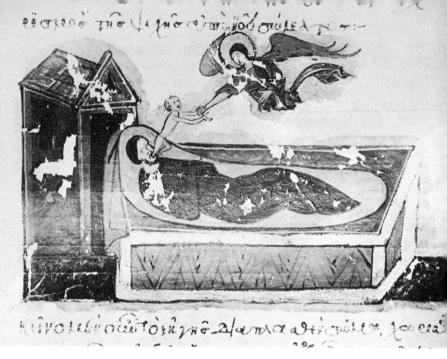

21A. THE SOUL LEAVING THE BODY

21B. A CRUCIFIED MONK

give thee thy reward." At these words, the old man's courage was restored and, with redoubled zeal, he went and established himself in a cell still further from the water than the first.'

An anchorite's behaviour should not be judged by human, secular standards: if an ascetic were seen walking in the desert, weighed down with heavy stones, or settling as far as possible from a spring, it was because he thought the angels and demons were watching him day and night, carefully recording his every hardship and relaxation and continually assessing even the least of his actions. One step more or less in the sand was one victory more or less for God or the Devil. The many disconcerting aspects of life in the desert, the natural ease and credulity with which the anchorite met every miracle and temptation, should therefore occasion no surprise. It is a phenomenon on which it has been customary not to dwell, as if all these wonders, diableries and apparitions of angels and archangels were a sort of literary farrago best passed over in silence. In doing so, one ignores the most significant and most precious part of this adventure: daily experience of the Invisible, of Evil and of spirits. It is impossible to ignore the enormous part played by the Devil in the mental world of the fourth-century ascetics without the whole of their behaviour appearing incomprehensible, just as it is impossible for example to neglect such a phenomenon of the previous centuries as belief in the imminent end of the world. The evolution of men and ideas within the realm of Christianity has nullified many aspects of Christian thought of the early centuries (such as the Apocalypse), and the present tendency is to minimize their importance. But it is not possible to dissociate elements which, in their day, formed an indivisible whole in the minds of the Christians. The name of Christ alone was then associated with the vision of his *parousia*, his Second Coming on earth, and at first this was the entire sense and originality of the Christian message: to proclaim the abolition of secular history and announce the advent of a new kind of man and a new City. The history of anchoritism as a whole fits in with this view of waiting for the new man, and one can understand the difficulties and the obvious discomfort experienced by the militant section of the Church in having suddenly to adjust itself to this world in suspense—when it became clear that the delay was protracted and that the end of the world was postponed *sine die*: the Church, in the fourth century, accepted the earthly City in place of the celestial City, and the responsibilities of history and temporal things. Louis Bouyer is therefore right when he states that 'the change from paganism to Christianity could not take place throughout the Roman empire without causing a certain widespread damage resulting in concentration upon the Apocalypse and the Devil. They are the outcome of the liquidation of a mass of complexes.'[1]

This also explains why anchoritism and monachism, which are historically coincident with this 'liquidation of complexes', are primarily a fight against the Devil, a daily, dramatic fight, undertaken as a real struggle and not as a symbolical contest. When the anchorites mentioned the Devil, they did so as if they referred to something experienced and not to a theological speculation, an experience which was all the more valuable for being the first of its kind. For, strange as it may seem, there is nowhere in the Old Testament a precise and traditional conception or experience of the Devil. The word itself, which is derived from the Greek *diabolos*, does not figure in the Bible. As for the term Satan, it stands for an individual Being, the incarnation of Evil, only in the New Testament, when a character named Satan comes to tempt Jesus on the mountain.

In the Old Testament, the word *satan* (or *satam*) is merely a legal term standing for the prosecutor in an action at law (as in Psalm 109, for instance) or for one who stands in the way. In only one passage of the Bible (Job, I, 6) is Satan mentioned by name as a personal Being, with the meaning of Adversary. When God has called together all his angels, Satan comes forward with the intention of testing Job's faith. Jehovah asks him: 'Whence comest thou?' and Satan answers: 'From going to and fro in the earth, and from walking up and down in it.' This expression was later enough to make Satan the Prince of this world or, as St Paul calls him, the 'god of this world'.

It is therefore essential to note that the 'creation' of the Devil, as understood today, coincides historically with Christian preaching and that the idea of a personal Being, the enemy of God, who seeks to obstruct man's salvation and the progress of Creation, is much more a Greek (and Egyptian) notion than a Hebrew conception. It was in particular the work of the writers of the New Testament and more especially the author of the Apocalypse, the first to combine in a single Being the hitherto different characters of Satan, Lucifer, the Serpent and the Dragon. The Devil was 'born' during the early centuries of Christianity and was almost contemporaneous with the first anchorites of the desert, which makes their testimony on this subject so valuable and also explains why their vision has persisted until the present time. The Devil was, in fact, born in the deserts of Egypt.

The character of the Devil is obviously complex, with multiple per-

[1] Louis Bouyer, *Saint Antoine et la Spiritualité du monachisme primitif.* (Editions de Fontenelle, 1950.)

sonalities and functions, since it combines Hebrew conceptions (Satan, Lucifer, the tempting Serpent) which are themselves related to Babylonain mythology, Greek conceptions (*daimon* and *diabolos*) and Egyptian ideas (the *n'ter*, evil spirits, phantoms and apparitions, which are nothing but the ancient pagan divinities of Egypt). It is, indeed, such a Being that appears in the literature of the desert and comes to tempt the ascetic: he appears as a *daimon*, a spirit haunting the lower regions of the atmosphere surrounding the earth, a *satan*, that is an Adversary in whom are combined all the forces of opposition to the power of God, and *n'ter*, a terrifying phantom torturer. Demon, adversary, phantom, the multiplicity of natures explains the Devil's many functions: a beguiling, tempting creature, representing all the enticement of the world and its beauty, but also a monstrous being who frightens and attacks the monk, a repugnant, repulsive bogey of a spirit. All the temptations and struggles of the Fathers of the desert ceaselessly alternate between those two representatives of diabolical power, Horror and Beauty.

In one case, the Tempter is obviously presented in human and even superhuman form: as a woman of astounding beauty or an angel of light. In the other case, on the contrary, he appears in predominantly human, even subhuman, shape: such as an animal (snake, wolf or dragon) or a hybrid, monstrous creature. What is the true face of Satan, that of a Beast or of an Angel?

THE VOICE OF THE AGES

It is very difficult today to imagine the vigour and sincerity of the Egyptian anchorites' belief in the Devil and demons. In an age when the tendency is to subject beliefs to rationalization and to see in the economy of the world only the interplay or exchange of impersonal forces, belief in Evil as a personified force, an identifiable Creature, provided with a name, a mind and sometimes even with a body, belongs to the superstitions of the past. And yet this irrational belief imposed itself for centuries upon the destiny of whole generations of Christians and played a defining part in that destiny, a part somewhat analogous to that of the oracles in pagan Antiquity, for instance. It is, some consider, a surprising, even incomprehensible, rôle in a race as logical and rational as the Greeks.

In fact, there is no contradiction in this. The moment the irrational becomes an integral part of the life of a man or a people, and intervenes as a permanent, not an occasional, element of destiny, it is absorbed quite naturally into the general economy of the system: the unforeseeable finally becomes part of the foreseeable, which explains why the oracles of Delphi never unduly disturbed the stability or the coherency of Athenian political life.

It was the same as regards belief in the Devil, in the life of the Christian communities of the desert. The moment the existence of invisible forces and beings called angels or demons was regarded as natural, the whole of everyday life was adjusted in relation to those forces and conformed to a logic very different from that of the secular world but having its own strict laws. Here, the supernatural is conceived as an integral part of the total of natural phenomena and that is why, in the desert, the unseen world so often becomes visible.

One may go even further than this and say that the existence of angels and demons was not only an object of faith with the Christians of the early centuries, but also an object of study: the inhabitants of the supernatural world were described and catalogued, their nature, their powers and their different rôles in Creation were defined. And thus catalogued, classified and dissected, this supernatural population became even more real to those who believed in it. The preciseness of the treatises on demonology was something astounding; all the evidence indicates that, to the investigators of those times, it was a matter of a complete—almost exact—science, with its vocabulary, its laws and even its experimental proofs. To believe in angels and demons was, as Henri-Irénée Marrou rightly states in an article on the Devil, 'not only an act of faith but participation in a science, a human science but based on reason and experiment. The Fathers spoke of demons as we should speak of evolution today: as a truth or, if one prefers it, a hypothesis, held without question by every educated person'.

That being granted, how did the majority of anchorites imagine demons and angels to be? Not as mere spirits but rather as creatures of substance, a substance much more tenuous than man's but palpable. As demons were only fallen angels from above, they were condemned to living in the regions of denser atmosphere near the surface of the earth and, preferably, even in the dark cone formed by the earth's shadow in space. The proof that they were creatures of substance is found in the fact that they needed food. In his *Exhortation to Martyrdom*, Origen wrote: 'In order to stay in the heavy atmosphere surrounding the earth, the demons must have the food supplied by smoke and they watch out for signs of smoke, blood and incense'. In other words, they fed on incense, as did the old pagan gods. Moreover, were they not, in fact, demons that lived inside those gods and gave the idols a semblance of life in order to delude the heathen? That was the belief of St Cyprian, who wrote in a revealing passage of his treatise *On the Vanity of Idols*:

'The demons hide within the garlanded statues and images. They inspire their prophecies, cause a stirring in the animals' entrails, control the flight of the birds, decide the fate of men and pronounce oracles mingled with a tangle of falsehood. They mar our lives and invade our sleep and our rest. They even insinuate themselves into our bodies, engender diseases, bring terror to our souls and twist our limbs to force us to worship them.'

This was a very logical assimilation, the historical motivations of which can be clearly seen: when the persecutions ceased and Christians had to combat the world deep within themselves, in their thoughts and desires, and not as martyrs in the arena, paganism carried the fight into its Christian adversary's own ground: it *took spirit form*, and its huge statues, its idols of stone and marble became aggressive phantoms, the demons of the new religion. And when one thinks that in Egypt these statues and idols were essentially zoomorphic divinities, it is understandable that the spiritualized, phantom images of an Anubis (jackal god), a Sekhmet (lioness) and a Sobek (crocodile) were in no way prepossessing. In the literature of the desert, such, in the main, was the origin of the conception of the Devil as a Beast and a Monster, that was to have such a 'vogue' with the passage of time: the divine animal from ancient Egypt, which loomed in the consciousness of Christian Egypt in the form of a demoniacal beast. And since the gods were hybrids, half animal and half human, the Devil in turn became a hybrid creature, a dragon, a centaur, etc.

Among these conceptions of the Devil as a Beast or a Monster, there was one which recurred with particular insistence: the Serpent. Let it not be supposed that this was a question of a purely biblical influence, although it would be a fairly logical assumption. 'The demoniac Serpent, as it appears in the literature of the desert, is nearly always a Dragon, a serpent with feet (sometimes even human legs), and is so represented in the bas-reliefs and funeral papyri of Ancient Egypt. It is a rabbinical tradition, the Serpent is provided not only with articulate speech but also with legs and feet; in appearance it reminds one of the camel or a primeval saurian.'[1]

The traditional Serpent—seen as a prehistoric Dinosaur, the Master of the Past or a Dragon—may, in the light of modern knowledge, be

[1] Albert-Frank Duquesne, *'En marge de la tradition judéo-chrétienne.'*

interpreted as a tempter: it represented the lure of the past, an affection for a successful but interim stage in the evolutionary process. The temptation was, in brief, a crystallization of the present time, amounting to a phenomenon of *spiritual inertia*. Contrary to the traditional idea that is held, it was a voice saying to the ascetic: 'You are on the right road. Stay where you are.' It was the voice of the Dinosaur from a world once flourishing but now over, the existence of which continued to haunt human imagination and which, in the shape of Dragon or Serpent with legs, stood in the way of the necessary evolution of man, that biologically and spiritually new man which the ascetic sought to become.[1] It was a voice from the depths of the past and therefore from the depths of Egypt: was Egypt not the ideal land in which Time stood still, in which the animal-headed gods were reputed to be immutable and to have existed since the beginning of the world? The Dinosaur was the voice of the ages, that is of ancient Egypt, from a hateful but inalienable past, difficult to admit but still more difficult to expel: the Devil, in Egypt, could only assume the characteristics of the ancient gods which persisted in their refusal to die.

'A WOMAN WANDERER OF THE DESERT'

From the assimilation of demons and ancient gods there resulted an 'advantage' to the ascetic: the demons shared the illusory power of the idols. Since, according to Clement of Alexandria, the idols were only 'a caricature of Divinity', the demons were themselves but a caricature of the angels. They have, indeed, no real power over the ascetic.[2] The continually changing appearances which they adopted in order to terrify were in themselves a proof of their unstable nature, and for that reason they rarely appeared alone, because, as Anthony said to his disciples, 'if they had any power, they would not come in bands. They would not appear to us as phantoms and would not transform themselves in order to deceive us; for those who do not lack strength have no need of illusions or noises to terrify us'. Above all, the demon could not penetrate the ascetic's consciousness: all his power and all his effort consisted in disclosing actions and forms of behaviour which he might then make use of against the ascetic. Many instances of this have been seen in the

---

[1] The Dragon, as the 'voice of the ages', is necessarily a twofold symbol. That is why René Guénon correctly observes in his *Renversement des symboles*, 'The Far Eastern Dragon, in reality a symbol of the Word, has often been interpreted by western ignorance as a diabolical symbol'.

[2] A limitation which also appears in Job (1, 6 and 2, 6) since, in order to unleash afflictions against Job, Satan needs the word of command from Jehovah.

present book: tempting him to take one step fewer in going to draw water, making him laugh by their combined pulling at an ordinary leaf on a tree, making a hole in front of his feet so that he could not kneel down and making him eat one olive more or less than the stipulated number. Such characteristics lay at the source of medieval demonology, necessitating the conclusion of a pact with oneself for the ascetic's undertaking to be well-founded and convincing: to the demon a simple internal adhesion was inoperable. This also offers an explanation of the weapons used against him: it was not enough for the ascetic to summon up resistance within himself. In order to vanquish the demon and show that he was not deceived by trickery, he had to perform certain specific actions—such as making the sign of the cross—or utter certain words, the rapid muttering of a passage from the Gospels. Only in that way could the demon see and understand that the ascetic was not to be tempted.

There were, however, moments in the life in the desert when the Devil appeared in a very different form: as a Tempter, with a halo of glory and light, like the 'most beautiful of all the angels' according to the traditional biblical conception.[1] The anchorites had no difficulty in accepting this dual personality of the Devil, the continual change from Horror to Beauty. And it is easy to understand that this second vision— infinitely closer to human experience—should have played a large part in the life in the desert. Here, the Devil presented a familiar countenance, so familiar that it became merged with the ascetic's repressed but ever-present desires. How many times in the constant struggle waged against hunger, thirst, sleep and all the demands of the flesh did he not feel tempted to give way or to offer less resistance? At such a time of continual tension between the anchorite and his desires, the least hesitation, the slightest relaxation, just a sigh or a careless glance at the world and secular life, anything might be a pretext for Satan to insinuate himself into the man's heart and mind. Everywhere he was on the prowl, in the desert, as a woman who had lost her way and was asking for a night's shelter, in the monk's or ascetic's cell, in his very heart, arousing in him pulsating desires, wandering thoughts, vague feelings of remorse—and indifference. Sometimes even, the Devil came from an earlier time, as in the wonderful temptation of St Pachon in which he appeared as a picture seen in childhood, a fleeting image of the past which had apparently been forgotten and which suddenly emerged from the subconscious, years later, in the solitude of the desert.

---

[1] The *only* truly authentic conception of the Devil in the very early days of Christianity: an attractive Being of exemplary beauty, intelligence and speech.

'Although I am of very great age,' said St Pachon to Palladius one day, 'and have spent forty years of my life in this cell thinking of nothing but my salvation, I still continue to be tempted. For more than twelve years, not a single day or night has passed without my being tormented or persecuted by the devil. One day, he took the form of a young Ethiopian woman whom I had seen gathering ears of corn in summer in the days of my youth. It seemed as if she came and sat on my lap, and she aroused in me such a desire for her as to offend God. I was extremely grieved and I struck her, after which she disappeared. More than two years later, my hand still smelt so offensive that I could not bear the stink of it.'

The stench that he left behind him when he went away was one of the demon's characteristics: it was generally a smell of sulphur or burning, which persisted for weeks or months. Smell played an important part in the lives of the ascetics, for it was the symbol of certain internal conditions: a man who smelled bad was a bad man, in a state of sin. Pachomius, who died 'in an odour of sanctity', had the gift of being able to smell out sin and even heresy from a distance, according to the peculiar smell of the visitors whom he received! Yes, souls had their smell no less than bodies, but not everybody was able to detect it, as witness this passage from the *Apophthegms of the Desert Fathers*: 'A saintly old man relates that one day, when he was walking in the desert, he observed two angels following him. After some time, they came across a corpse. The old man held his nose because of the stench and the angels did likewise. "Did you also notice the stink, then?" he asked them. "No," the angels answered, "we cannot smell the odour of bodies, but only the stink of souls."'

To return to the Devil as the Tempter, the temptation suffered by St Pachon was not the only one of its kind. The Devil appeared very frequently in the form of a woman of wonderful beauty, lost in the desert and seeking the hospitality of some solitary. Thus, in the temptation of John of Egypt (according to the *History of the Monks* by Rufinus) which is a model of its kind, the ascetic gradually succumbed to the fascination of the lost Woman, with an ease that is surprising in so hardened a recluse who had lived for more than thirty years in a cave:

'One evening, the Tempter of men took the form of a very beautiful woman who, as a wanderer in the desert and worn out with fatigue, drew near to the cave of John of Egypt and, feigning exhaustion, went inside. She clasped him round the knees and begged him to have pity on her: "Night caught me unawares in this desert where I had come to hide:

allow me, I implore you, to rest a little in a corner of your cell so as not to be devoured by wild beasts." John of Egypt, moved to pity, took her into his cave and asked her the reasons which obliged her to wander in the desert in that way. She gave him false but cleverly invented reasons and proceeded to talk, radiating her poisonous charms and flattering him with envenomed words, telling him by turns how miserable a creature she was and how unworthy of his help. So the solitary was touched by the sweetness of her words. This was followed by still pleasanter talk accompanied by laughter and caresses, and the woman was bold enough to fondle his beard and his chin; finally, she went so far as to kiss him on the head and neck in a very familiar manner.

'How can I continue? She got the better of that soldier of Jesus Christ and made him her slave. For he began to be deeply stirred and to feel a great urge within him, to give way to unbridled passion, and the memory of his past exertions could do nothing to restrain him. Therefore, when he would have given full rein to his shameful desire, the demon in female form, whose imaginary body was made of nothing but air, vanished from his grasp with awful howls and, as the unhappy man went in shameful pursuit, he left him bewildered with a cruel mockery. And a great crowd of demons collected to witness this spectacle with much shouting and laughter.'

The temptations were, however, often less spectacular. The Tempter was not always to be seen, but was often nothing but a voice, an impression, even a thought, insistent and insidious, drawing a man towards the world and causing him to doubt himself. Thus, during the long hours spent in solitude, there were moments of sudden weariness when anguish and disgust laid hold of the ascetic. This torpor was most often felt about midday, when the desert radiated an intolerable heat, when time itself appeared to stand still and life suddenly seemed to be devoid of meaning. This feeling the desert Fathers knew very well and they called it *acidia*, meaning indifference, distaste, apathy of heart and mind. 'It is especially about the middle of the day that he torments the monk,' wrote Cassian in his *Institutions of the Monks of Egypt*, 'as though with regular bouts of fever. Many monks have therefore named him the noonday demon.' The anchorite begins by 'feeling horror for the place in which he lives, distaste for his cell and disdain for his brethren. He feels incapable of returning to his cave, of working or of praying.' Then, as the hours pass by, 'when the middle of the day approaches, weariness and hunger weigh more heavily upon him. The anchorite feels as exhausted as if he had just completed a long distance through the desert or several days' fasting. He cannot stop looking towards the horizon in search of some visitor. He goes out, he comes back, he keeps looking towards the sky, towards the sun which appears to him not to be moving!'

Acidia was a disease of solitude, of ascetic life in the desert, a disorder in the man himself—giving up the struggle and the quest of the new man. What was the extent of this disorder? If it originated in the roots of a human being, in the depths of his personality, then it was inseparable from that personality. It would therefore form part of the ascetic's personality or at least part of the dark,[1] inactive side of his nature. Certain texts gave a literal interpretation of this disorder as an illness which could be eliminated from the body and the soul of the ascetic by the application of remedies, by prayer and fasting. So we find this strange episode in the *Coptic Life of Shenute*, showing the demon, in the form of an ailment, sordid and active, suddenly leaving the ascetic who was in the grip of fever. 'It happened,' said the ascetic to Shenute, 'that in the evening, when the light had faded, my body began to shake in a very unpleasant manner. I thought that all my joints were protruding through my flesh and that I was near to death. And then something began to leave my body, something that stank like a putrefying corpse, and it spread out over the bare rocks like smoke, blew away and was gone.'

If the 'stench of death' within the bodies of the ascetics did not quit them, if in spite of their fastings and their struggles they were doomed to be haunted all their lives by Anubis and the Serpent, by the Woman and by Acidia, what name may be given to the demon that dwelt within them and held them down to earth, what kind of face, exactly, did the demon have? The answer can be guessed, and certain texts, few but reliable, confirm it. This answer was amazing—but not unexpected (for it was the Evil One's cleverest trick). Any ascetic in the desert, watching a visitor coming towards him and having the foreboding or the certain knowledge that it was the Devil, sometimes discovered when this Visitor came within view that *it was none other than himself*, his own double come to meet him from the distant horizon.

---

[1] The demon often appears in the form of a 'little black man' or a 'terrible little Ethiopian', coming from the ascetic's head or body. The demon was often thought to be housed in Ethiopians as they were black.

CHAPTER 9

THE SUBSTANCE OF THE ANGELS

'Desire not to see with the eyes of the body the angelic Powers or Christ or his Angels on pain of losing your sanity.'

EVAGRIUS PONTICUS '*Concerning Prayer*'

If life, as it was conceived by the Copts, was just a continual reckoning between Evil and Good, the balance had sooner or later to be declared and the higher powers had to present man with the 'bill'. This they did usually at the time of his approaching death. If there was a debit balance, man had to pay, and in the last chapter it was seen what form the payment took. If, on the other hand, there was a credit balance, man was rewarded and went to paradise. He did not always go there directly, and each man's stages of progress and rewards varied according to his degree of purity. 'If the dying man is of very high degree, by virtue of his past activities, three angels of superior rank come for him and take him to God. If he is of average virtue, angels of lesser degree are sent for him. God acts in this way because, if he sent highly placed angels for a man of small achievement, they might treat him in a manner usual with earthly authorities.' The hierarchy is also to be found among the angels themselves, for it is stated 'that the three angels sent to the dying man are of different rank from one another and that each obeys the orders of the next one above him'.

There was no need of hooks to withdraw the soul of a virtuous man, nor was a spirit-horse necessary to bear it away. When a man was 'about to give up his spirit, one of the angels stood near his head and another by his feet, apparently rubbing him with oil until his soul should leave his body, while the third spread out a spiritual cloth to receive the soul with fitting honour. As for the saint's soul, it was observed that it was of beautiful appearance and as white as snow.' Then came the solemn march through the bright regions of the beyond towards the presence of the Lord. As soon as the soul had left the body, 'one of the angels held two corners of the cloth from behind, while the second grasped it from the front, in the manner of earthly men lifting a body. Meanwhile, the third angel was singing to the soul in an unknown tongue. Even father Pachomius did not understand their song,[1] recognizing only the word "Hallelujah" at times. And thus the angels moved away through the air towards the east, taking the soul with them. They did not move like men walking, but glided along like a stream, for they were spirits. They carried the soul up towards the heights so that it might see from one end of the earth to the other and look upon the whole of Creation, glorifying God who made it. After which, they indicated to him his resting-place in accordance with the Lord's command.' There, he was met by all the saints (which reminds one of the funeral customs of ancient Egypt, when all the gods received the dead man in the sky on his way towards Osiris) and 'they came to meet him, in proportion to his deserving qualities. For some, the saints came even to the Gate of life and embraced them. For others, they came only so far, as required by the merits of the deceased. For others again, they remained where they were, awaiting the dead men's approach, before rising and embracing them. Finally, there were some who did not deserve to have the saints rise and embrace them.'

WORKERS OF FIRE

But paradise can sometimes come down to earth. The life led by the anchorites in the desert was already an anticipation of the celestial life and it was natural that this anticipation should show itself in certain signs. In this world of constant illusions, in which the demon assumed the likeness of an angel the better to mislead the solitaries, the importance of precise and definite indications to show the ascetic that he was on the right road can readily be understood. There existed a sort of 'temptation by angels' just as there was a temptation by demons. Many texts mention the disappointments of some anchorite or other guilty of thinking too soon that he had attained hesychia and prematurely considered himself to be an angel:

'Father John one day told his elder brother that he wished he were like the angels, who do no work and have nothing to do but praise God, and so saying he took off his coat and left for the desert. When he had been there for a week, he came back to call upon his brother and he knocked at his door. "Who is it?" cried the brother. "It is John", was

---

[1] This passage, like that of the previous chapter, on hell, is taken from the *Life of Pachomius.*

the reply. "John has become an angel," retorted the brother, "and is not now to be found among men." Whereupon, as the other still continued his knocking and calling out that he was John, he left him to spend the night outside. Finally, with the coming of daylight, he opened the door and said, "If you are an angel, what need have you for the door to be opened in order to come in? And if you are a man, why are you not working like other men?"'

The angels, just as much as the demons, were constantly present in the desert and were just as numerous. They continually intervened in the life of the ascetic, to keep watch over him, to record his progress and his setbacks, to protect him from the demons and acquaint him with messages and instructions from the Lord. Guardian angels, recording angels, angels performing the functions of soldiers, messengers, liberators and escorts of souls—all these many specific angelic functions should cause no surprise since, to the desert Fathers, the unseen world was as real—and therefore as systematized as the visible world.[1] The cohorts of angels and demons were to them countless, so much so that they would soon have blotted out the light of the sun if God had not, as it happened, made them invisible to human eyes.

'The Christians of the early centuries laid stress upon this numerical aspect, *anarithmetos*, of the angelic host. It was commonly held by the Fathers that the ratio of the total number of men past, present and future, to that of the angels was 99 : 1. To this problem was applied the parable of the lost sheep (humanity) and the ninety-nine faithful sheep (the good angels).'[2]

In that respect the desert Fathers did no more than continue the beliefs already widely held among the Fathers of the Church and Christian writers of the early centuries. To these writers, all living creatures, whether man, animal or plant, had their own angels. According to Origen, the angels preside over the elements, the birth of animals and the growth of plants. In St John Chrysostom's view, 'they administer the world, the nations (thereby showing that history is made, not by men, but by angels), inanimate creatures, the sun, the moon, the sea and the earth'. Clement of Alexandria and the Cappadocian authors,

---

[1] This is confined to the angels of the tradition of the desert. All those mentioned in the Old Testament might be added: the *Cherubim*, ancient Babylonian genii guarding the temples and palaces, the *Destroying Angels* sent by Jehovah against Sodom and the Egyptians, and many more.

[2] Henri-Irenée Marrou.

St Gregory of Nyssa and St Gregory of Nazianzus, even speak of 'City Angels'. In short, the beliefs of the day attributed to angels a whole collection of causalities and natural phenomena, such as the movement of the planets, the growth of plants and other living things, and even the march of history. Modern science has obviously rendered such beliefs a little outworn, although the question is not in fact quite as simple as it would appear. To explain the rising of the sun or chlorophyllian absorption by reference to the intervention of an angel satisfied, in those times, a need for the logical, not for the irrational. It is by no means certain that, if such an outstanding intelligence as Origen were suddenly transferred to our epoch, he would have found his belief in angels incompatible with the findings of modern science. He would perhaps have called Gravity the angel who continually reveals his extreme benignity by keeping the Earth moving in space and Electron the angel who ensures the rotation of particles of matter around the atomic nucleus.[1]

But the speculations of writers are of less importance here than the rough and ready way in which the anchorites believed in angels and regarded the part they played in the daily life of the desert. Every angel, it has been seen, had a mission, a specific function, which explained both his attributes and his appearance. In the language of the age it may even be said that in the desert the angels and demons were functional creatures; functional in appearance and even in their nature, since some of them—such as the angelic torturers described in the last chapter—were so created by God for the purpose of performing one particular task, which made them incapable of pity. Therefore, as the ascetic saw them, the angels had an appearance exactly corresponding to their function. Pachomius's disciple Theodore saw one night, for instance, while he was praying, an angel watching over all the brethren in the monastery. Now, this angel, 'had the appearance of a soldier of the king. In his hand he held a shining sword of fire and was dressed in a sticharion, for at that time he was not wearing his chlamys. Large medallions adorned this beautiful and brilliant sticharion. The belt he wore was a hand's-breadth wide, red and flashing.'[2]

There was the angel, red and armed because he was allocated 'military' guard-duty or the task of fighting the demons. There was, in contrast,

---

[1] The quite recent discovery of particles of anti-matter would only have confirmed this angelic conception of the universe, in his view: to each electron angel (a spirit charged with positive energy and will) there would be a corresponding anti-electron demon (a spirit charged with negative energy and will).
[2] The chlamys was a short mantle covering the breast-plate worn by officers. The sticharion was a pleated robe worn by priests.

the angelic messenger of God, the bearer of the divine Word, a dazzling white angel whose brightness was sometimes greater than that of the sun itself.

When he was 'assigned' to, or rather created for, humbler tasks, such as keeping watch upon an ascetic's movements or utterances, the angel dispensed with his wings, his sword and his brilliance. He assumed a human form, such as that of the young man who counted the anchorite's steps in the sand, as already mentioned. Sometimes he even took on the appearance of the ascetic himself, becoming his angelic double as the demon became his diabolical double. So it happened that, one day, when he was asking God's advice as to how he should spend his time, St Anthony saw seated in the desert before him a man who was like him in every detail and who was busy weaving mats. Such were the forms and functions of angels in the desert. Whether as soldiers with swords, dazzling winged messengers, silent young men walking in the desert or angelic doubles, indicating the road to be followed, the angels intervened in the ascetic's life just as they came into the life of the world; they pointed the way, even shaped the future of men and things and were, in Tertullian's phrase, 'workers of fire'.[1]

The life in the desert was not, because of the familiar presence of angels, only the anticipation of a future paradise; it was also a reminiscence, a revival of a lost paradise. The anchorite, it has been said, lived both before and after history. But what did *history* mean to the mind of a Copt? It meant: the temporal world and Sin. To the Christian, history and the consciousness of history came about with Sin and the consciousness of Sin, and the nightmare of history was, in his view, only an aspect of the great nightmare of original Sin. In so far as he wished to escape history, the anchorite had therefore to live before and after Sin, or at least to strive to do so, for nobody, on pain of grave heresy, would have dared to affirm that fasts and the life in the desert could blot out the effects of original sin. But, at least, the purifications in which he was engaged in the desert mitigated those effects. They permitted the ascetic for brief moments to live as 'before the Fall', to live the life of Adam in paradise. They did even more than this, making it possible for him to be a new Adam. 'Through the virtue of the Holy Ghost and spiritual regeneration,' said Macarius the Elder in one of his *Spiritual*

---

[1] 'Workers' who, on occasion, became so completely incarnate that they were materially indistinguishable from human beings. 'Have you not read,' wrote Tertullian in his treatise *On the Body of Christ*, 'that the angels of the Creator changed into human forms in such a way and appeared so authentically flesh and blood that Abraham washed their feet?'

Homilies, 'man rises to the dignity of the first Adam, for such a man is deified.' These brief moments when the Eternal impinged upon the present, when man was deified and became a new Adam, were the age of miracles.

Before these miracles are examined, one thing should be made clear: it is not here a question of miracles *in the desert.* It would be a serious mistake to attempt to consider the miracles without relating them to history and a definite cultural environment. Miracles, like temptations, are historical phenomena, that is to say relative phenomena, which first meet the needs of such an environment and then disappear naturally as soon as the environment or the need ceases to exist. In particular, a miracle is always meaningless in isolation. Primarily, its occurrence supplies evidence, a proof of the truth and power of faith. It is intended less to astonish than to attest and prove, and this fact explains why different civilizations have not all had recourse to the same miracles to demonstrate the truth of God and why some have entirely excluded them. Could one claim today to convert atheists by exterminating dragons? Every age has had its miracles, the 'answers' to its own questions, and it is impossible to study them, to understand them, to appreciate their purpose and their impact on the human psyche, if they are considered apart from the age and setting in which they occur. Just as with angels and demons, it may be said that miracles are functional phenomena.

These few remarks link up with those in the early chapters concerning the conception of aretology. This term and this form of *edifying and ideal dissertation* correspond closely to the modern notion of functional discourse. The miracles with which the literature of the desert is crowded were not exclusively intended to testify to the intrinsic power of the saints as much as to their extrinsic power; they were to cause astonishment, but with the purpose of *edification.* Whose edification? That of the Christian readers of the lives of the saints, in order to strengthen their faith, and also of possible heathen readers, so as to persuade and convert them. (Very many texts, indeed, tell of spectacular conversions of pagans after a miracle has taken place, which gives rise to the thought that the miracle may have been invented *a posteriori* in order to justify a conversion difficult to explain historically.) There was undoubtedly an aretological, and therefore literary, basis for certain miracles, such as those which reproduced in the lives of saints the feats already performed by magi in the lives of pagan sages: walking on the waters, controlling wild beasts, annihilating serpents and dragons, commanding obedience from inanimate objects—all these miracles forming

22. THE DORMITION OF ST. EPHRAEM

23A. RUPESTRIAN MONASTERIES IN CAPPADOCIA

23B. A HERMITAGE ON
MOUNT ATHOS

part of an ancient aretological resource, tinged with magic, which owed nothing to Christianity and which was simply borrowed for the *Lives* of the saints from earlier heathen records.

THE ANIMALS OF THE DESERT

Miracles have their own logic. If, in fact, some anchorites succeeded in recapturing, if only for a very brief moment, the innocence lost with the Fall of Man, the implication is that the life in the desert 'reproduced' that of Adam in paradise. Food from heaven, and never wanting, a state of innocence knowing no shame or nakedness, the fellowship of animals—all the privileges of man's early existence—were found once again in the desert.

The theme of manna from heaven occurs frequently. Several instances of it have already been seen: the anchorite who found a white loaf of bread on his table every day, St Mary the Egyptian who lived for seventeen years with only two small loaves, etc. Many other examples could be given. This miracle, it will be noted, was rather to be 'taken internally' and intended for the edification of the anchorites themselves, for it was encountered only among particularly virtuous ascetics who had gone to extremes of fasting and mortification.

The second theme, that of rediscovered innocence, is not strictly a miracle. It is rather a matter of the logical consequence of a state of inner relinquishment which was interpreted as a physical 'relinquishment', a nakedness of which the ascetic was quite unaware. Moreover, conditions of life in the desert made it necessary for some anchorites to live in an 'Adam-naked' state, and, indeed, John Moschus quotes several cases of nudism: Sophronius the browser, mentioned earlier, 'who lived quite naked for seventy years near the Dead Sea', or the anchorite George, who with no clothing of any sort roamed the desert for thirty-five years. This nudity obviously gained symbolical importance very quickly, for it was considered as a divine favour, a special form of grace reserved for a very small number of ascetics and associated with other privileges. 'When I was at Raithu, years ago,' a monk told John Moschus, 'I was in church one Thursday in Holy Week, in the company of all the Fathers, when I observed two anchorites entering. They were naked but I was the only one who noticed that they were so. When they had partaken of the sacrament, they left the church and went away.' The monk begged them to take him with them, but they answered: "You cannot live with us. Stay here, where you are well suited." They said a prayer for me and, before my eyes, they walked upon the waters of the Red Sea and passed over it on foot.'[1]

But the most frequent miracle was that of the 'obedient animals', with which the anchorites lived in perfect harmony. Here again, the theme no doubt has some basis of truth. It could happen that some hermit or other lived on good terms with some placid-natured animal or that there was in the desert some buffalo-child or jackal-child, as with Onuphrio and Aphu the Buffalo mentioned earlier, whose way of life gave rise to this theme. But that was not the main point, for the repeated use of the theme indicated other preoccupations: as John Moschus says, one was concerned to show 'how animals were subject to Adam's will before he disobeyed God's command and was driven from the earthly paradise'.

The aretological animal stories were, then, meant for the edification of the reader or listener. The principal role was played by the lion, first because that creature was the beast most commonly to be seen in the deserts of Egypt, Palestine and Syria, and also because of the traditional symbolism attaching to it: if the king of beasts bowed before the anchorite, the whole animal Creation thereby rendered to man the homage due to him.

The best of relations, and the most friendly, existed between lions and men in the desert. There, the lion was the friend of man, understanding, obedient and, if need be, helpful to him. Thus, as Moschus relates, when a lion appeared in the region where Julian the Stylite was living, and caused trouble to many people, the stylite 'called his disciple to him and said: "Go south from here for two miles and you will find a lion resting. Say to him, 'The humble Julian sends you word to leave these parts.' " The disciple went to the place, found the lion and delivered the message, and the lion left at once'.

As for Simeon the Elder (not the stylite but the one mentioned by Theodoret, walking on the Sinai road), he was in the habit of having lost visitors escorted to the nearest town by 'two lions in his service. Instead of looking fierce, these lions gazed fondly at the saint as if they recognized him as their master'.

The lion's attachment and devotion to its master may go even further, as is borne out by the admirable story of the lion of St Gerasimus, as recounted by John Moschus. Gerasimus was an anchorite living in a laura near the Jordan. To do his bidding he had a very faithful lion

---

[1] In an entirely different connexion it is noteworthy that in Alexandria in the second century there existed Gnostics called *Adamites*, who used to meet naked in their houses and in caverns.

which he had once cured of an injury and which had remained with him ever since. This lion's main task was to watch over the laura donkey whenever it went in search of water in the river. But, one day, some camel-drivers succeeded in laying hands on the donkey, and the lion, 'having lost the donkey, came back sad and crestfallen to the laura and Gerasimus. The latter thought the lion had devoured the donkey and said: "Where is the donkey?" Just like a man, the lion hung his head and remained silent. The monk said: "You have eaten the donkey! By the blessed God, what the donkey did you shall do henceforth." And from that time, whenever Gerasimus commanded it, the lion carried the pack-saddle with its four water-jars'.

Every day for five years the lion went to the river to fetch water and for that reason was given the name of Jordan. Then Gerasimus died 'and went to meet his Lord. That day, by God's bidding, the lion was not at the laura. He returned there some time later and looked for the monk. Seeing the lion, the monks' disciple said: "Jordan, our monk has left us fatherless. He has gone to the Lord. But come and eat." But the lion would not eat. He kept looking in all directions for Gerasimus, uttering loud groans. The other Fathers patted the lion's back and said: "Gerasimus has gone to the Lord and is no more with us." But Jordan only cried and wailed the louder and, by voice, look and gesture, showed his grief at seeing the monk no more. At last, the disciple took the lion to the place where the monk had been buried, about half a mile from the church. Then he knelt before the grave and said: "This is where he lies." Then Jordan beat his head violently against the ground and, with a mighty roar, fell dead upon the monk's grave'.

Of all the lions in the desert, it was clearly those of the Jordan that showed the greatest qualities of kindness and politeness. On a narrow path by a river, a lion would deliberately go and lie down in a thorn-bush to let an anchorite pass. Another, going to drink at the river, noticed a monk lying across the lion's usual path—a monk who had found no better way to expiate a sin than to give himself up to be devoured by a lion—and, 'standing up on his hind legs like a man, stepped over him without even touching him'. But it was perhaps a matter of time rather than of place. In going round the lauras, hermitages and monasteries, the stories of obedient lions, the oldest of which go back to the fourth century, added new and picturesque details and finally made the lion an almost human character capable of thought, tears and laughter. The lion was so depicted, moreover, by Byzantine painters and sculptors: in the form of a human-faced animal which had lost its natural ferocity in order to live among the ascetics and, in its own way to benefit from the word of God. It was an animal with soft, intelligent eyes.

As well as stories of lions, leopards, hyenas and jackals, which are of biblical inspiration, the animal literature of the desert contains other miraculous stories of pagan, even Egyptian, inspiration. In general, these are all the miracles in which figure crocodiles and dragons.

The crocodile is a typically Egyptian animal, and the theme of the obedient crocodile is merely a Christian transposition from a number of magical tales from ancient Egypt. Some of these are met with in Lucian of Samosata's book, the *Philopseudes*, already mentioned, in which are described the adventures of a young man sent by his father to Egypt to pursue scientific studies. Going by boat up the Nile, he met an Egyptian sage named Pancrates. Now, this man, 'of excellent learning and well versed in Egyptian doctrines, performed an endless number of wonderful feats every time the boat came inshore: he would go swimming among the most fearsome beasts, which treated him with respect and stroked him with their tails, and *would ride astride the crocodiles*. In short, he was a man beloved of the gods.'

This 'miracle' has an almost identical counterpart in Christian literature of the desert in this amusing episode from the life of St Helenus:

'Arriving one Sunday at a monastery, St Helenus observed that the office for the day was not being performed. He was told: "It is because the priest lives on the other side of the river and has not dared to make the crossing because of a crocodile which is frightening him." The saint went to the water's edge and called upon God for help. The crocodile immediately appeared and came towards him. The creature offered its services to the saint and carried him on its back to the other bank of the river. The saint found the priest and begged him to come to the solitaries. He called out and the crocodile appeared, humbly offering to carry them. Saint Helenus got on to its back and urged the priest to do likewise, but the latter was so frightened that he fell over backwards and made off. Saint Helenus went back across the river alone, on his crocodile.'

The theme of the obedient serpent and dragon was also Egyptian but it was rather rare, since the dragon soon became a demoniac creature to be destroyed rather than subjugated. And yet Rufinus, in his *History of the Monks*, relates the case of St Ammon 'who, every time he was away from his cell, was robbed by thieves, who took away the bread which was his only food'. So, one day, 'he went into the desert and, having ordered two dragons to follow him, told them to guard the entrance to his cell', and when the robbers came 'they saw the dragons posted as sentries, and they were so terrified that they fell senseless to the ground'. Whereupon, the thieves were converted and 'soon became so highly virtuous that they performed the same miracles as St Ammon'!

The subjection or destruction of dragons was, indeed, one of the commonest and most easily accomplished miracles of the desert. Whoever spent some time in fasting and in prayer, quickly acquired, it seems, the power to reduce these terrible creatures to ashes. This facility no doubt means that the dragon was one of the Devil's roughest incarnations and therefore one of the easiest to expose and combat. Yet the dragon often appeared in the texts as a very real animal, spitting fire and venom, a monstrous dinosaur which terrified all the ascetics. What was to be done, then, if a dragon was by chance encountered in the desert ? One had to avoid feeling afraid, wait until the dragon came near, then make the sign of the cross and blow on the creature. That was what St Marcian did, for instance, in the Syrian desert and 'the breath that came from the saint's mouth was as a flame that scorched up the dragon so that it fell to pieces as a reed would have done if consumed by flames'.

The spectacular character of these 'miracles' and the ease with which they were performed obviously risked giving the ascetic a feeling of vanity. Certain anchorites, like Nisteron mentioned in the *Apophthegms of the Fathers*, therefore made haste to disappear as soon as they saw a dragon, not 'from fear of the animal but, on the contrary, to avoid the demon of vanity and the temptation to destroy the animal'. Others, however, had no such scruples. Not only did they destroy dragons all day long, but they did so preferably in the presence of strangers. Thus, Rufinus, when passing through the desert with other pilgrims, was the compulsory and terrified witness to a happening of this kind. The monk who acted as their guide observed in the sand the tracks of a huge dragon and decided to follow them and find the creature. He was 'carried away by impatience and delight at the prospect of this encounter and the opportunity to demonstrate the power of the faith'. It was no good Rufinus and his companions telling him that they took his word for it; the monk would not relinquish his intention and, 'having taken up a position at the entrance to the beast's lair, he waited for us so as to kill the creature in our presence and refused to leave until he had put his plan into execution'.

LIVING IN THE TIME OF CHRIST

If the miracles of obedient lions and stricken dragons revealed the hold that biblical symbols and Egyptian marvels had over the mind of the

Copt, there were others of more strictly Christian inspiration. In his desert life the anchorite did not strive only to discover lost innocence or to re-establish the state of things before the Fall of Man; he also lived in the continual presence of Christ. His Birth, Life, Crucifixion, Resurrection and Ascension were to him ever-present events, made real by each religious service and festival. Therefore it is normal to see occurring in the literature of the desert a certain number of miracles which reproduce those performed by Christ in the course of his life on earth: the healing of the paralytic, the blind and the insane, the miracles of the loaves and fishes and water changed into wine, the raising of the dead— all had their place in the desert. But in that setting they had a particular meaning, for their purpose was not so much to amaze multitudes or convert heathens as to prove the ever-present power of God. Every miracle accomplished in the desert brought up to date the identical miracle first performed by Christ and seemed like a return to his time. Stress must be laid on the value and function of the miracles which abolished all sense of time and enabled the ascetic to exist in a world where he lived continually in the age of Christ. Since Christ had known temptations and performed miracles, nobody in the desert could become a saint if he too did not know temptations and perform like miracles. His life in the desert was a symbolized repetition of the life of Christ, even to his crucifixion. This was borne out by the theme of the *crucified monk* which occurred so frequently in the ascetic and mystical literature of the desert; a sameness in miracles implied a sameness in suffering.

Nevertheless, the different miracles performed by the desert saints were sometimes very unlike their evangelical models. The reason is that the cultural setting had changed in the meantime; the fourth-century Copts were not the first-century Jews. In this sense every miracle is a 'historical' fact: the miraculous happening may remain the same, but its meaning and application vary. To take an example: the raising of the dead. In the Gospels, the raising of Jairus's daughter and Lazarus are 'pure' miracles, in the sense that they are immediately presented as such to prove to the Jews the greater glory of God (in the case of Lazarus, at least). In the writings of the desert, on the contrary, the miracle of the raising of the dead was never performed for its own sake but always for secondary and practical reasons. A dead man was made to speak in order to denounce a criminal or to provide valuable information that might save a living person. The resurrection itself became an epiphenomenon, a sort of last resource to which the saint was obliged to turn in order to reach his desired objective. Once the information had been obtained, more often than not he let the 'risen' man relapse into death and bothered no more about him!

Thus, in the *Life of Macarius the Elder*, Macarius was seen to revive a dead man in order to confound a heretic who denied the resurrection of the dead. On another occasion, he saved the live of an innocent person accused of murder, by questioning the dead man, who answered from the depths of his tomb and cleared the accused person of the charge. As the crowd, both amazed and angry, begged Macarius to ask the name of the real murderer, the saint answered: 'I shall take good care not to do so. It is enough for me to save an innocent man without becoming involved in discovering who is guilty'! From this it is clear how far resurrection, properly considered, was a secondary phenomenon: it did not even occur to Macarius to take advantage of the occasion to keep the risen man alive! Still clearer evidence is to be found in a passage from the *Life* of St Mucius, quoted by Rufinus, in which St Mucius raised a man from the dead merely to discover whether he liked his shroud! This man was, in fact, a young disciple of St Mucius, who had asked him to bury him with great care if he should die before the saint. 'As the young man died soon afterwards, St Mucius buried him with many garments and said in everybody's presence: 'Is that enough, my son, or shall I add more?' Then the dead man, whose face was already covered and swathed in bandages, spoke up: 'It is enough, father.' All those present considered this to be an extraordinary miracle, but the saint returned to the desert, so great was his concern to avoid any suspicion of vanity.'

To resuscitate a dead man with the sole purpose of discovering whether he is sufficiently clad seems so absurd that it may be wondered if it is not a matter of an incident belonging to another legendary cycle to which a resurrection has been added. This cheapening of resurrection is made even clearer in a passage from the *Life* of St Sisoes (St Anthony's disciple) in which the saint brought a child back to life *by mistake*, believing that he was just sick! Here, the miracle showed a power quite unknown to the saint himself, who acted without being aware that he did so.

Among the other miracles concerned with death, there are many that have to do with what might be called the 'preservation of the saints' bodies'. An instance of this has already been seen in the life of Onuphrio, with the body of the anchorite falling to dust, but, in the time of John Moschus, this legendary cycle had become traditional and enriched. A monk told John Moschus:

'One day, when I went into a cave, I found a kneeling anchorite, with

199

his hands raised up to heaven and his hair trailing on the ground. I bowed down before him, saying: "Pray for me, father." He did not answer. Then I went up to embrace him, but as I touched him I saw that he was dead and I went away.

'A little further on, I saw another cave. I went inside and I saw a monk. He asked: "Have you been into the other cave?" I told him that I had done so and he said: "Well, the monk has been dead for fifteen years." Now, he was as well-preserved as if he had fallen asleep but an hour earlier. I went on my way praising God.'

THE SUBSTANCE OF THE ANGELS

All the miracles described so far corresponded to a certain necessity in the life of the desert: to live a life of friendship with animals, to raise the dead and heal the sick, was to abolish all notion of time and become the contemporary of Christ. When one intends to study the miracles, it is first necessary to establish in what ideal time a miracle was placed and what exemplary, primordial age it brought into the present, whether it was the age of Adam, of Christ or of the Martyrs. The miracle established a universal unity, through time, between the ascetic and all men, past and present. Macarius conversing in the mountains with a Greek's skull is a striking example. In all, what the ascetic lost by taking to the desert, namely contact with men of his day and society, he regained by virtue of that brotherhood which—beyond the scope of death and time—made him one with all men of the past, since Adam. The anchorite was never alone in the desert: there were first the angels and the demons, then the dead with whom he frequently spoke—the saints and martyrs of early Christian times and also the dead of a distant past, Greek, Roman and Egyptian, whispering in the darkness of the tombs. All these surrounded the ascetic and constituted his true society, his millions of unseen companions.[1]

There were in the desert, however, certain miracles which implied no abolition of the sense of time—no return or revival of the age of Adam or of Christ. These miracles were all those which referred to certain powers of the ascetic (physical powers generally) and which changed the conditions of his material existence or even the properties of his corporeity. In brief, they concerned his relation to Space and physical environment: instantaneous transportation from one place to another, levitation, seeing through opaque objects and immobilizing a

[1] And also, of course, the men of the future, those who will be born before the Day of Judgement and whom he will find in the life beyond.

man or an object from a distance. For the sake of convenience these will be referred to as 'kinesic miracles'.

The first type of kinesic miracle, levitation and transportation, is very rare in the literature of the desert. (Levitation is the phenomenon of raising oneself into the air a distance ranging from a few inches to several yards.) This type is mentioned only three times: in the *Lives* of St Ammon, Mary the Egyptian and Shenute. It was said of St Ammon that, one day, having to cross the Nile which was in flood, 'he requested his disciple Theodore to withdraw to a distance so that he should not see him naked when he crossed the river. Theodore did as he was asked and, as Ammon felt ashamed at the idea of seeing his own nakedness, he was suddenly transported to the other side of the river'.

As for Mary the Egyptian, her levitation was witnessed by the monk Zosimus. He related that, at the end of his first interview with the saint, she 'turned towards the East, raised her eyes to heaven, held out her hands and began to pray just by silently moving her lips.' Not a word of her prayer could be heard and Zosimus, as he stated later, was dumbfounded and remained silent with downcast eyes. But when he looked up again, he saw that Mary was raised a full cubit above the ground and that she continued to pray while suspended in the air. He was filled with such great dread that, bathed in sweat, he flung himself to the ground not daring to speak except to say within himself: 'Lord, have mercy upon me.' This reaction by Zosimus should be noted, for it is unique in its way. It was neither astonishment nor fear that prevailed, as it usually did, but almost a feeling of anguish in the face of the inexplicable, as if the phenomenon escaped the saint herself and was a trick of the Devil.

Shenute's levitation took place during the last years of his life when his many 'expeditions' against the heathen temples had resulted in his appearing for trial by the court of Antinoë. When the judge had read out the indictment, Shenute was about to begin his defence, when 'he was suddenly taken and lifted up above the court to a height from which a man speaking might still be heard from the ground, as we learnt from his own truthful lips'. And while, at his feet, the crowd which had come to see and hear the Man of God cried out and called to him, 'our holy father remained suspended in the air. And after some time he was gently lowered until he reached the ground. He was immediately seized by the crowd and taken to the church.' And the record adds: 'It was his own truthful lips which spoke of these things, but briefly, to avoid the praises of men.'

Levitation is perhaps one of the only really disturbing phenomena of the desert by reason of its infrequency and the obvious embarrassment and discretion shown in the texts which mention it; which is a little strange when one thinks of the eagerness with which writers of the age made the most of the slightest miracle. Somewhat akin to levitation is the phenomenon of telekinesis, or transportation over a distance, which includes both the movement of an object and the movement of the subject himself. The *Lives* of the desert saints contain several instances of ascetics who made the journey from Egypt to Rome or Byzantium, and back, in a single night. John of Egypt, the recluse of the Lycopolis cave, appeared in the presence of the emperor Theodosius at the very moment when the latter was thinking of sending a eunuch to consult him! Still more curious were the miracles that were the reverse of kinesic, consisting of depriving a man or an object of all movement. Two of these are mentioned in the *History of the Monks* by Rufinus: that of St Theon who, 'from a distance bound some thieves who had come to rob him and who were held at his door for a night and a day quite unable to move', and the much more famous instance of St Apollo, who halted a whole crowd of heathens engaged in a ritualistic ceremony, so that they could not move at all. Over and above its solar character, it was clearly an example of a literally amazing aretological miracle for the purpose of converting heathens.[1]

Two cases of distant immobilization are likewise indicated by Theodoret in his *Religious History*. The first is that of St Acepsimas, the recluse who lived in a tree-trunk with his body laden with chains and who was mistaken for a wolf by a shepherd. The shepherd was about to throw a stone at the saint but his arm was rendered powerless and remained so all night.[2] The second case occurs in the *Life* of St Maysimus who brought to a standstill the chariot of a wealthy pagan of Antioch who was ill-treating his peasants.

Fairly numerous are the instances of this kind of miracle also found in the work of John Moschus. St Adolas, for example, the recluse who lived in the hollow of a plane-tree in Mesopotamia, halted a barbarian who was preparing to strike him. Likewise, the bland account given by a Saracen: 'I had gone hunting on Anthony's mountain. While I was walking there, I saw a monk who was sitting and reading. I went up to him with the intention of robbing and possibly killing him. As I drew near he stretched out his right hand in my direction saying: "Stop." Unable to move, I stayed as I was for two days and nights. At the end

[1] See page 105.
[2] See page 153.

of that time I said: "In the name of your God, let me go." He answered: "Go in peace." And I went.'

Finally, there was a whole series of miracles which were less dramatic but could not pass unnoticed in the desert. These come under the heading of what would now be called parapsychological phenomena: telepathy, premonitory dreams, fulfilled prophesies, etc. All these phenomena were evidently common currency in the life in the desert, so common in fact that they were hardly thought of as miracles and were most often mentioned incidentally or by chance.

When careful thought is given to all these miracles, it is seen why they do not fall within any of the preceding categories. It is, in fact, because all these powers conferred upon the saint by God's favour are not the revival of the early state of man before the Fall but, on the contrary, the foreshadowing of the new man as announced in the Gospels. They define—to a lesser degree of course—the state of the man of the future, after the Resurrection and the Last Judgement. In these miracles the saint's body is a hallowed body, which escapes earthly laws, both as regards their continuance and their severity, his flesh becomes a new flesh, a 'deified' flesh, to use Macarius's phrase. If the saints translate themselves from Egypt to Rome with such ease, if they suspend themselves above the earth and communicate with living people by means of telepathy, it is because in body and in mind they already anticipate the angelic state. And it was indeed to a change in the actual state of their flesh, to becoming 'deified' (or biologically new) men, that the most lucid and perfect desert anchorites aspired. Asceticism, fasting and mortification led to a first stage in the modification of the ascetic's flesh, in rendering it insensitive to cold and heat and pain, but also in making it more capable of resisting all forms of temptation and the allurements of the demoniac world. 'Just as mud, dried hard in the sun, can no longer be polluted by swine,' wrote John Climacus, one of the greatest of the ascetic writers, in his *Ladder to Paradise*, 'so our flesh, dried and hardened by austerity can no longer be endangered by the violence of demons.' And the pseudo-Macarius echoes this sentiment in his *Spiritual Homilies*: 'When the apostle says: "Rid yourself of the old-style man", he refers to the whole man and means: "Have eyes different from his, another head, different ears, hands and feet." ' Here, it is not strictly a question of miracles, since the slow transformation of the flesh and the body is due to man's extended effort, to his fastings and continual macerations. But the new physical state so acquired, the deified body which to some extent escapes the laws of society, becomes very nearly a miraculous state. In short, between the life of Adam in paradise before the Fall and the future life in the Kingdom of Heaven, the miracles of the desert cover *the whole range of man's condition, past, present and to come.*

'Why asceticism?', was the question asked at the beginning of this book. A new reply can now be given: not only because asceticism is the rejection of the material world and a repudiation of the state in which man finds himself, but also because it leads towards the 'new man', capable of overcoming the problem of space, of treating suffering with contempt and of passing through centuries of time—a man, in fact, having the substance and the powers of the angels.

CHAPTER 10

'TO BE LIKE THE ANGELS'

'A man cannot be considered a saint until he has purified the clay of his being.'

PSEUDO-MACARIUS, 'Spiritual Homilies'

'A disciple came to Macarius the Elder one day and said: "Macarius, what must I do to save my soul?" Macarius answered: "Go and insult the dead." The disciple went to the cemetery, he insulted the dead and came back to Macarius. "What did the dead say?" asked Macarius. "They said nothing," replied the disciple. Then Macarius told him to return to the cemetery and bless the dead. The disciple did so and came back to Macarius. "What did the dead say?" asked Macarius. "They said nothing," replied the disciple. "Be like the dead," said Macarius. "Judge nobody and learn to keep silent."'

This pretty well sums up what might be called the 'teaching' of the desert. The great anchorites did not write and they spoke little. They have left practically nothing behind. Accident of history is not entirely responsible for this silence. If the refusal to give any sort of instruction does not exactly mean that they were like dead men or stones, it indicates that everything that has come down to us under the names of Anthony and Macarius is almost entirely apocryphal. The saint's task in the desert, was to suppress all that he discovered. The only definite teaching on the part of the anchorites was this silence itself, in which they were voluntarily enveloped.

It is therefore far from easy to estimate what was gained by the experiment. What did the great anchorites experience, learn and know, deep within themselves? How far did they succeed in their quest for the new man? To what extent were the many powers attributed to them by the miracles probable or possible? Beyond all question, something new was created in the deserts of Egypt in the fourth century: a new way of living and thinking, which attracted thousands of men to the desert but no trace of which remains today.

What we are endeavouring to discover here will never be revealed by excavating and finding remains of any sort. All evidence goes to show that the experiment undertaken by the desert Fathers was performed at a double level: a collective level, the reality and importance of which are borne out by history and archaeology, and an individual level which can only be discovered from well-authenticated texts and sayings.

Along the lines of this book it has been seen that the experiment did not concern only the spiritual destiny of those who undertook it but, with some ascetics, became even a biological experiment for the shaping —by fasts, macerations and vigils—of the future man, the man new *in mind and body* as indicated in the Gospels, the man who was 'dead' to the old world. This 'death' is confirmed by all literary sources. Anthony, Macarius, Pachomius, Poemen, Ammon and many others were really 'dead' to the world and society. Were they born again elsewhere? What was the land of their rebirth and how was it reached?

The only honest way to answer such a question would be to consult the texts again; not the texts written about the desert Fathers, like all those which have so far been quoted, but those from the saints themselves. For the most part, these texts are non-existent. From St Anthony, who is reputed to have dictated to his disciples a large number of letters in Coptic, only one may be authentic: that on *True Penitence*. From Pachomius, only his *Rule* (known through St Jerome's Latin translation) and a few letters, two of which are written in the 'angel's language' and therefore indecipherable, are all that remain. From Macarius, the great luminary and pneumatophore, there is an abundance of material: more than fifty *Spiritual Homilies*, but unfortunately they are entirely apocryphal and the work of a Syrian writer of the fifth century, elsewhere referred to as the pseudo-Macarius. The only certain testimony to the teaching of Macarius the Elder is contained in the few *Sayings* or *Apophthegms*, some of which have already been quoted in this book.

There is also another reason for this silence: the great anchorites, those who in Coptic are called: *the elders in asceticism*, in Greek the *gerontes*, and later on in Russian the *startsy*, taught much more by example than by the spoken or written word. It should not be forgotten that at this time hardly any of the monks and hermits of the desert could read and that instruction was exclusively oral and at times entirely visual. There are hundreds of anecdotes to prove that the true 'lessons' of the desert consisted not so much in speaking as in demonstrating. Thus, a certain anchorite named Zeno accepted a disciple and spent two years with him in the same cell without even enquiring what his name was or where he came from. In order to teach him how to weave mats, he contented himself with showing the method without uttering a word. Nowadays, this wonderful gift, possessed by former races, of *learning by observation* of the work of others, has been lost. In the Egyptian deserts, if a man could not use his eyes and his ears, there was no point in his going on: the gateway to more complex and loftier truths was permanently closed. The continual references in this book to literal interpretation of symbols by the anchorites of the desert have their ultimate confirmation in this: it was entirely from the result of their sensory experiences that the disciples were set on the road to more difficult truths. Thus, to two disciples who asked him whether the frequent visits he received did not prevent his praying, father Joseph made no reply. He went alone to the back of his cave and returned dressed in rags and walked about without a word. Then he went back again and this time he returned wearing clothes normally reserved for feast-days and continued his walking in silence. The disciples understood from this that, whether he were poorly or richly clad, the ascetic remained essentially the same man, and it mattered not at all whether he spoke or held his tongue. It is what is in a man's heart that matters; his appearance is of no consequence. All this was expressed and communicated *without a word*.

Some will consider that such a method of teaching was very elementary and that the average spiritual level of the anchorites must have been extremely low. That is both true and false, for this 'language' of action and example could always be interpreted in its most figurative and abstract sense. It was employed by all the great religions and is found in almost all myths. It made it possible for the few ascetic texts of the desert, like those of Evagrius Ponticus and John Climacus, to express the highest experiences and the most lofty mystical states by reference to the visible, solid world.

'The monk in a state of hesychia is he who aspires to contain what is ethereal within a vessel of substantial flesh. The cat watches for the mouse and the spirit of the hesychast is on the look-out for the invisible mouse. Do not scorn my comparison, for by so doing you would show that you do not yet understand solitude,' wrote John Climacus, the monk of Sinai, in the seventh century.[1] The same might be said of the literal interpretation of symbols by certain ascetics. By smiling at it we should expose our ignorance of the Desert.

The Egyptian wilderness bequeathed to posterity nothing but the Devil. Most certainly, not all the ascetics could investigate the reasons

[1] *The Ladder*, 27th rung.

Mt. Athos

Byzantium

Hadrianopolis

Nicomedia

Nicaea

Ancyra

R. Halys

CAPPADOCIA

Nyssa
Caesarea

Ephesus

Nazianzus

St. Simeon

Edessa

Antioch

Aleppo

Damascus

M E D I T E R R A N E A N

S E A

Alexandria

Jerusalem

Gaza

St.Hilarion

WADI NATRUN

St. Macarius

St. Anthony

Sinai

THEBAID

R. Nile

St. Pachomius

Thebes

E.G.M

R.Arazes

Lake Van

Lake Urmia

Nisibis

Mosul

R.Tigris

Ctesiphon

R.Kerkhek

Seleucia

R.Karun

R.Euphrates

EASTERN CHRISTENDOM

Principal monastic and
eremitic centres

Stylites

for their existence in the desert with the lucidity of an Evagrius Ponticus or a John Climacus, but if only a few of them had thought about the conditions and the consequences of their experience, their testimony would have been invaluable.

We should not be surprised by the term 'experiment' as used in connexion with fasting and anchoritism; the anchorites' way of life in Egypt and Syria certainly constitutes a unique experiment, in the scientific sense, upon the behaviour and reactions of the body and the mind when they were subjected to precise material influences. Nobody today has ever in any way, scientifically speaking, attempted an experiment comparable with that of a Simeon Stylites remaining shut up without food for forty days or a Macarius staying for forty days curled up in a hole in the desert. What is more, to these extraordinary material conditions—which it is always possible to re-establish—were added a certain mental tension and a phenomenal will and faith which it would be quite impossible to reproduce and which wholly determined the trend and the aims of those times spent in a restrictive setting. Since it is impossible, in a laboratory, to combine both the physical and mental conditions of this experiment, the changes in metabolism operating in an organism subjected to such tests cannot be exactly estimated. With the most sensitive of the desert anchorites—a Macarius, an Anthony, a Pachomius or a John of Egypt—everything took place as if they were surrounded by 'experimental conditions' that were always the same and capable of freeing the psyche, if only for a few minutes, from its bodily confines and permitting it immediately to enter a visionary world. Fasts, privations, mortification, staying motionless in the dark or cooped up in a confined space, chains, wounds which are allowed to fester and suppurate, all these could easily be shown not to have been practised by chance. For most of them it was often a matter of empirical methods, always the same through the centuries, which corresponded to well-established ascetical technique.

It must be admitted, however, that it would be of little avail to repeat experimentally today the undertaking of a Macarius or a Simeon Stylites, without the essential atmosphere of faith and fervent devotion and the cultural environment in which it took place; for the ascetic, in the course of these undertakings, was sustained and borne along by a general admiration and devotion, his task being judged less for its own sake than in relation to those which had gone before. The ethnologist Claude Levi-Strauss has clearly shown, in one of the essays in his *Structural Anthropology*, how in some archaic societies an individual subjected to certain social pressures, such as hoodoo for instance, 'offers no resistance to the breakdown of his social personality'. The victim, he writes, 'gives way before the combined action of the intense terror which he feels and the sudden total withdrawal of the many systems of reference made available by complicity on the part of the social group'; in short, he dies what might be called a social death. But why should the great ascetics' survival of the incredible hardships which they imposed upon themselves not have been due to an analogous but opposite process, *with the complicity of the group extolling the forces of survival*? The authenticity of certain ascetic exploits cannot be judged by referring, as some have done, to the behaviour of a twentieth-century man living under entirely different conditions as regards food and climate and—what is most important—sustained by the positive, exalting influence exerted by the social group, whose support helps in the saint's physical survival, just as in other circumstances it assists in the removal and the death of a condemned man. In other words, the miracle, by which is meant the survival of such trials, may here be considered as a phenomenon of a *cultural nature* made possible by the action of forces which, although imperfectly understood, are in any case of social, rather than individual, origin. Who can even say whether, in such a situation, the absence of pain, and physical insensitivity are not themselves phenomena of cultural origin?

'To be dead to the world', the fundamental objective of asceticism in the desert, therefore meant being dead in body and in mind. The body must be dead and cease its *normal* reactions, it must overcome hunger, thirst, fatigue and sleep. 'I am killing my body because it is killing me', was the reply given by St Dorotheus to Palladius when the latter questioned him on the reasons for his asceticism. And if he was 'killing' his physical self, it was obviously in order to create another self, to 'purify the mortal clay of his being' and to attain to that state which the ascetical writings call *apatheia*.

In its primary sense, apatheia (from the Greek *a* and *pathos*) means: that which is lacking sensitivity. It is a matter of *physical* condition leading to an identical state of mind. Insensitivity then gives place to impassivity. The apathetic knows no more anger, fear or desire, he has cut himself off from the world of emotions and is no longer ruled by the dictates of his heart. The heart, Macarius says, 'is a tomb. When the Prince of Darkness and his minions occupy it, when the powers of Satan are abroad in your minds and thoughts, are you not dead to God?' The emotions, as he happily expresses it, find their nourishment in the 'pastures of the heart'. In order, therefore, to deny the emotions and prevent the heart from 'ruling and controlling the whole body', one must be ever watchful of oneself and prevent sin from 'running through the heart and mind as water runs through a canal'.[1]

It was this *apathetic* man that the ascetic sought to become—a man, says John Climacus, who set the silence of his lips against the turmoil in his heart and whose body would in consequence remain beyond the reach of suffering. This new *apathetic* body must not, however, be confused with the glorified bodies of the ascetics who walked on the water, rose into the air or crossed the Nile without their even being aware of it; those were miraculous bodies representing—in the beliefs of the Desert —an ultimate bodily state in accordance with the Last Judgement. Just before this state, as John Climacus says in his *Ladder*, comes the apathetic state, half-way in fact between man and angel. James of Nisibis, praying motionless until, without realizing it, he became buried beneath the snow, Shenute, praying in the field with his arms raised and, being bitten by a snake, concluding his prayer before killing the creature, clearly had bodies in a state of apatheia.

Attainment to such a bodily state was indeed indispensable if one was to achieve the ultimate asceticism, hesychia. This word has been met with on several occasions but it must now be defined in greater detail. To give it the meaning of 'tranquillity', as is generally done, means nothing. Like apatheia, hesychia was a double state: a state of living and a corresponding state of mind. It represented a complete availability of the mind, brought about by 'silence of heart and thought', a kind of unawareness of oneself as apatheia was a state of physical unawareness. In this state of hesychia, no feeling, no thought or notion, beset the ascetic, nor even any shape or appreciable image. 'When you pray,' wrote Evagrius Ponticus, the fourth-century Egyptian ascetic, in his *Treatise on Prayer*, 'do not picture the Godhead within yourself, do not let your intelligence receive the impression of any shape at all; remain in an unsubstantial state in the presence of the Unsubstantial, and you will understand.' What will the ascetic understand? 'That when the intellect has done away with the old-style man and by the grace of God the new man has replaced him, he will, at the time of prayer, see his state like a sapphire, the colour of the sky. That is what the ancients to whom it was manifested on the mountain called the "place of God".'

Here it can be seen how ascetic writers like Evagrius Ponticus, Macarius, John Climacus and Diadochus of Photike, came in the end to an experience fundamentally at variance with that of the other, and cruder, ascetics of the desert. The marvellous and the supernatural, angels and devils, had no place in such experience; they were even

[1] Pseudo-Macarius: *Spiritual Homilies.*

regarded with suspicion. What mattered to these mystics was the purification of their hearts and minds and the eschewing of all imagination, not giving themselves up to imaginings and consequent ambiguous effusions. They explicitly denied all possibility of incarnation of the Unsubstantial and Invisible, whether diabolically or angelically inspired. 'If there should appear to some desert ascetic a light or a figure of fire, let him be on his guard against accepting such a vision. It is plainly an illusion sent by the Enemy, for as long as we occupy this mortal body we are exiled from God and cannot behold him or any of his heavenly wonders', wrote Diadochus of Photike, the fifth-century mystic, in one of his *Hundred Gnostic Chapters*. The vision of Christ and the angels was to be banished from the ascetic's experience, for it could lead 'only to madness and to suicide'.

A true ascetic in a state of hesychia could not be near both to God and to the vision of God. He had, without regret and even with joy, to give up the notion that 'God in his glory might appear before his eyes'. He had to renounce Christ and the angels![1]

Among all who thus renounced Christ and the angels there was one, mentioned by Theodoret, who showed how far hesychia was, as John Climacus said, 'an unconcern for all things, rational or not' and to what extent the hesychast 'had no thought for his own person'. This was St Salaman, who lived as a recluse near a town in Syria and who had acquired such a reputation for holiness that even in his lifetime the people of the nearby villages were already quarrelling over his body. One day, indeed, 'the inhabitants of his native town, crossed the river by night, got into the cottage where he lived and carried him off willy nilly. They took him into their town, built him a house exactly the same as his own and shut him up inside it, while the holy man himself remained silent all the time and spoke not a word to anybody.

'A few days later, the people of the town where he lived before crossed the river in their turn, broke into his house and took him to their own town. The saint did not offer the slightest resistance or make any attempt either to stay where he was or to leave, so truly dead to the world did he appear to be'!

There were paradoxes also in asceticism. An ascetic who, by dint of fasting and prayer, was completely 'dead to the world', had no longer to fear or desire the world. He had no need to run away. The disdain and

---

[1] This is also clearly expressed in the work by Evagrius Ponticus quoted at the head of the previous chapter: *The Substance of the Angels.*

fear of the world, which were the cause of the first departures for the deserts, in the end became purified and used up in their own fulfilment. So ended the vast cycle begun with distaste for the world, continued with a love of solitude and concluded with the extinction of all sentiment. Man had reached the supreme stage of asceticism where his inner cleansing was so thorough that he could, in the words of Diadochus of Photike, 'without sin and even without risk, give himself up to good living and licentiousness, since he was no longer subject to passion and so could indulge in forbidden pursuits'! After years spent in solitude he could therefore return to the life of the towns, his family and his friends. He left the desert and mingled with the crowd. And in that crowd he could not be distinguished. Consider St Alexis, returning to his family after seventeen years' absence: nobody recognized him, not even his mother or his wife, for he was both himself and yet another person. Henceforth, he could live wherever he wished; what did it matter if the woman who was speaking to him as to a stranger was in reality his own wife? Now he was an ascetic beyond asceticism itself and he could, without breaking the hesychia, indulge in laughter, singing and reminiscence. Thus, at Antioch in the seventh century, Evagrius the Scholastic tells an analogous story in his *Ecclesiastical History*: it concerns Simeon Salus, the saint who feigned madness and debauchery, the better to prove to all that he was dead to the world. 'For (says Evagrius) there are some ascetics who have raised themselves so far above the level of the passions through a long time spent in the exercise of virtue that they return to the towns, mix with the crowd and pretend to be out of their minds so as to scorn vainglory, which Plato says is the jacket that is always the last to be taken off.' This is undoubtedly an allusion to Simeon Salus, who was known as the mad saint and the dissolute saint because he even went to the extent of appearing to have dealings with courtesans. 'He always acted in the presence of everyone as if he were out of his mind. Whenever he was hungry he would go into the taverns and eat anything he found there. One day he was even seen to enter a courtesan's room, stay for a long time shut up with her and then come running out looking furtively around him so as to increase suspicion.' And Evagrius adds in respect of the ascetics who were dead to the world: 'They go into public baths and bathe indifferently with all and sundry. They have so conquered passion and triumphed over nature that no glance or touch can arouse them to any dishonourable action. They are as men among men and it seems as if they are as women when they are in the company of women. The Grace of God combines in them the most contrary elements, even life and death, which are otherwise incompatible. In brief, they are Contestants who have no body and who fight with no blood to spill.'[1]

More than three hundred years before Simeon Salus, St Anthony had left his Theban village to go and live in the desert and had opened the road to solitude. And now the experiment reached an unexpected conclusion in this return to the world. Who would have thought that that man in a tavern in Antioch, laughing and talking and carousing with loafers and loose women, was a saint?

---

[1] Such is also the case with Serapion, an 'elder in asceticism', who lived at Skete and went one day to Rome where he met a virgin, 'fierce and silent and anxious to follow the road to God'. To prove that they were 'dead' to the world, they both walked naked through the city, with their clothing over their shoulders!

EPILOGUE

If a traveller today thought of going to Egypt to visit the places where Anthony, Macarius and Pachomius lived, he would find little to resemble a 'field of the saints'. Of the great undertaking by Anthony and Pachomius, of the hundreds of monasteries and the thousands of monks established along the Nile, exactly how much is left today? Four monasteries in the Wâdi-Natrûn and two on Mount Colzim. The first of these, the Deir es-Suriani, the Deir Macarius, the Deir Amba Pshoi and the Deir Baramus (Deir meaning 'monastery' in Coptic) were visited and studied in detail in 1920 by Evelyn White, who made them the subject of an important study entitled *The Monasteries of the Wâdi Natrûn*, which appeared in New York in 1926. The present buildings, the oldest parts of which go back to the ninth century, were constructed on the spots where the great anchorites of Nitria lived. Some of them, such as the Deir Macarius, contain eleventh-century frescoes. The Deir es-Suriani possesses one of the oldest libraries in the East, including fifth- and sixth-century manuscripts. The presence of such a library is due to the fact that in the ninth century the monasteries of the Wâdi Natrûn, under the influence of monks who came from Syria and Mesopotamia, became the centre of important literary and religious activity; all texts in Sahidic were translated into Bohairic, and collections were made of all works of Syriac literature, Christian and secular, from the Bible and the writings of the Fathers of the Church to translations of Archimedes, Aristotle and Galen. But this activity and literary effulgence dwindled in the thirteenth century and the monasteries of the Wâdi Natrûn suffered a decline. There were already fifty of them in the fifth century, in the time of Sulpicius Severus, and a hundred by the tenth century, but when the Arabian historian Makrizi visited them in the fifteenth century he found no more than seven, four of which still remain today inhabited by some hundred and fifty monks.

The present monastery of St Anthony is situated at the foot of Mount Colzim on the site of the first community of disciples founded by Anthony. But the existing buildings are evidently of later date. Jean Doresse, who has made a detailed study of the architecture and history of this monastery, observes that in the eleventh century the buildings looked much as they do today. The frescoes which adorn the inside of the main church themselves date from the eleventh century; they depict saints on horseback (a very common subject in Coptic art), pictures of anchorites and a few scenes from the Old and New Testaments produced at a rather later date, for they show a marked Byzantine influence. As for the monastery of Paul of Thebes, situated about an hour's walk from that of St Anthony, it is archaeologically and historically less interesting, although the monks always point out, in the principal courtyard, the cave where it is supposed Paul of Thebes lived.

These monasteries are now the only ones in Egypt that are occupied. On going up the Nile from Cairo, the traveller would come upon no more than ruins; first, those of Sakkara and Bawit, which long stayed buried in sand and have preserved intact a large part of their frescoes dating from the sixth century and constituting the oldest known record of Coptic painting. Then, much further south, near Sohag, the famous White and Red monasteries, founded by Bgoul and Shenute of Athribis, only the outer walls of which remain. Finally, near the former Khenoboskion, are the few deserted monasteries visited by Jean Doresse as already mentioned.

Palestine and Syria present a similar scene. Of the hundreds of lauras, hermitages and monasteries that were dotted about the deserts of the Dead Sea, Calamon and Jericho, nothing remains today. There are still many monasteries to be found in Palestine, but they are all orthodox institutions, Greek or Basilian, and therefore foreign to the spirit and tradition of Coptic and Syriac monachism. Only the ruins of what is called Qal'at Sim'ân (Simeon's Castle) still bear witness to the importance and popularity of stylitism in fifth-century Syria. These ruins represent the most valuable evidence available today on the art and architecture of Christian Syria. They are valuable in the first place because of their importance as a group of buildings: basilica, martyry, guest quarters, monastery, offices and gardens, occupying nearly three thousand acres; and then because of their originality, the basilica of St Simeon being the largest and best-preserved of the cruciform churches in Christian Syria.

In the fourth century also, monachism and anchoritism reached Mesopotamia and Asia Minor. The *Life of the Blessed Ones of the East* by John of Ephesus, written in the seventh century, and then, in the ninth and tenth centuries, the *History of the Superiors* by Thomas of Marga and the *Book of Chastity* by Jesudenah, all three works being in Syriac, were to the history of Mesopotamian monachism what the *Lausiac History* and the *History of the Monks* were to Egyptian monachism: chronicles and biographies, more often fabulous than not, covering the whole of the history of the monks and hermits of Mesopotamia from the sixth century to the ninth as well as the Nestorian heresy. This heresy originated in Syria soon after the rise of Monophysism and spread throughout the East (where Nisibis and Ctesiphon became the great literary and religious centres of the Nestorian Church), and reached even to China in the eleventh century by way of the silk trade!

The history of monasticism in Asia Minor and Greece does not, strictly, form part of that of Monophysite and Nestorian eastern monachism. It was above all the work of Basil of Caesarea (known also as Basil the Great) who, after a long stay with the monks and ascetics of Egypt and Syria, and together with his friend Gregory of Nazianzus, drew up the two *Monastic Rules* which became the basis for all subsequent monachism. While recognizing the importance of the Pachomian Rule, Basil in fact made some departures from it on essential points. He attached less importance to renouncing this world and much more to a love of the next, and made much of the service of men. It was Basil's rule (the *Asceticon*) that gave inspiration to Benedict of Norcia in Italy in the sixth century, and through him western monasticism followed paths very different from those of Egypt.

In relation to the 'God-possessed', mention must be made of Cappadocia, because it played a very important part in the history of anchoritism. In Basil's day there were in existence in Cappadocia important anchorite colonies. They had become established in one of the strangest places on earth, a region to the west of Caesarea, between Caesarea and Argeus. Within a triangle of about fifty thousand acres the very porous soil had, from very early times, undergone erosion and the action of the rains so that only the hardest parts remained. These formed a whole fantastic landscape of peaks, domes, cones and monoliths pointing to the sky. 'There are stones of all shapes and sizes carved by the elements or by the hand of man into holes and hollows, and with door and window spaces worked in the bare rock. Occasionally, where the outer walls have fallen, one's gaze can roam casually through the cells and winding passages of an intricately contrived monastery. There are ruins wrought by nature and ruins brought about by man. The winter rains fill the hollows, freeze and expand and split the rock. Sometimes, like locusts, there are devastating swarms of humans. So, near to me, turns the wheel of life and death.'[1]

It was here that the first anchorites were installed. Later, they came together in lauras and monasteries, the oldest of which go back no doubt to the sixth century. The ascetics' instinct for seclusion and introversion

---

[1] Georges Séféris: *Trois jours dans les églises rupestres de Cappadoce.* (Institut Français d'Athènes, 1953.)

could be given free rein here. These rocks and monoliths of soft stone could easily be worked; so the monks became troglodytes carving from the rock their beds and tables, their churches and large rooms, some of which could hold more than fifty people. The Arab invasions of the seventh century compelled them to live completely shut up inside these caves and peaks with heavy round stones rolled across the entrances. It was not until some time later, about the ninth century, that the first frescoes made their appearance. These admirable paintings, like those of Bawit and Sakkarah in Coptic art, are the oldest examples of popular Cappadocian art free of Byzantine influence. These rupestrian monasteries prospered until the fourteenth century, then gradually fell into decline until the eighteenth century, when they were completely abandoned. Was not this, rather than Egypt, the setting for an undertaking unique in the history of *collective reclusion*?

Nearer to us, there exists another eremitical centre, which has survived until the present day. Mount Athos is situated in Greece, some sixty miles east of Salonica, at the eastern extremity of Chalcidice. Its history is much the same as that of the other eremitical regions. One day in the tenth century, a man decided to give up the world and went in search of a place where he could spend the rest of his life in seclusion. He came to Mount Athos and installed himself in a cave on the southern side of the mountain. There he stayed for fifty years, living on grasses and roots for which he had to contend with wild animals. A passing hunter came across him in his retreat and other anchorites came and settled round about him, meeting together in a laura once a week. So was created, in the eleventh century, the first laura, which was to produce the oldest and most beautiful of the monasteries of Athos, the *Great Laura*. This story continued for a thousand years, the lauras and monasteries increasing in number without preventing the anchorites from living apart on the southern side of the mountain. Athos, in the twelfth century, became the new Mount Colzim, the new Amanus of the Christian East. At the far southern edge of the mountain, between the Great Laura and St Anne's skete, live the last anchorites of our epoch. Like Anthony, Macarius and Onuphrio, they are illiterate and, like them again, they are dressed in rags and spend their time in the sun, weaving mats, making strings of shells and praying. They too, see almost nobody. They live on rainwater, bread which is brought to them once a week and a few vegetables. Like Anthony and Macarius also, they are very old; one might even say that they were born old, with their emaciated faces and very long beards. They have the timeless old age of the hermits portrayed in the frescoes of the monasteries of Athos. Their names are Athanasius, Pachomius, Philaretus, Gerasimus and Chariton. Each of them lives on a narrow ledge of rock or in a cave, a few dozen yards from his neighbours but never sees them; the mountain is steep in this part and one must seek the help of chains in order to go from one hermitage to another but, for a long time now, they have not had the strength to do so. In front of them is nothing but the sea. But for twenty, thirty or forty years they have never left these rocks, the sea and sky sufficing for their meditations.

These meditations are not always as peaceful as one might think. Mount Athos shelters not only the last anchorites of our time, but also all that inevitably went with the anchorite at all times and in all places: the last temptations, the last miracles and the last apocalypses. On Mount Athos one still believes in the imminent end of the world with the same intensity and ingenuousness as in the early centuries of our era. As evidence of this there is the Rumanian hermit, encountered by chance on a beach, away from all the other anchorites. Although he is a fisherman, he no longer fishes in the sea, for, according to him, there are no more fish in it. To explain this mystery he took me inside his chapel: olives were drying on the ground, like a bright carpet right up as far as the iconostasis, and fishing-nets hung rotting on the walls. 'Yes,' he said, 'the sea has emptied itself of fishes, for the world will soon be no more.' There he waited, by the seashore, for the end of the world. Already he could hear the rending of the sky, as of a great heavy curtain, and the angels' trumpets, so loud 'that you will have to stop your ears'. Since that day, the Apocalypse smells to me of ripe fruit and rotting nets.

NOTES TO THE ILLUSTRATIONS

Frontispiece. THE MEETING OF ST ANTHONY AND ST PAUL OF
THEBES

'*I am he whom you have sought with such difficulty.*' (p. 71). This
painting of the Sienese school is the work of Sassetta and illustrates the
principal events in the meeting of St Anthony and St Paul of Thebes,
as they are described by St Jerome. Reading from top to bottom:
Anthony's departure ('*At daybreak, St Anthony began to walk, not knowing where.*'), then the encounter with the Centaur ('*He saw a creature
which was half horse.*'), finally the arrival at the cave of Paul of Thebes.
From the Sienese painting of the Quattrocento.
(Photo: Michaelides.)

2. ST ANTHONY'S DESERT

This desert scene of light and shade lies between the Red Sea and
Mount Colzim (the present-day Gebel-el-Galaza region). It was such a
landscape that was familiar to Anthony in the last years of his life,
when, from his cave on the mountain, he '*witnessed strange sights, endless
visions of a heaven peopled by angels.*' (p. 66).
(Photo: Hassia.)

3A. ST ANTHONY'S MONASTERY

St Anthony's monastery at the foot of Mount Colzim as it is today.
The photograph is taken from one of the lower ridges of the mountain.
It is here a mere stretch of sand but it recalls Jean Coppin's words:
'*From this spot we could observe the Red Sea lying to the east, but because
it was so far distant it looked to us like a cloud resting on the ground.*'
(p. 65).
(Photo: J. Doresse.)

3B. ANCIENT TOMB IN UPPER EGYPT

'*One evening, in the deserted village where he lived, Pachomius went
underground.*' (p. 76). It was undoubtedly in some deserted tomb such
as this, in the neighbourhood of Thebes in Upper Egypt, that Pachomius
underwent his first trials of seclusion.
(Photo: Hassia.)

4A. DEATH OF ST PAUL OF THEBES

The painter has meticulously adhered to St Jerome's account. On the left, the meal in the desert: Anthony and Paul of Thebes break the bread miraculously provided by the crow. (*'They saw a crow swoop gently down, placing before them a whole loaf of bread.'*) (p. 71). On the right, Paul of Thebes buried by Anthony with the help of two lions. Detail from a work entitled *The Anchorites of Thebaid*, by Starnina, a painter of the Sienese school, born *circa* 1413. Florence.

(Photo: A. Martin.)

4B. ST ONUPHRIO

'See, I too am flesh and blood.' (p. 96). Detail of a Serbian fresco from *Serbian Painting in the Middle Ages*, by R. Petkovic.

(Photo: Michaelides.)

4C. SHENUTE OF ATRIPE

The figure on the right is Shenute and that on the left is St Anthony. *'Shenute's eyes became deep-sunk and very dark because of the copious tears he shed.'* (p. 132). Painting from an Ethiopian manuscript of the Abbadie collection, No. 135.

(Photo: Rigal—Bibliothèque Nationale.)

5A. ST MACARIUS AND ST ONUPHRIO

'He went up to them and touched them, so as to see whether, after all, they were not spirits.' (p. 122). The seeming lack of physical substance in the great desert saints, their flesh and their expression suggesting that they were already *'half-way to the next world'*, have rarely been so forcibly depicted as in this fresco from the Cozia monastery. From *Religious Painting in Wallachia and Transylvania*, by I. D. Stefanescu.

(Photo: Michaelides.)

5B. ST MACARIUS THE ELDER

'On the face of the ascetic, that hesychia, that silence of heart and mind.' (p. 118). Fresco by Theophanus the Greek (fourteenth century) from the Church of the Transfiguration in Novgorod. From the *History of Byzantine Painting*, by Lazareff.

(Photo: A. Martin.)

6A. ST PAUL THE SIMPLE

From the Menologium of Basil II, Vatican Library.
(Photo: Michaelides.)

6B. A DESERT ANCHORITE

'The places where they live like dead men in their graves.' (p. 155).
Detail from the *Anchorites of Thebaid*, by Starnina.
(Photo: A. Martin.)

7A. ST HILARION

From the Menologium of Basil II.
(Photo: Michaelides.)

7B. ANCHORITES

Miniature from the story of *Barlaam and Josaphat*, illustrated by
S. Nedersessian.
(Photo: Institute of Byzantine Studies.)

8C. MONASTERIES OF THE WÂDI NATRÛN

*'In these desert areas where the sun's rays reflected by the soda deposits,
were unbearable.'* (p. 109). Deir-el-Suriana and Deir-Macarius Monasteries in the Wâdi Natrûn.
(Photo: Mme Hassia.)

8A.B. 9A. DESERT ANCHORITES

*'Fasts, nightly vigils, prayers in the full heat of the sun or meditations
in the gloom of a cave; in the desert day follows day without change.'*
(p. 111). Scenes from life in the Egyptian deserts. Details from the
Anchorites of Thebaid, by Starnina.
(Photo: A. Martin.)

9B. MACARIUS THE YOUNGER

Here shown in his cave in the Desert of Cells. Engraving from the
Vitae Patrum.
(Photo: Michaelides.)

10. THE DESERTS OF THEBAID AND SKETE

Detail from '*The Deserts of Egypt and Thebaid, showing the exact spots where the Desert Fathers lived*'. Michalet, Paris, 1693. (Photo: Hassia.)

11. ST MARY THE EGYPTIAN

'*What he saw was a woman whose body had been blackened by exposure to the fierce heat of the sun.*' (p. 148). St Mary the Egyptian is here depicted receiving the communion from Zosimus. The artist has faithfully adhered to the original text by making Mary the Egyptian look like an old man '*with hair as white as wool but so short that it came down only to her neck.*' Fresco from a monastery on Mount Athos. (Photo: Dr Bénardeau.)

12A. ST SIMEON STYLITES

Here is seen the ladder which enabled visitors and disciples to converse with the saint. Eleventh century menologium from the monastery of Esphigmenon on Mount Athos. (Photo: Institute of Byzantine Studies.)

12B. ST ALIPIUS

Miniature from the Menologium of Basil II. (Photo: Michaelides.)

13A. ST DANIEL

Miniature from the Menologium of Basil II. (Photo: Michaelides.)

13B. AN UNKNOWN STYLITE

From *The Icons of Cyprus,* by T. T. Rice. (Photo: Michaelides.)

14. THE BASILICA OF ST SIMEON STYLITES

The famous basilica built at Qal'at Sim'ân, where Simeon Stylites ended his days. In the centre is the Martyrium built around the remains of the saint's pillar. From *Central Syria. Civil and religious architecture from the first to the seventh century,* by M. de Vogue. (Photo: A. Martin.)

15A. ST BARADATES

A static. Engraving from the *Lives of the Holy Fathers of the Desert*, 1761.

(Photo: Michaelides.)

15B. ST THALELAEUS

A recluse. (*Ibid.*)

15C. ST MARON

A recluse. (*Ibid.*)

15D. A DENDRITE (Tree-dweller)

'*The gentle life of a bird in the branches and the wind, a bird possessed of God and the thought of Heaven.*' (p. 168). Detail from Starnina, *The Anchorites of Thebaid.*

(Photo: A. Martin.)

16A. LIFE OF ST EPHRAEM

The various details of the life of a desert anchorite are here set out according to a fixed sequence: manual occupation, reading of the Scriptures, prayer. '*He might just as well have led another person's life without anything being changed at his death.*' (p. 155). Detail from a fresco in the monastery of Docheiarion on Mount Athos. G. Millet collection.

(Photo: Institute of Byzantine Studies.)

16B. ST JAMES OF NISIBIS

Miniature from the Menologium of Basil II.

(Photo: Michaelides.)

17. THE TEMPTATION OF ST ANTHONY

The Temptation of St Anthony is an inexhaustible pictorial theme. Unlike Jerome Bosch, the artist here keeps fairly close to the account given by St Athanasius: '*The four walls of Anthony's cell gaped open and the demons crowded in.*' (p. 61). Detail of the *Temptation of St Anthony*, by M. Grünewald, Colmar Museum.

18A. THE TEMPTATION OF JOHN OF EGYPT

'*The Tempter of men took the form of a very beautiful woman who, as a wanderer in the desert*—.' (p. 184). This episode fron the *Life of John of Egypt* is exactly reproduced by the artist. Here the Demon is shown in his most tempting guise, that of Beauty. Detail of a fresco attributed to P. Lorenzetti, Camposanto de Pise.
(Photo: Alinari.)

18B. THE TEMPTATION OF ST ANTHONY

'*The phantoms of the old Egyptian gods pestered Christian Egypt.*' (p. 61). Here is depicted temptation by Horror, the Demon's other aspect. Painting by Sassetta, from *Sienese Painting of the Quathocento.* (Photo: Michaelides.)

19A. AN ANCHORITE'S TEMPTATION

This is probably an episode from the life of St Bessarion who is seen crossing the Nile '*with the water coming over his ankles*'. On the opposite bank is a dragon which the saint is about to annihilate. Here, the temptation takes the form of the *physical* struggle on the part of the saint against natural and demoniacal obstacles (the river and the dragon). Detail from *The Anchorites of Thebaid*, by Starnina.
(Photo: A. Martin.)

19B. THE TEMPTATION OF ST ANTHONY

'*At the very time of the ascetic's leaving the world for ever.*' (p. 62). Here Sassetta has depicted St Anthony's temptation during his journey to the Pispir fortress. Gold and silver appear in his path. A remarkable painting; for the first time St Anthony's temptation is considered as coming from *within*. There are no monsters, no horrors, but a lonely road, with bare trees, motionless animals, a whole world *in abeyance*, a pictorial barrenness expressive of a corresponding emptiness in the ascetic.
(Photo: Michaelides.)

20A. THE BEAR AND THE ANCHORITE

'*The fellowship of animals, the privilege of man's early existence.*' (p. 193). An anchorite and a bear, as visualized by Starnina, *The Anchorites of Thebaid.*
(Photo: A. Martin.)

20B. PARADISE

'*Living like Adam before the great nightmare of original Sin.*' (p. 191).
Detail of a fresco from the monastery of Coutloumousi on Mount Athos.
(Photo: Dr Bénardeau.)

21A. THE SOUL LEAVING THE BODY

'*The saint's soul was of beautiful appearance and as white as snow.*'
(p. 187). Detail from a miniature of the story of *Barlaam and Josaphat*,
by S. Nedersessian.
(Photo: Institute of Byzantine Studies.)

21B. A CRUCIFIED MONK

'*A sameness in miracles implied a sameness in suffering.*' (p. 198). Miniature from the Menologium of Basil II.
(Photo: Michaelides.)

22. DORMITION OF ST EPHRAEM

'*A silent question posed in the presence of the mystery of holiness and
death.*' (p. 157). Detail from the *Dormition of St Ephraem*, monastery of
Docheiarion on Mount Athos.
(Photo: Institute of Byzantine Studies.)

23A. RUPESTRIAN MONASTERIES IN CAPPADOCIA
(Photo: Yan.)

23B. A HERMITAGE ON MOUNT ATHOS
(Photo: J. Lacarrière.)

BIBLIOGRAPHY

ABBOTT, N. *The Monasteries of the Fayoum* (Chicago, 1937).

AMELINEAU, R. *Voyage d'un moine égyptien dans le désert; Vies de saint Antoine, de saint Pacôme et de saint Macaire; Mémoires publiés par la Mission archéologique française en Egypte; Monuments pour servir à l'histoire de l'Egypte chrétienne* (Musée Guimet); *Les Sermons de Schnoudi* (Trans.); *Etudes sur saint Pacôme et le cénobitisme égyptien; Contes et romans de l'Egypte chrétienne* (1888); *Les Apophtegmes coptes de Macaire* (Trans.); *La Vie copte de l'apa Bgoul* (Trans.); *Les moines égyptiens.*

D'ANDILLY, A. *Apophtegmes des Pères du désert* (Trans.); *Vie de sainte Marie l'Egyptienne* (Trans.).

ANTHONY. *Life of St Simeon Stylites.*

ST ATHANASIUS. *Discourse against the Arians; Discourse against the Pagans; Vie des saints Pères du Désert* (Lyon, 1654). (Trans. by d'Andilly.)

BASIL OF ANCYRA. *On Virginity.*

VAN DE BOCK. *Matériaux pour servir à l'archéologie de l'Egypte chrétienne* (1901).

BOUYER, L. *Saint Antoine et la spiritualité du monachisme primitif* (Abbaye de Wandrille, 1950).

BREMOND, H. *Les Pères du Désert* (Paris, 1926).

BUDGE, W. *The Wit and Wisdom of the Christian Fathers* (Oxford, 1934); *Story of Holy Fathers* (Oxford, 1934).

CASSIAN. *Institutions of the Monks of Egypt.*

CHAPOT, V. *L'Empire romain* (La renaissance du Livre).

CLEMENT OF ALEXANDRIA. *Protreptic; The Pedagogue.*

CLIMACUS, J. *L'Echelle du Paradis* (Trans by J. Gouillard).

ST CYPRIAN OF CARTHAGE. *Letter to Dimitrianus.*

DELEHAYE, H. *Les saints stylites* (Brussels, 1923).

DIADOCHUS OF PHOTIKE. *A Hundred Gnostic Chapters.*

DORESSE, J. *Deux monastères coptes oubliés: saint Antoine et saint Paul de Thèbes dans le désert de la Mer Rouge* (Revue des Arts, 1952); *Les livres secrets des Gnostiques d'Egypte* (Plon, 1958).

DRAGUET, P. *Les Pères du Désert* (Paris, 1949).

ELIADE, M. *La nostalgie du paradis; Mythes, rêves et mystère* (Gallimard).

ST EPHRAEM. *Eulogy of the Mesopotamian Solitaries.*

EPIPHANIUS THE GNOSTIC. *On Justice.*

ERMAN, A. *La religion des Egyptiens* (Payot).

EVAGRIUS THE SCHOLASTIC. *Ecclesiastical History*; *Traité de l'Oraison* (Trans. by P. I. Hausherr).

FESTUGIÈRE, A. J. *Les Moines d'Orient* (Editions du Cerf, 1961); *Antioche, païenne et chrétienne, Libanios, Chrysostome et les moines de Syrie* (Bibliothèque des Ecoles Françaises d'Athènes et de Rome, 1959).

FLICHE & MARTIN. *Dictionnaire de théologie catholique.*

GOGUEL, M. *Apocalypse et eschatologie* (Revue d'Histoire des Religions, 1932).

HADRIAN. *Letter to Servianus.*

HANOTAUX, G. *Histoire de la nation égyptienne.*

HAUSHERR, I. *Les grands courants de la spiritualité orientale* (Orientalia Christiana Periodica, 1935); *Petite Philocalie de la Prière du Coeur* (Trans. by J. Gouillard).

HEUSSI, R. *Der Ursprung des Mönchtums* (1936).

ST HIPPOLYTUS. *Commentary on Daniel*; *Treatise on Antichrist.*

HOLLARD. *Deux hérétiques: Marcion et Montan* (1935).

HUXLEY, A. *Heaven and Hell.*

JEANMAIRE, H. *Dionysos* (Payot).

ST JEROME. *Vie de Paul de Thèbes* (Trans. by d'Andilly); *Vie de saint Hilarion* (Trans. by d'Andilly).

DE JOURNEL, R. *Introduction au Pré spirituel de Jean Moschos* (Editions du Cerf, 1947); *Textes ascétiques des Pères de l'Eglise* (1947).

DE LABRIOLLE, P. *L'Origine du monachisme* (Fliche & Martin).

DE LABRIOLLE, M. *Le montanisme et la crise montaniste* (1913).

LADEUZE, P. *Etudes sur le cénobitisme pachômien* (1898).

LAGIER, C. *L'Orient chrétien de 35 à 1204* (Paris, 1950).

LAVAUD, B. *Antoine le Grand, père des moines* (Fribourg, 1943).

LEFORT, L. T. *Les premiers monastères pachômiens* (Le Muséon, 1939); *Les vies coptes de Pachôme et de ses premiers successeurs* (Louvain, 1943).

LEISENGANG, H. *La Gnose* (Payot, 1951).

LIBANIUS. *Pro Templis.*

LOT, F. *La fin du monde antique* (La Renaissance du Livre).

LUCIAN OF SAMOSATA. *The Syrian Goddess.*

(PSEUDO-) MACARIUS. *Homélies spirituelles* (Trans. by J. Gouillard).

MARTINEZ, P. *L'ascétisme chrétien pendant les trois premiers siècles* (1913).

MOSCHUS, J. *Le Pré spirituel* (Trans. by R. de Journel. Editions du Cerf, 1946).

MUSSET, H. *Histoire du christianisme en Orient* (Jerusalem, 1948).

NEWMAN, J. H. *Apologia pro Vita sua.*

PALLADIUS. *Histoire lausiaque* (Trans. by d'Andilly).

ST PAUL. *Epistle to the Ephesians; Epistle to the Thessalonians.*

PEETERS. *Le tréfonds oriental dans l'hagiographie byzantine* (1950).

PUECH, H. C. *Le manichéisme, son fondateur, sa doctrine* (1949); *Introduction à la vie de saint Antoine par saint Athanase.*

QUEFFELEC, H. *Saint Antoine du désert* (1950).

RESCHE. *La doctrine ascétique des premiers maîtres égyptiens au IVe siècle* (1935).

RUFINUS OF AQUILEIA. *Histoire des moines d'Egypte* (Trans. by d'Andilly).

STEIN. *Histoire du Bas-Empire.*

SULPICIUS SEVERUS. *Dialogues.*

TATIAN. *Diatessaron; Discourse to the Greeks.*

TERTULLIAN. *Against Marcion.*

THEODORET OF CYRRHUS. *Histoire religieuse* (Trans. by d'Andilly); *Vie de saint Syméon stylite* (Trans. by d'Andilly).

TOYNBEE, A. *Christianity and the other Religions of the World.*

VISA. *La Vie copte de Schnoudi* (Trans. by R. Amelineau).

WELTER. *Histoire des sectes chrétiennes* (1950).

WHITE, H. C. E. *The monasteries of the Wâdi Natrûn* (New York, 1926-1933).

ZILLBORG. *Considérations psychiatriques sur l'idéal ascétique.*

Etudes Carmélitaines: *Limites de l'Humain; Magie des Extrêmes; Satan.*

Revue de l'Orient chrétien (1899, IV).

The Gospels.

INDEX